*If You Want
What We Have*

If You Want
What We Have

SPONSORSHIP
MEDITATIONS

JOAN LARKIN

▨ HAZELDEN®

Hazelden
Center City, Minnesota 55012-0176

1-800-328-0094 (Toll Free U.S., Canada, and the Virgin Islands)
http://www.hazelden.org

Library of Congress Cataloging-in-Publication Data

Larkin, Joan.
    If you want what we have : sponsorship meditations / Joan Larkin.
    p.   cm.
    Includes index.
    ISBN 1-56838-192-1
    1. Twelve-step programs—Religious aspects—Christianity—
Meditations.   2. Devotional calendars.   I. Title.
BL624.5.L37   1998
616.86'0651—dc21   97-48995
                                                           CIP

01 00 99 98   6 5 4 3 2 1

Book design by Will Powers
Typesetting by Stanton Publication Services, Inc.
Cover design by David Spohn

Editor's note

Hazelden offers a variety of information on chemical dependency and related areas. Our publications do not necessarily represent Hazelden's programs, nor do they officially speak for any Twelve Step organization.

The Twelve Steps are reprinted with permission of Alcoholics Anonymous World Services, Inc. Permission to reprint and adapt the Twelve Steps does not mean that AA has reviewed or approved the contents of this publication, nor that AA agrees with the views expressed herein. AA is a program of recovery from alcoholism *only*—use of the Twelve Steps in connection with programs that are patterned after AA, but that address other problems, or in any other non-AA context, does not imply otherwise.

Acknowledgments

I owe an enormous debt to my sponsors. My first and most profound experience of sponsorship was in my early years of recovery, when I spoke each day with Francis B. I met Francis in my second week of recovery, and he remained my sponsor until his untimely (but sober) death seven years later. His only requests were that I call every day and that I promise to call first if I were considering a slip. With only a year more of recovery than I had, Francis listened, laughed, and gave, with willingness, good humor, and common sense. He made it clear that he was human and in recovery from an addiction—he was not a guru. He frequently acknowledged his gratitude to his own sponsor and others, saying, "Everything I have has been given to me."

Thanks, too, to Jennifer H., for being there at the beginning and opening the door. Thanks to Denis O, for unwavering love for the program; to Tom T., for morning phone calls; to Greta N., for taking the first look. Special thanks to Doug A., for friendship, faith, and inspired research, and to editor Kate Kjorlien, for patience, toughness, and clarity. Many, many others helped make this book possible. My thanks to all of you, beginners and old-timers, whose sharing keeps showing me the way.

. . . my lifetime
listens to yours.
MURIEL RUKEYSER

Introduction

This is a book of daily readings based on the developing relationship of a sponsor and a sponsee over the period of one year in Twelve Step recovery. For each day of recovery, a question or concern raised by a newcomer is followed by a response from his or her sponsor. Their down-to-earth exchanges are meant to suggest the daily give-and-take of conversations between two recovering people. Whether the sponsee's questions are practical or spiritual, simple or not so simple, all are treated respectfully.

Although this book focuses on concerns that are typical of early recovery, it is meant to be of use not just to newcomers but to those who have spent time in recovery—perhaps especially to sponsors, who may not always think that they have the answers. These readings aren't necessarily intended to have all the answers, either, but to serve as the basis for further reflection. Some of you may read them on your own; others may want to read and discuss them with a sponsor or sponsee. They may help you to speak about certain issues you would otherwise have difficulty raising on your own. While they are meant to supplement a sponsor-sponsee relationship, they cannot replace the face-to-face contact of real sponsorship.

Some of these meditations use the words "sober" and "sobriety." They aren't intended to limit the framework of these conversations to recovery from alcoholism, but instead to suggest the fullness, dignity, and joy of all lives in recovery. If you are more comfortable with such words as "clean" or "abstinent," by all means substitute them. "Drug" and "drug of choice" are words used to denote not only substances (including food and alcohol) but also "process addictions" such as compulsive debting, gambling, or sex.

Recovery is often compared to a journey. In fact, many journeys take place during a life in recovery. The sequence of this book is intended to suggest the shape of some of these concurrent journeys as they unfold:

1. One journey is the evolving relationship of two recovering people. I hope that the honesty and clarity of the questions and answers will serve as a reminder of the mutual trust and compassion that are necessary to the process of recovery.

2. Another is the recovering person's journey from fear and resistance to faith and commitment. Recovery unfolds at a different pace for each individual. The questions and concerns on any given day are rarely identical. So it's a good idea to take the same approach, reading these pages, that one takes to stories heard in meetings: "Identify; don't compare." Please don't assume that because a particular question is raised on day 10 or day 110, you ought to be facing the same question on that day. The index can help you find your way to a specific issue.

3. Still another is the journey through the Twelve Steps. Each month, one of the Steps is discussed just as if the reader were ready to take that Step. In reality, of course, some may take Step Four in the fourth month, some in the eleventh month, and some only after the first year is long past. Whether or not you're ready to take the Steps, you can begin to familiarize yourself with them throughout the first year by attending Step meetings. Conversations about the Steps are included here in that spirit. Please use the pages that discuss particular Steps as the basis for whatever reflection or action is right for you now.

When a meditation quotes directly from one of the Twelve Steps, the words used are taken from the Steps of Alcoholics Anonymous. I have done this for the sake of simplicity—not to suggest that the wording used in one particular program is definitive.

Whatever your own particular experiences have been, whether you believe that they have been gentler or harsher than those alluded to in this book, whether your early recovery is a smoother or a bumpier ride than the one suggested here, my hope is that you will identify with many of the questions raised in these pages. In the tradition of Twelve Step recovery, you are welcome to take what you like and leave the rest.

1

Whatever happens at all happens as it should.
MARCUS AURELIUS ANTONINUS

Newcomer

I came to this meeting, but I don't know if I belong here. I just don't know.

Sponsor

We have a saying: "Nobody gets here by mistake."

For many of us, this means that something inside us knows we need help and that we're in the process of becoming willing to accept it. Some of us are drawn here thinking, at first, that we've come because of someone else's problem; then we discover that we've also come for ourselves. Some of us sense immediately that we belong here; some come to this feeling over time; some never feel they belong. Our arriving at the first meeting can seem mysterious until we realize how unlikely it is for a person with no relationship to addiction whatsoever to show up here.

Since you can't decide whether you belong here or not, why not stay? Consider it a gift that's been offered you, a chance to explore your relationship to addiction. You are entitled to be here. The only "qualification" for membership is a desire to quit our addictive substance or behavior. Unless you cause a disruption, no one's going to ask you to leave a meeting. Relax, sit back, and listen. See if you identify with any of the feelings that you hear people share, whether or not their specific life experiences mirror yours. If you keep coming, more will be revealed in time.

Today, I am where I'm supposed to be.

2

*We know the truth, not only by the reason,
but by the heart.*

BLAISE PASCAL

Newcomer

I'm not sure I qualify to be in this program. I wasn't that bad—I hear stories that are so much worse than mine.

Sponsor

There's a joke about a group of friends standing at their drinking buddy's graveside with his widow, all of them shaking their heads and saying, "I don't understand it—he wasn't *that* bad."

Who qualifies for a Twelve Step program? The answer doesn't lie simply in the quantities of a substance consumed or in the frequency of an unwanted behavior. More telling is whether or not we have a choice. It's useful to make a list of times we remember using in spite of intentions not to and a list of times when using took us places we never meant to go, made us do things we never meant to do. Perhaps we'll recall many such situations, perhaps only a few. The number is less important than our willingness to look back at our memories, and the feelings accompanying them, without censoring ourselves. Something inside us brought us here; it's up to each of us to take an honest look at what that was.

Today, I look honestly at times when I have been
powerless over this addiction. I acknowledge
the ways it has made my life unmanageable.

3

A man takes a drink, the drink takes another,
and the drink takes the man.
SINCLAIR LEWIS

Newcomer

I've heard Alcoholics Anonymous members say, "It's the first drink that gets you drunk," and Overeaters Anonymous members say, "Don't take that first compulsive bite." It seems a little extreme. Don't Twelve Step programs allow for the possibility of doing things in moderation?

Sponsor

There are numerous stories of addicted people who started with the idea that they'd have "just one" of whatever it was. Hours, days, or weeks later, they were still in the middle of a binge. Most of us, when we were active in our addictions, promised ourselves repeatedly that we'd be moderate, though we'd already accumulated plenty of evidence that we lacked the desire and the capacity for moderation. Once we started using, no matter how seemingly insignificant the beginning, we were under the control of our addiction. We experienced a craving that no quantity of a drug or repetition of an addictive behavior could satisfy.

There are people on this planet who leave wine unfinished in their glasses and food uneaten on their plates. There are people who can do in moderation what people filling the seats at meetings couldn't stop doing, once they started. But we are not those people. If we've suffered from an addiction enough to come here for treatment, why would we want to keep playing with denial?

Today, I'm strengthened by accepting my need to take special measures to protect my health and recovery.

4

Later is now.
ROSEANNE BARR

Newcomer

I guess I do have some addiction problems, but right now is a terrible time for me. I know you'd like me to be more involved, use the program more, but I need time—there's something else I have to deal with first. I've tried talking about it at meetings, but no one really has much understanding of my particular problem.

Sponsor

I do respect the fact that there are pressing problems in your life and that you are going to have to face them. Addiction is, in one sense, a response to underlying issues we all have to deal with. And in addition to our inner problems, many of us enter recovery in the midst of some crisis—serious illness, separation, overdue taxes, even homelessness are situations some of us have had to face while newly recovering. I agree that your problems are real ones. But putting off recovery is not likely to help you with them. It may make things worse.

While I may not be able to help with the specifics of your situation, I can be here to share my experience, strength, and hope as a person in recovery. Recovery is the foundation of my life today. I make it my highest priority, and as time goes on I find the help and strength I need to resolve everything else I have to deal with. If you, too, have the willingness to face your addiction and show up for your recovery, I'm willing to be here.

Today, I let go of all obstacles to recovery.

5

Life is not made up of yesterdays only.
CARL JUNG

Newcomer
I heard a bunch of jargon at the meeting I went to last night. I didn't understand any of it. What does "ninety in ninety" mean?

Sponsor
I can understand your bewilderment at unfamiliar program phrases and customs. In the beginning, it may feel as if we're participating in a culture that's new to us. I'm glad I can help, and if I'm not here to translate, almost anyone you see at a meeting would be happy to explain unfamiliar expressions.

"Ninety in ninety" is an abbreviated way of saying, "Go to ninety meetings in ninety days." One of the strongest suggestions this program makes to newcomers is to attend a meeting every day for at least the first three months. Intermittent attendance, a few meetings here or there, won't provide enough information about whether we belong here or not. Ninety days of meetings can make it clear.

At first, it may sound like a lot. But when we think of the time we have given to our addiction—pursuing it, trying

to control it, acting on it, feeling sick and guilty about it—
then an hour or an hour and a half doesn't seem like too
much of a commitment. Meetings create a sense of belonging to a community and a solid basis of support over
time. It's such a good use of time: an hour in a room with
my peers gives me a reserve of strength and hope for an
entire day.

Today, I am part of a community of people in recovery.

6

It's not what you were, it's what you are today.
DAVID MARION

Newcomer

I get the general idea of "ninety meetings in ninety days."
But aren't there any exceptions? Some days, like on the
weekends, I have time to go to more than one, but later in
the week, when I'm exhausted from work, I'd sometimes
rather go to a movie or go to bed early.

Sponsor

No one takes attendance; no one expects perfection. But
why deprive yourself? In this program, we stay away from
addiction a day at a time. At the beginning of recovery, especially if we're going through a process of detoxification,
twenty-four hours can seem endless. Going through a whole
day of early recovery on our own may be bewildering and
anxiety-producing. Why "white-knuckle it" when help is
available at a meeting?

Anticipating a meeting at the lunch hour or at the end
of a workday gives me a kind of safety net. Knowing

throughout the day that I'm headed for a place where recovery is the top priority can help me through hard moments—I anticipate the meeting, instead of my preferred drug or compulsive behavior. Some of us prefer to begin the day with an early-morning meeting that helps us face the hours ahead calmly.

Each new day offers us new challenges, new opportunities for our addictions to flex their muscles. Going to a meeting can strengthen our spirits and help ensure our continuing recovery.

Today, I further my recovery by going to a meeting.

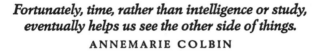

Fortunately, time, rather than intelligence or study, eventually helps us see the other side of things.
ANNEMARIE COLBIN

Newcomer

I don't think these meetings do enough. Some people come in with their health in terrible shape. Someone should be evaluating them! I think I should be getting vitamin B shots. I'm angry that such important things are being ignored.

Sponsor

You may very well need extra vitamins; nutrition sounds like something you might be ready to look into. You may want to see a doctor, a nutritionist, or both. I support you in your desire to get help with the ways you have neglected your health. And I understand that you feel angry at not being taken care of.

One reason that this program works for me is that it respects my decision to seek help, if and when I choose to, from the people and institutions I trust. It doesn't get into the business of dispensing medical advice, diets, vitamins, or exercise plans, any more than it tells me where to pray, how to earn a living, or whom to vote for. The group doesn't hire experts to come tell us how to run our lives, and we don't have to be covered by insurance to come to a meeting. Each of us here is an expert on just one thing: our own experience of addiction and recovery. You might say that we're specialists!

Today, I appreciate the gift of my experience.
I add one new thing to my knowledge of how to
take care of my health—physical, mental, and spiritual.

8

. . . that they may solve their common problem . . .
ALCOHOLICS ANONYMOUS PREAMBLE

Newcomer
When they say we're here to solve our common problems, I'm really put off. Adults should be able to handle their problems on their own, shouldn't they?

Sponsor
We don't go to meetings to solve our "problems," but rather our "problem"—singular. Meetings address the problem none of us could solve on our own: the disease of addiction.

I can identify with your discomfort at the thought of accepting help from a group of people. I've always wanted to think of myself as independent. Talking about what's bothering me feels like I'm risking my pride, my privacy, and my autonomy.

Deep down, though, I care a great deal about what other people think of me. I'm afraid that if they really get to know me, they'll find out I'm not good enough. I'm afraid they'll want more from me than I'm capable of giving. I'd rather believe that I don't need others than risk being challenged or let down by them.

I'm not alone in having these fears and resentments of others. Most of us who've resorted to addictive substances or behaviors have problems in our relationships with other people.

When, through the help of other recovering people, we solve our common problem of addiction, we become truly independent. We're free of our deadly attachment to a drug. We're free to acknowledge our connections with other human beings.

Today, I add the word "help" to my vocabulary.

9

Which way lay safety? Which way life?
JACQUES LUSSEYRAN

Newcomer
What would be the harm of using in moderation? The rest of the world does it. I have to admit that I feel deprived, even somewhat resentful.

Sponsor
When I was free to use in moderation, how moderate was I? Was my relationship with certain substances and behaviors

easy and comfortable, one that created no problems for me or others? Was it easy for me to stop, once I got started? Was it easy for me to stay stopped, if I chose to? It's easy to slip back into denial about the seriousness of my problem, once I've gotten some momentary feelings of control.

Some of us consumed our addictive substances in smaller quantities than others did. Some of us are taller or thinner or shorter or younger; some spent more years in school; some can enjoy strawberries without breaking out in a rash. I can easily point to the differences between me and others; there are plenty!

Or I can go to meetings, listen, and see if there are feelings with which I identify. The addictions that call to us will always be there, if we decide to go back to them. For today, there's no hurry to return to old habits. Let's keep an open mind, as we go through today without putting our recovery at risk.

> I look honestly at my previous life and remember
> what feelings and situations got me here.
> For today, I give myself the chance for recovery.

10

The war is over.
SAYING HEARD AT MEETINGS

Newcomer
I'm trying to understand the First Step, and I'm really stuck on that word "powerless." I'm not weak; I don't want to be called powerless. It really insults my intelligence.

Let's take a look at this part of the First Step together. It doesn't simply say, "We admitted we were powerless." Far from it. It says that we were powerless *over* something. We recognized that a specific substance or behavior had proved stronger than our determination not to consume it or engage in it. Choosing recovery does not mean that we are weak, but it does offer us an opportunity to surrender. Accepting the truth that we have an addiction is an easier way for us to change our addictive behavior than continuously fighting with it. When I resist, my enemy just seems to get stronger. So instead, I accept that there are some things I can't control. That acceptance becomes a source of enormous power.

Today, I empty my hands and let go of my weapons.
I admit that addiction has played a role in my life.

11

May you live all the days of your life.
JONATHAN SWIFT

Newcomer

I'm confused about the wording of the second part of the First Step. When people say, "My life had become unmanageable," they don't all seem to mean the same thing. For some it's a big deal if they have a messy house or unpaid bills; another person says he has lost everything, but seems totally calm about it. I don't know if my life is unmanageable or not. Just what is "unmanageability"?

Sponsor

People who manage offices, theaters, restaurants, classrooms—you name it—are responsible for lots of planning and decision making. Periodically, they have to reevaluate. They may ask, "What results did we get from taking the actions we took? What can we do more effectively?" Managing our lives is similar. Life used to just happen to me; I *reacted* to events, often feeling like a victim. When I acted on impulse, then looked for reasons for what I'd done, I wasn't managing anything. Today, I can see the range of choices available to me, now that my life isn't dedicated to serving my addiction. In recovery, we're responsible for finding out how we want to live, where, and with whom— what our true preferences are. Our disease made our lives unmanageable, but we are no longer victims when we take back the responsibility for our decisions in recovery.

Today, I am free to make decisions that help bring about the life I want for myself.

12

Let the counsel of thine own heart stand.
APOCRYPHA

Newcomer

I've told one or two old friends that I've started going to meetings of a Twelve Step program. One of them is very dubious about it. When I talked about being addicted, she said she'd never thought of me as having a serious problem. Maybe she's right—she's known me for a long time.

Sponsor

It's ultimately our own deep discomfort that tells us we have a problem. Our friends, our families, and even our doctors may have told us that they want us to get help—or they may have said that they don't believe we have a serious problem. Do they know the whole truth about us? We may have hidden our addiction from them. They may not be adequately informed about what addiction is. Or they themselves may be in denial, in order not to have to look at their own relationship to addiction.

Friends who aren't facing a life-and-death disease may not understand that what I'm doing here is saving my life. They may think that I'm exaggerating my problem or that I'm simply caught up in a trend. Such opinions appeal to me at times, when I'd rather not have to face what I know to be true in the depths of my being.

We can't let others "vote" on our decision to enter recovery—it's up to us to know our own truth and respect it.

Today, I own my need for recovery.
I don't argue about it, with myself or with others.

13

The day is a gift of the universe.
KATHLEEN CULVER

Newcomer

I don't want to disappoint the people who count on me, but I'm afraid to promise that I'll stick to this recovery stuff forever. I don't know if I can do it. Frankly, I feel suffocated by the idea of never using anything ever again, of going to meetings for years—I can't imagine spending my whole life in recovery.

Sponsor

The span of a whole life is impossible to imagine. We have no idea how long we're going to live, what unforeseen things will take place in our lifetime, or even how a small choice we make today may in some way change the person we grow to be tomorrow. If I try to imagine doing anything "forever" or "for my whole life," I'm overwhelmed. Fortunately, no one here is asking me to promise that. The program suggests only that we get through one day—today—without using an addictive substance. Yesterday is over. Tomorrow is not here yet. My whole life is now, and now is all that need concern me. Sometimes even a twenty-four-hour period feels overwhelming, so I break it down into hours and go through the day an hour at a time. Some days I've even had to think in terms of just one minute at a time. Using substances we're addicted to comes naturally to us; a day in which we choose recovery instead is a highly successful day.

> **I let go of yesterday and tomorrow.**
> **I choose recovery for today.**

14

The truth can be spoken only by someone who already lives inside it.
LUDWIG WITTGENSTEIN

Newcomer

Some of the expressions people use to talk about recovery sound sickeningly sweet to me. On my first day, someone

I'd never seen before said to me, "Welcome to our fellowship." It makes my skin crawl when they say that kind of thing. And all those slogans! They make me wonder if people in recovery can think for themselves.

Sponsor

I can identify with you. In early recovery, I felt uncomfortable when people reached out to me. I had been impatient and cynical for a long time; I was suspicious of positive statements and looked down on people who made them. My habit of finding fault came in handy when somebody challenged my old ways of thinking. It was easier to criticize others than to look at myself.

It's funny: when I was active in my addiction, I rarely complained of how tedious and repetitive my life had become. I had surrounded myself with people who enabled my addiction. I must have sounded like a broken record as I justified my addiction in spite of the consequences. Today, my focus is no longer on likes and dislikes. Instead of dismissing people without really looking or listening, I can go deeper and see what's true for me in whatever they are saying.

In recovery, free of the need to make snap judgments, we can begin to listen in a new way.

Today, I listen without judging. I cultivate respect and tenderness for others and for myself.

Very little is needed to make a happy life.
MARCUS AURELIUS ANTONINUS

Newcomer

I'm having a horrible day. I have way too much to do. This morning I felt overwhelmed, but I went to a meeting as you told me to. Instead of making me feel better, the meeting made me feel worse: I got upset at what someone shared and started to cry. Now I have a headache and I can't concentrate on what I was supposed to do. How will I ever get this stuff done?

Sponsor

What you experienced at the meeting was not to blame for your sadness. More likely, whatever triggered your tears was already inside you, waiting for something to release it. Most of us who are in recovery have a lot of stored-up grief. Tears are beneficial and cleansing.

There are days like this, when we feel sad, distracted, overwhelmed. Some days—especially in early recovery—are unexpectedly emotional. On such days, we may have to accept that it's enough simply to breathe, eat three meals, drink water, and abstain from using our drug of choice. And, yes, to go to a meeting. Meetings remind us that when an alcoholic stays sober, an overeater eats moderately, or a perfectionist knows that he or she has done enough, a significant victory has been achieved. For those of us living with addiction, one day without addictive behavior is a precious step forward on our journey.

I am willing to revise my goals for this day. I give myself the gift of keeping it simple for one day of recovery.

I am of old and young, of the foolish
as much as the wise. . . .
And breathe the air and leave plenty after me,
And am not stuck up, and am in my place.
WALT WHITMAN

Newcomer

I've been told to make program calls, but I hate bothering other people, and I don't like them bothering me. I can't bring myself to ask people for their telephone numbers in the first place, and though a few people have offered me their numbers at meetings, I haven't used them. How can I make phone calls to people I don't know? Especially when I don't really have anything to say other than that I feel terrible and don't know why!

Sponsor

New recovery is a little bit like starting to walk after having been paralyzed. In recovery, we're moving muscles that we haven't used before. It's uncomfortable. It's work. But because we want to get better, we need to stop making excuses. I follow suggestions and use the tools of the program. I let go of my self-centeredness and see that making a program call is a gift: it offers someone else the opportunity to share his or her recovery. I recognize, too, that in the adult world, people can tell me when they aren't available to talk; I don't have to figure it out for them! I can be honest about where I'm at today, too—I don't have to have my act together before I make a program call.

Today, I allow others to further their own recovery by
sharing their experience, strength, and hope with me.

I have had just about all I can take of myself.
S. N. BEHRMAN

Newcomer

I can't sleep. I'm too exhausted to concentrate during the day. At night I'm tortured by thoughts of sickness, death, debts, people I've hurt or who've hurt me. I'm uncomfortable physically, mentally, and emotionally. I bring it up at meetings, but no one takes me seriously. People just say, "It gets better" and "Keep coming back."

Sponsor

Whether our addictions involve a substance or a behavior, we go through a period of detoxification. Though some things may improve fast, most of us don't heal overnight. Those who say "It gets better" and "Keep coming back" are speaking from experience and compassion. All of us, when we're new, go through some version of what you've just described.

In time your body will readjust. Meanwhile, there are things you can do to reeducate your body about when it's time to slow down. You can prepare for rest by dimming the lights, turning off the phone, playing slow music, or taking a warm bath by candlelight. In bed, you can take time to breathe and consciously relax your body, moving your attention very slowly upward from the toes as you picture every part of your body slowing down and letting go. You can do the same with thoughts, and visualize erasing them as they arise. You may still not sleep, but you can commit yourself to not indulging in worry or self-centered fear.

Today, I accept that detoxification is part of healing.
This, too, shall pass.

18

A good listener is not only popular everywhere,
but after a while he gets to know something.
WILSON MIZNER

Newcomer

I feel impatient. *What am I doing at this meeting?* The speaker's concerns are entirely different from mine. He has cancer, and his doctor has told him that he has eighteen months to live. He says that he is not afraid of dying and he wants to die sober. I am impatient; my health is not a problem right now, and I don't feel like I'm dying. I hate to say it, but *what good is this going to do me?*

Sponsor

When I am at a meeting, for the brief space of an hour I have nowhere I have to go, nothing I have to do. I can choose to relax, breathe, still my racing mind, listen. Sometimes a speaker addresses exactly what is on my mind. Other times, I have to listen hard for a feeling I can identify with or a principle I can practice. If I listen intending to hear something that I can take away with me, even if it's just one thing, I always find that it is there. After listening to someone who is facing illness and possible death, for example, I take away with me the new knowledge that there are recovering people who do not look at personal tragedy as an excuse for using again. Their priorities have changed. Are you willing to reconsider your priorities?

Today, I listen without judging. I take responsibility for hearing one thing that relates to my own recovery.

*. . . I always come to why, to
the unfair, painful
part of life.*
MALKIA CYRIL

Newcomer

Today, I went to a meeting, but I could hardly hear the speaker. She spoke softly, and the fan was making too much noise. During the discussion period, she called on people by name; they must have been her friends. No one noticed me during the coffee break, and I left the meeting feeling worse than when I came in. I thought people in this fellowship were supposed to reach out to newcomers!

Sponsor

When I was active in my addiction, I "medicated" myself when I felt uncomfortable with other people. In recovery, I have had to learn new skills. Developing friendships, both in this fellowship and in the "real" world, takes time. Some of the people I see at meetings are still coping with problems like the ones I walked in with: shyness, anger, self-centered fear. When I feel lonely, instead of waiting to be rescued, I introduce myself to the person next to me. I sit as close to the front of the room as possible, focus on listening to the speaker, and thank him or her at the break. I put my hand up (high, as if I meant it!) and, if called on, let the group know something about me. If I don't get called on, I refrain from resentment and plan to keep coming and attempting to share. We can trust that, over time, if we're willing to reach out to others, people will begin to know us.

Today, I do not blame others for my feelings.
I take one step toward sharing myself with others.
I let go of needing instant results.

20

For sometimes, were the truth confess'd,
You're thankful for a little rest.
DANTE GABRIEL ROSSETTI

Newcomer

I can't stop thinking about the mess I've made of my life. I rush around all day trying to get things done, then I run to a meeting, grab some cookies and coffee, and try to listen. I feel impatient and annoyed at what people are saying. Sometimes I even fall asleep at the meeting. I leave wondering if it's worth it.

Sponsor

Mood swings are a signal that something needs taking care of. The slogan "HALT (Don't get too Hungry, Angry, Lonely, or Tired)" is a reminder to pay attention to basics. We have bodies that need regular food and rest. When I deprive myself of a meal, I get cranky and depressed. Being overtired is a mood changer for me, too. When I try to revive myself with coffee and sugary snacks at night, I may have trouble sleeping afterward. My spirit has needs, too, that I'm learning to recognize and nourish. For a long time, I was used to masking my anger and loneliness with addictive substances. To change this habit, I allow recovering people into my life. Sometimes speaking to just one other person can break the cycle of isolation that addiction thrives on. But even if we do everything perfectly, we may still fall asleep in a meeting sometimes. We needn't worry; even if we don't catch every word, a meeting is a safe place to be.

Today, I respect the basic needs of my body and spirit.
I nurture my recovering self with food, rest,
and conversation with others.

Get rid of the poisons.
M. F. K. FISHER

Newcomer

I'm trying to take your advice not to get too hungry, angry, lonely, or tired, but sleep is still a problem for me. When I get into bed, my mind starts racing. I toss and turn; it's as if I'm being flooded with adrenaline. Then I'll pass out for a while, and the dreams I have are horrible—they're like hallucinations. When I get up, I feel exhausted.

Sponsor

In the first few weeks of recovery, especially from physical addictions—alcohol, food, drugs, cigarettes—sleep disturbances are likely to occur. Our bodies are still undergoing a process of detoxification and rebalancing. When we feel as if we're being flooded with adrenaline, that's probably exactly what's happening. Night and day may be turned around. Sleep problems vary from person to person, depending on former addictive patterns. Some may sleep a lot, with dreams that feel hallucinatory; others may feel as if they've been lying awake for days. When we used our addictive substance or behavior, we were numbing ourselves so that we wouldn't have to feel certain things. Those feelings don't go away just because we've entered recovery.

The extremes you're experiencing will level off as recovery continues. Bodies have a natural tendency to heal. One morning, you will wake up refreshed, surprised to realize that you've had a night's rest. You can help the process along by avoiding caffeine or heavy eating at night, by drinking plenty of water, and by beginning to add some form of gentle exercise to your day. A walk or some gentle yoga or stretching can do more than you'd think to help your body detoxify and regain hormonal balance.

**Today, I cooperate with the natural process
that is healing my body and spirit.**

22

Over and over, we begin again.
BANANA YOSHIMOTO

Newcomer

Yesterday was such a difficult day. But here it is, morning again—somehow, I've gotten through another twenty-four hours, and without a drug. I wish I'd known yesterday that things wouldn't feel so bad this morning.

Sponsor

Yesterday, we did the best that we could. Yesterday is over. We have slept. We think we know some of what today will hold. We may boil water in the same kitchen, take the same route to work, see some of the faces we usually see. At the meeting we attend, we'll hear the familiar readings, take comfort from hearing the words we've heard before. Perhaps our shoulders, hunched with any tensions we're experiencing, will drop at the sound of those accustomed words, and we'll relax.

Along with the predictable, there may be a thousand unexpected experiences: a new color in the sky, a smile answering our own, a phrase of music, a sense of willingness rising within us to do something differently.

Let's take some deep, slow breaths and begin the day with faith that whatever it brings, we'll be present for it.

This day is a gift that recovery has given to me.

23

The more you can experience the interconnectedness of all beings, the healthier you will be.
ANDREW WEIL

Newcomer

I'm spending a lot of time traveling, because I don't like going to meetings in my neighborhood. What if someone who knows who I am happens to see me going in, or even shows up at a meeting?

Sponsor

Of course, you can travel to other neighborhoods if you want to—it's not going to hurt anyone. But I wonder if your fear is justified. Most people I know are thinking about their own lives, not about mine. In the unlikely event that a neighbor sees me walking into a church or community center for a meeting, he probably won't know just where in that building I'm going or why, unless he's been to the same meeting!

I appreciate having meetings in common with people in

my neighborhood. Though I'm certainly not required to become friends with them all, I feel strengthened knowing that we share a program of recovery. Once, in early recovery, feeling in danger of having a slip, I recognized another recovering person coming down the street toward me. We nodded to one another and moved on. I didn't know her well, but seeing her reminded me of my own connection to the program and of what a gift recovery has been in my life. Perhaps your example will save someone else's life one day, whether you know it or not; meanwhile, you're saving your own.

> Today, I let go of self-centered fear.
> As someone who shows up for recovery,
> I'm willing to be a power of example.

24

A friend is a person with whom I may be sincere. Before him I may think aloud.
RALPH WALDO EMERSON

Newcomer

Someone from where I used to work showed up at the meeting I went to last night. I was uncomfortable, and I avoided looking straight at him, but I'm pretty sure he saw me. What happens to my anonymity now? I don't want the whole world to know my problems.

Sponsor

I'm glad that you've raised this question; it's an important one. What, exactly, is "anonymity" with respect to Twelve Step fellowships? The root of the word means, literally, "without a name." I honor the tradition of anonymity by not mentioning your name in connection with the name of this program. I may decide to tell someone that I've been at a meeting, but I will not say that I saw you there. And I must never talk to anyone about what you've shared here. That won't change after I've been here ninety days, or a year, or twenty years. I never have the right to break your anonymity to people in the community, even your close friends or family—that choice is yours and no one else's. We all share this trust, and most of us are surprisingly good at honoring it. Anonymity gives a sense of freedom essential to recovery. If you bump into this person again, maybe you'll just nod a greeting, or maybe you'll reassure him that he can trust you to respect *his* anonymity!

Today, I have no room in my life for gossip or self-consciousness. I feel joy at seeing others participate in recovery.

 25

Day in, day out
I hunger and
I struggle
SAPPHO

Newcomer

I have so many problems. I have debts. I feel anxious and shaky at work. Meanwhile, friends and family members expect me to be the same person I've always been. I'm totally overwhelmed.

Sponsor

In recovery, we have a future to look forward to. Over time, we learn new ways to approach situations that trouble us. But we can't do anything differently if we're still in the throes of our disease. We cannot rush recovery.

You can learn to treat yourself gently, as you would a baby or a kitten, or a sick or injured person lying in a hospital bed. You wouldn't yell at such a person, *Get up! You have work to do! Stop wasting time!* You'd be tender and understanding. You would not begrudge a baby, or someone recovering from illness, time for rest, food, or medicine. Taking some time for meetings is essential to the healing process. Prayer and meditation can help calm you when you feel overwhelmed.

We are entitled to take time for recovery.

Today, I treat myself tenderly and patiently.
I deserve to recover. I allow myself time for healing.

26

This is a "we" program.
SAYING HEARD AT MEETINGS

Newcomer

Why must I have a sponsor? Can't I do this on my own?

Sponsor

Sponsorship is a strong suggestion—not a rule. Yes, some people do stay in recovery without a sponsor. And no, we can't recover on our own.

There are great advantages to taking the program suggestion to maintain a relationship with a sponsor. Recovery is a major change—it's one of the most difficult, most courageous things we can do in our lives. A sponsor, someone who's survived the ups and downs we're facing in early recovery, can serve as a guide and mentor. He or she can answer our questions and help us through the Steps, giving us the benefit of his or her experience. With a sponsor present to witness our recovery process, to offer perspective and support, we may have a gentler ride.

When I was active in my addiction, I avoided the intimacy of relationships in which I might have to open myself to others or trust them. Even at times when there were many people in my life, I managed to avoid "people situations" that made me uncomfortable. A sponsor-sponsee relationship can be the start of learning that human beings can depend on one another.

Today, I'm not alone in recovery.

27

I took the portion that was given to me and gave it to him.
THE BABYLONIAN TALMUD

Newcomer
Are there any rules about how to find a sponsor?

Sponsor

Some meetings have interim sponsorship programs. An interim sponsor works with a newcomer temporarily—a few weeks to a few months—while he or she looks for a regular long-term sponsor. Sometimes, an interim sponsor becomes the newcomer's regular sponsor, if they both agree to it.

Long-term sponsorship is a relationship of trust, one that's likely to have a significant impact on the process of recovery. It's not a good idea to choose impulsively. When we attend meetings, we listen closely as people qualify or share. We'll hear people who have the serenity and sober experience we ourselves want. If we hear someone we think we'd like to ask to be our sponsor, we try phoning or going out for coffee with him or her first. We take a little time. We soon know whether or not we have the willingness to share and to listen. We sense whether this is someone whose guidance we can trust.

Sponsors should have a minimum of one year of recovery. It's suggested that a sponsor's gender not be that of his or her sponsee's sexual preference; for example, a heterosexual woman generally shouldn't choose a heterosexual male sponsor. It's a suggestion, not a rule, meant to keep the way clear, so that sponsors and sponsees don't get distracted from their goal. The goal is continued, quality recovery—for both the sponsor and the sponsee.

Today, I welcome a sponsor-sponsee relationship
that encourages and supports my recovery.

Sincerity is the foundation of the spiritual life.
ALBERT SCHWEITZER

Newcomer

I started out with a temporary sponsor. She was the one who spoke to me first. She seemed to like me and to have real concern for how I was doing as a newcomer. At first, we talked a lot. She knew what being a newcomer was like and said some things that went pretty deep.

Then she became hard to reach. She took her time returning my calls, and when I finally asked if something was wrong, she said she thought I should get a regular sponsor. I was angry and hurt. We'd worked together so well at first.

Sponsor

Some people prefer working with newcomers, helping them through the roller coaster of early recovery, but aren't available as long-term sponsors. Whatever the underlying reasons, it's a preference—just as some parents take more naturally to parenting very young, dependent children, while others have an easier time with kids who can walk and talk and read books. There's nothing wrong with that—it's just a fact.

Of course, it helps if a sponsor is clear with us from the beginning about the limits of his or her availability. Confusion sets in when people send us mixed signals. I don't know all the specifics of what occurred between you and your interim sponsor, or whether there was a clear understanding between the two of you at the outset. But what is perfectly clear is her last message: when she suggested that you find another sponsor, then stopped returning calls, she let you know that she was no longer available to you.

I respect your desire to extend the relationship with your temporary sponsor; I, too, can still feel the power of my first attachments in this program. But when someone says no to us, it's wise to believe what they say. It's freedom.

Today, I remember that many people are willing to help me on my path.

 **29**

They try to pass along something they themselves have not yet received.
LEWIS HYDE

Newcomer
What do I do if someone I don't know offers to be my sponsor?

Sponsor
Sometimes, a volunteer sponsor is the best thing that could happen to a newcomer who's floundering or confused and who would do well with strong guidance. Sometimes it's not such a good thing. What are the motives of someone who walks up to me and announces, "I'm your sponsor"? How do I know the difference between someone whose offer of service is sincere and someone who has the wish to control me? Or worse, who wants to prey on me—sexually or in some other way?

Control is an issue for most of us in recovery. As a sponsor, I have to be careful about my impulse to try to "fix" another person. It may make me feel powerful to think I've got the answers; it may distract me from my own unsolved problems. Overresponsibility can be an addiction, too.

If I have doubts about what someone in recovery is offering me, I can take some time to talk and to listen. I can trust my instincts. If I listen, I may discover that I already have the answer inside me.

Today, I'm grateful for the unconditional love offered by others in recovery. I trust my ability to make good choices as I form relationships with people I meet, here and elsewhere.

 *30*

How easy it was to underestimate what had been endured.
MARGARET DRABBLE

Newcomer
I heard someone share that it was her anniversary and that she wanted to celebrate by stepping in front of a car and killing herself. How can someone talk that way at a meeting? I don't want to listen to it.

Sponsor
The first thing I notice about this dramatic statement is that it was made at a meeting. As desperate as the person who made it may have been feeling, she did not act out her addiction, but instead showed up and shared. I've walked into meetings feeling depressed, despairing, angry, rebellious, alone, or misunderstood, and when I've been willing to share my state of mind, have felt sudden relief.

Not knowing the person who shared, and not being experts, we can't really know how seriously to take such a statement. From one person, it might be a sign that compassionate professional help is needed; from another, it might be just a bit of self-indulgent humor or a bid for attention. People come to meetings in many different frames of mind, with different life experiences, and with recovery of varying lengths and quality. Some make everything they experience sound like high drama; others are reluctant to expose depths of real pain. And, of course, there are many people with strong recovery who use the tools of the program to help them "ride the waves" of life's problems with relative ease and even joy.

Rather than focus on your discomfort with someone else's sharing, why not keep the focus on yourself and your own recovery work?

Today, I say a prayer for those who are still
sick and suffering, in or out of this program. I give my
attention to the work that's mine to do in recovery.

 *31*

I like to think that at birth, everyone is allotted
a quantity of alcohol to last for her whole life,
and that by the time I was in my twenties,
I'd already consumed my entire quota!
WOMAN IN RECOVERY

Newcomer

I can't get my mind off what I'm missing. I think that at this point I could control myself and just use moderately. Ordinary people have a glass of wine when they eat dinner at a restaurant, or have a beer on a hot summer day. Why do I have to deprive myself?

Sponsor

Frankly, I can't imagine a better way to torture myself than making the decision to have just a little. I'd be preoccupied with that little bit all day long: waiting beforehand for the right time to have it, then resenting its being over, afterward. For me, how could just a little ever be enough? And how could I keep from rationalizing, after a while, having just a little bit more? My biochemistry and my mental obsession make me crave certain substances whenever I have them. Other people may not react this way—but I'm not other people. My susceptibility turns something that may be safe for others into poison for me. There is one simple way for me to keep from craving more of this poison, and that is to avoid it altogether. Over time, deprivation takes on a new meaning—we no longer have the desire to deprive ourselves of this experience of recovery.

For today, I stop my craving by not feeding it.
I make room for a new, better life.

32

To accept a favor from a friend is to confer one.
JOHN CHURTON COLLINS

Newcomer

I've been okay for the past few days, so I haven't called you. I feel as if I'm calling you too much. I don't know what you could possibly be getting out of it.

Sponsor

I identify with your fear of imposing on other people, so I want to say first that I'm grateful for your phone calls. They help me to stay sober, just as much as they help you. They remind me, every day, of our addiction, and they remind me of the ways we're growing and being healed.

When we stay in daily touch with a sponsor, it helps to keep us from "slipping through the cracks." Though I go to a meeting, make coffee or put away chairs, say hello to a few people, even put up my hand and share, there may be parts of my recovery process that I don't understand, don't like to talk about, or don't get to talk about in depth. I can share more deeply and at greater length with my sponsor. My sponsor knows me pretty well by now and is likely to bring up recovery issues I'd rather evade or bury. Calling our sponsors isn't always easy, but it's part of our commitment to ourselves and our recovery.

**Today, I'm willing to know others
and to be known by them.**

 *33*

Argue not concerning God.
WALT WHITMAN

Newcomer

It's obvious from what I hear people saying in meetings that God is a pretty important part of Twelve Step programs. What if I don't believe in God or a Higher Power?

Sponsor

We don't need religion in order to recover. The only requirement for membership is a desire to stop using our preferred addictive substance or behavior. To recover, we have to put down what we're addicted to, and we have to come to meetings. Not easy, perhaps, but simple and clear.

Whether or not we believe in God, most of us recognize that we don't live entirely independently. The phrase "a Power greater than ourselves," from Step Two, is a reminder to me that I don't run the universe. Whatever I believe about God's existence, I have to accept that I myself am not God—if I'm going to recover. I can't control my addiction on my own. Willpower stopped working for me some time ago. I owe this newfound willingness to recover to someone or something that isn't my intellect or will.

Those who reject traditional concepts of God can still point to something inside—what some call their "better self," their "sense of right and wrong," their "higher self," or their "spirit"—that got them here. The desire for wholeness has somehow proved stronger than the impulse toward self-destruction.

Today, I accept that I'm not all-powerful.

34

For extreme illnesses, extreme treatments are necessary.
HIPPOCRATES

Newcomer
I keep hearing people refer to this problem as a disease. I'm not sure I buy that. I've stopped, haven't I?

Sponsor
The "disease debate" reminds me of the old saying, "If it looks like a duck, if it walks like a duck, if it quacks like a duck—then it must be a duck."

We know from experience that our addiction, untreated, is a craving so powerful that we have no choice but to put it first, before our goals and ideals, before work, health, and love. Willpower and promises may curb our addictive use for brief periods, but our physical craving and mental obsession return. Lives are shattered in the process. Some of us die.

Yet we persist in thinking that our addictive behavior is a moral issue. If we could just pull ourselves together, we could stop for good. Good intentions and inspirational messages haven't worked for us, but we try them again and again. We forget that recovery isn't about stopping, but about *staying* stopped.

We can look at it as good news that we have a disease. Accepting this helps us become willing to make the radical changes in our spiritual, mental, and physical lives that are required for our survival. We're grateful for the "medicine" of meetings, literature, phone calls, sponsorship, and service. It's helping us create new, healthy selves.

Today, I'm grateful for the lifesaving principles of this program.

 *35*

No one knows what he can do till he tries.
PUBLILIUS SYRUS

Newcomer
I feel as if I have no energy. When I get home from work, I force myself to go to a meeting, but all I really want to do is sleep.

Sponsor

At the end of active addiction, we were exhausted. Our bodies were used to brief, intense pickups—from drugs or cigarettes, from foods containing large amounts of caffeine and sugar, from the high of acting out behavioral addictions—after which we "crashed." The boost to our physical or mental energy was brief. Low blood sugar, depression, and renewed craving were the other side of this depleting cycle.

For me, exhaustion returned after the "high" of early recovery. I badly needed rest. This meant sleep, nutritious food, and, in my case, vitamin and mineral supplements. To my surprise, it also meant exercise.

How can we think about jogging around a track when we're feeling exhausted? If we haven't been exercising regularly, the key word to remember is *gentleness*. We can begin with a few minutes of gentle stretching in the morning. We can put on sneakers and walk for a short time each day. Or we can choose some other activity that appeals to us and that feels more like play than work. Surprisingly, regular physical movement increases our feelings of energy and well-being—sometimes more effectively than napping. It helps our digestion and circulation, balances our body weight, strengthens our bones, and helps us feel centered and refreshed.

Whatever we choose to do to get our bodies moving, gentleness and consistency are the keys.

Today, I nourish my body and spirit with gentle exercise.

They are dead even while they are alive.
LAWRENCE KUSHNER

Newcomer

What exactly is a blackout? I can't figure out whether I've had them or not.

Sponsor

The term "blackout" usually refers to a period of time when we acted under the influence of an addictive substance, but later couldn't remember or account for what we did. Many recovering alcoholics, for example, whether their drinking was daily or periodic, speak of having had to make phone calls "the morning after" to find out what they said or did the previous night. Blacking out as a result of drinking is one of the warning signs of alcoholism; it can last a few minutes or several days. Some have found themselves in strange beds, or even in foreign countries, with no memory of how they got there. Some people have killed during blackouts.

We don't have to be using alcohol, drugs, or other substances to experience the blackout phenomenon. Some of us use the term more loosely to name a state in which, demoralized or compelled by our addiction, we behaved as if we weren't "all there"—took unnecessary sexual risks, for example, or spent money we didn't have, lied, forgot commitments, or acted in other ways we were later ashamed of. We say of such moments, "I was in an emotional blackout" or "I behaved as if I were in a blackout."

Today, I look at places my addiction took me
without my full consent. I'm grateful for my ability
to make conscious choices in recovery.

This disease is like an elevator going down;
you can get off at any floor.
WOMAN IN RECOVERY

Newcomer

What does it mean to say, "I've hit bottom"? People seem to mean different things by it. I've heard some who have been homeless, others who have lived luxuriously. And a whole lot of people seem to have had pretty ordinary lives with typical human problems.

Sponsor

I've heard it said that if you stay in recovery, your story gets worse as time goes on. For me, that means that as I cleared up and listened to recovering people tell about their lives, I gradually remembered more about my own: places I'd forgotten my addiction had brought me to. Actual places, yes—but even more important, places in my soul. Feelings of uselessness and despair, feelings that somehow, somewhere, I'd lost the dreams I'd once had for my life. Whether you and I consumed the same quantity of what we're addicted to, whether we had trust funds or were living on the street, spiritually we arrived at the same place. Instead of comparing my story with yours, I think about what, exactly, brought me here. No one gets here by mistake.

Today, I remember what got me here.
I know that I'm in the right place.

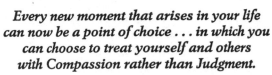

38

Every new moment that arises in your life
can now be a point of choice . . . in which you
can choose to treat yourself and others
with Compassion rather than Judgment.

DAVID HARP

Newcomer

I wince every time I hear the words "God as we understood Him" and "Higher Power." When meetings close with the Lord's Prayer, I feel like I'm being railroaded. I don't fit into the same religious slot that other people seem to take for granted.

Sponsor

All of us qualify to be here, but not because of any religious identification or belief. Most of us are tolerant of differences, but, being human, some of us forget that not everyone shares the same religious context. Whatever an individual member has to say about the role of his or her Higher Power, the only requirement for membership is the desire to stop using the addictive substance that got us here.

Once I heard a member say, "This meeting is my church." I'm glad that notion works for her. By the same token, I've always been grateful that this program is *not* a church—otherwise, I might have to rebel against it! We're not required to subscribe to a particular set of religious beliefs or rituals. In recovery, each of us is free to explore what we believe.

Today, I respect others' rights to their beliefs,
just as I respect my own. I bring my love of openness,
inclusiveness, and harmony with me wherever I go.

39

But let me think away those times of woe;
Now 'tis a fairer season. . . .
JOHN KEATS

Newcomer

I feel trapped and miserable. I don't want to pick up my addiction, but, frankly, my life feels bleak without it. I'm not like those goody-goodies who do everything right and spout program. I'll never be like them. What's the point of being in recovery, if I feel this bad?

Sponsor

In recovery, I make the decision not to change my mood with an addictive substance or behavior today. And I can make other decisions as well. Recovery is the freedom to make choices. I can choose to remain isolated with feelings of fear, anger, and loneliness, or I can choose to share my feelings with another recovering person. I can arrange to go to a meeting. I can make phone calls—even short ones—to people whose numbers I have asked for. If I only reach answering machines (some days are like that!) I can choose to leave messages asking people to call back. I can let go of results, knowing that I've done my part. If I'm feeling stressed, I can light a candle or just sit quietly for a few moments to relax and breathe. I may read a page from some program literature.

We can choose to put yesterday and tomorrow "on the shelf" and just let ourselves be, for this moment.

Today, I make choices that support my recovery.
I have the willingness to be happy.

40

Example is always more efficacious than precept.
SAMUEL JOHNSON

Newcomer

It's devastating to me to watch old friends and family members whose lives are still being screwed up by this disease. How can I convince them to join me in recovery before it's too late? I'm sad and frustrated. Life's so unfair! Why am I in recovery, while they're still suffering?

Sponsor

Recovery is a gift that somehow, against all the odds, has been given to you. You can refuse it, trash it, or think yourself out of it. Loss of recovery not only would be your loss, but would also be a loss to all who could be helped by your example. You have a responsibility to maintain it each day, to nurture it by going to meetings, by using the tools that have been given to you, and above all by not picking up addictive substances and behaviors.

Friends and family members who need recovery but who don't want it yet may be able to see the changes in us over time. Even though we'd like more than anything to persuade them to do themselves a favor and join us in recovery right now, we need to accept that this approach doesn't work. Could anyone have persuaded you?

I am entitled to the gift of my recovery.
I cherish this gift, not by preaching or trying to rescue
others, but by making recovery central in my own life.

41

As we advance in life, we learn the limits of our abilities.
JAMES FROUDE

Newcomer

If I hear "This is a 'we' program" one more time, I'll get sick. I don't like groups, I don't like the idea of depending on this program, and I don't like the idea of depending on a Higher Power to take care of me. I've always been a strong person. I cherish my independence.

Sponsor

Let's take a look at some different kinds of dependency. Of course, there are dependencies that aren't appropriate; they keep us from growing, just as our addictions did. For example, a parent's continuing financial support of a grown child who is capable of earning a living on his or her own enables a mutual dependency that's probably unhealthy for both parties.

There are other kinds of dependency that most of us accept without hesitation. When we strike a match, we expect a flame; when we put seeds into the earth, we trust that plants will grow. Dependency isn't enslavement. If we're diabetic and depend on daily insulin to regulate our blood sugar level, we don't regard ourselves as weak. We're grateful that the means exist to keep our disease in check. The same is true of Twelve Step programs for those of us who acknowledge our addictions. We can count on these meetings being here when we need them. We can count on the fact that if we follow the program, we will not have to depend on addictive substances and behaviors.

Today, my willingness to depend on
this program gives me freedom.

Rest in natural great peace.
NYOSHUL KHENPO

Newcomer

I keep hearing people say that giving up the addiction itself is only the beginning of the process. Today, I'm feeling upset and downhearted. I don't know if I can face the literature on the Steps yet.

Sponsor

As we prepare to continue on the path of the Steps, we can do an exercise that helps quiet our mental agitation and gently begins to restore our sense of connection with positive forces in our lives. We start by finding a comfortable position, either sitting or lying down, with our spines straight but relaxed. We can close our eyes, if that helps us concentrate. We take several deeper, slower breaths. Then we take a few minutes to think of positive aspects of our lives. One by one, we make mental note of things we're grateful for. If we can't think of any, we begin with air, water, food, then see what else occurs to us. As each blessing comes to mind, we picture it clearly and see ourselves benefiting from it. We breathe it in, and breathe out heartfelt gratitude. This is an exercise we can do any time of the day or night, even in situations when we're not alone. It need only take a few moments.

Cultivating gratitude can help change our belief that what lies ahead will be burdensome. When you're ready to begin exploring the Steps, you may even feel the joy and excitement that accompany an adventure.

Today, I feel life's richness and beauty. I let it fill me.

43

***When God wants to be what is not God,
man comes to be.***
KARL RAHNER

Newcomer

I listened to a long reading from the AA Big Book that was all about atheists and agnostics, and how, if they expect to stay in recovery, they have to recognize the evidence that God exists. I didn't find the God argument very convincing. Sometimes I think that the program literature is incredibly illogical and old-fashioned.

Sponsor

Yes, there are days like that. I, too, have sat in meetings saying, "No, no, no" to everything that I heard said about God. Though I may resist certain ideas, it helps me to remember that this isn't a debating society. I don't have to agree with everything I hear, but I'm not in this program to make intellectual arguments against the existence of a Power greater than myself. The intellect I'm so proud of today neither prevented me from engaging in addictive behavior nor led me to recovery. I'm here to address my addiction, and my path is the path of my spirit.

Each of us knows what our own experience of a Higher Power is. We don't find this Power through argument—our own or anyone else's—but through going deep within. We know that when we entered recovery, we surrendered our heavy task of trying to be God. Our egos are no longer in charge.

Today, I don't have to be my own Higher Power.

44

*The business of being human among other humans
is holy business.*

CATHERINE MADSEN

Newcomer

I keep hearing that this isn't a religious program. So why is the word "God" everywhere? It's in the Steps, and I hear people use it when they share in meetings. When they say "HP," doesn't it mean the same thing? And then there's all this prayer and "spiritual awakening" stuff. How can you say it isn't religious?

Sponsor

There is a big difference between the religious and the spiritual. This is a spiritual program. When I see in Step Twelve the words "having had a spiritual awakening as the result of these steps," I think, not of a voice from the mountaintop, but of the ways my spirit has come alive—how I've become capable of living in the here and now, connected to my fellow human beings, conscious of so much I used to miss out on.

The program makes suggestions, not rules. There are no priests or rabbis, no prescribed beliefs, no blasphemies, no excommunication. "God as we understood Him" and "Higher Power" are terms meant to allow each of us his or her own understanding of the energy that sustains us. This program is not about what we believe, but about what actions we take—how we stay away from addictive substances, how we help others to stay on the path of recovery.

**Today, I know that many things other than
my own will are sustaining me.
I don't have to be in charge of my own recovery.**

45

Newcomer

Step Two begins, "We came to believe . . ." I'm uncomfortable with the idea that sooner or later I'm going to have to have the same belief in God that everyone else here has.

Sponsor

I'd be uncomfortable with that, too. Step Two isn't about sticking around until your beliefs are similar to others' beliefs. I can assure you that not everyone here shares the same spiritual beliefs or practices. Far from it.

I didn't come here seeking to embrace a particular, prescribed belief, but I did come here seeking something. Addiction was in charge of my life. It had been a long time since I'd felt that I could truly believe in myself, in my connection with others. I was exhausted, scared, unhappy. Some people call this "rock bottom." Some call it a spiritual crisis.

When I could admit that I wanted to stop my addictive behavior and that I hadn't been able to stay stopped on my own, something changed. After coming to some meetings, I felt less alone, and I felt hope. I could look within myself and acknowledge that something in me wanted to live. The life spirit at the center of my existence was waking up. I wanted to be whole again.

In Step Two, we begin to accept that healing is possible, and that, in fact, it has begun.

Today, I look inward and see light and health.

46

No one should have to dance backward all their lives.
JILL RUCKELSHAUS

Newcomer

When I was active in my addiction, I often felt smart and strong. Now that I'm in recovery, I feel little and weak and depressed. I'm afraid I'm never going to feel like a full human being again.

Sponsor

Many of us have similar fears at the beginning of recovery. Back in the early days of being active, we were convinced that we had the key to living. There were behaviors we engaged in that lent us feelings of power and control. We may look back wistfully at those days when we felt stronger, smarter, more important. We wish we could have those feelings again, without paying the penalty.

But we need to remember the deprivation or panic we felt when we had to do without whatever magic "pill" we depended on to put us together each day. We can't forget the times when addiction only made bad situations worse. We don't want to repeat the crash we experienced when the drug or addictive behavior stopped being effective and our self-doubts came back.

Strength, intelligence, and competence don't, in fact, depend on addictive substances and behaviors. They are ours. They are returning to us over time in recovery, and in much more dependable ways.

Today, my gifts are emerging into the light.

**One must have a good memory
to be able to keep the promises one makes.**
FRIEDRICH NIETZSCHE

Newcomer

What's the point of pretending that I'm giving up my drug of choice one day at a time, when I know I have to quit for the rest of my life? Isn't it hypocritical?

Sponsor

There's nothing hypocritical about living in the present moment. It's an old and honored spiritual path. To be fully awake and alive in this day, using our senses to experience what's going on right now, not avoiding our feelings, not playing games with our minds, is a profound achievement. Living in the future isn't living; it's keeping our minds so busy that we can't be here. The role of our addictions is escape; its opposite is living in the here and now.

At some time, we've probably promised ourselves or others that we were never again going to act out our addictions. We weren't able to keep these promises; in the past, we didn't know how not to use.

Limiting our focus in recovery to a twenty-four-hour period makes the challenges we face seem more manageable. We can get through twenty-four hours, no matter what. At the end of it, we can rest. It doesn't mean that we'll forget all about recovery tomorrow—only that we are willing to live in recovery now.

**Today, I commit myself to living
this one day of recovery fully.**

The road to Hades is easy to travel.
BION

Newcomer

I hear people say, "This is a progressive disease," and I understand that from my own experience. I did get progressively worse—I had my ups and downs over the years and hit what I now recognize as a bottom. But how can people say that the disease keeps progressing even when we're in recovery? What does that mean?

Sponsor

Many relapses follow a predictable course: At first, we hang on to the illusion that control is now possible—a little time in recovery has proved that we don't have to act out our addiction. We think we can behave like "normal" people and "have a little" now and then. It may take only a few hours or days for this illusion to collapse, or it may take weeks or months; most of the stories we hear suggest that the return of active addiction comes quickly. Perhaps our "clean" systems succumb more readily, perhaps our need to anesthetize the guilt of relapsing leads to stepped-up use, or perhaps we're in rebellion against what we learned in recovery: the "I'll show them" reaction. The reasons seem less important than the fact that most people who relapse after a period of recovery find that they've gotten worse, not better, at handling the addiction. Though there's no guarantee that someone who has had a relapse will find his or her way back, some do return to recovery and share with us what they've learned.

Today, I cherish this chance at recovery,
letting go of any need to test it.

49

Body and Spirit are twins.
ALGERNON SWINBURNE

Newcomer

I want to be responsible, and I'm trying to clear up the paperwork and phone calls I'm behind in, and the messes I've made. But I can hardly sit still. I start feeling a sensation of pressure in my chest and throat. I worry that I could be having a heart attack.

Sponsor

When I first entered recovery, I didn't realize what a profound impact the substances I'd been using had had on my central nervous system. Cleansing my body of their effects, rebuilding my strength, and restoring balance took time. I was anxious all the time, and my nerves were shot. For me, a checkup by a medical professional familiar with the effects of addiction was reassuring and informative. In my case—and this was just for me—I needed nutritional supplements and regular exercise. But I still felt scared and sad a lot of the time.

Feelings are a part of life. We don't have to "fix" them; they're just feelings. They pass through us without harming us, if we let them. As we go through the work of early recovery, it's not unusual for intense emotions to arise. They seem to flow more easily when we share them with others. If chores seem daunting, we can work on them a little bit at a time. It's okay to ask for help.

My body, mind, and spirit are going through
huge changes as I recover. Today, I share my feelings.
I request and accept help.

50

Faith needs her daily bread.
DINAH CRAIK

Newcomer

I still don't feel very serene when I wake up in the morning. I start worrying as soon as I'm awake, usually about someone I'm afraid of or have a resentment against. I guess I'm having trouble staying in the present.

Sponsor

You're not alone in what you're experiencing. Some of us describe morning anxiety as "the committee in my head" or "the disease." I've heard people in early recovery say, "My disease gets up before I do; it's already sitting at the foot of my bed when I open my eyes."

Some of us make a program phone call first thing in the morning; even a few minutes' talk with another recovering person can help put our morning fears in perspective and help us face the day with lightness. This works both ways: both the caller and the person called are nourished by the contact.

While we're still in bed, we can gently stretch our bodies any way that feels comfortable, then take several slow, deep, complete breaths. We can begin our day by reading and meditating on a page of program literature or other spiritual literature that appeals to us. And we can spend a few moments in prayer. For many years now, I've begun my day offering thanks for the day and for all the days that have led to it. I turn over anything that worries me, affirming that my Higher Power will show me how to handle whatever the day offers.

Today, I center myself in prayer.

> *There are moments when everything goes well;*
> *don't be frightened, it won't last.*
> **JULES RENARD**

Newcomer

Yesterday, I had a pretty good day. I woke up feeling rested after a night's sleep. The weather was just the way I like it. I enjoyed the food I ate. I finished the work I was supposed to do. I went to a meeting and was asked to share. It was a little bit like being in love—with recovery! Today, nothing is going my way. I woke up late. I feel rushed and pressured. This weather depresses me. A good friend misunderstood everything I said. I showed up at a meeting, and nobody even said hello.

Sponsor

When I was active in my addiction, dramatic highs and lows were the pattern of my life. I needed my drug of choice to manage my moods. Even without it, I may continue to experience mood swings. Recovery doesn't happen in a day, a week, a period of months; it's a gradual, ongoing process. Just as consistent rest and good nutrition restore my body to health and balance over time, consistent use of the tools of the program helps put me on an even keel mentally and spiritually. As I maintain new, sober habits, the off days have less power to throw me. Sometimes I even remember to laugh at myself or to reach out and help another human being. We choose not to take self-prescribed mood changers today; cultivating a sense of humor and helping out at meetings are among the "legal" mood changers that work, when we remember to use them.

Today, I don't expect to have it made.
I accept the unique challenges of this day
as if they were gifts. I am consistent in using
the tools of recovery I've been given, no matter what.

52

*Living entirely turned in on oneself is like trying to play
on a violin with slackened strings.*
JACQUES LUSSEYRAN

Newcomer

I went to a meeting today feeling angry, rebellious, and bored. I hated sitting there, and I hardly listened. It was the round-robin kind of meeting where the discussion goes from person to person: you get to share without raising your hand. When it was my turn, I said how resentful and different I felt, how I hated everything about the program and didn't think it could help me. People nodded, some laughed, and the speaker said, "We've all been there." I felt relieved. Often, I don't start feeling okay until almost the end of a meeting. I wish I didn't have to keep going through this.

Sponsor

As an addicted person, I have a special talent for letting negative thoughts and feelings take over. It's as if my mind were a balloon filled with heavy, dark stuff; left to my own devices, I keep blowing it bigger, filling it with more of the same. It takes another person, someone who lives outside of my mind, to prick the balloon and let my tired old thoughts escape. Suddenly, reality looks completely different. That's one reason to get to some small meetings where we're more likely to have a chance to share. And it's always a good idea to stay through a whole meeting; in an hour, things can change! I've noticed that even when I share my most unacceptable feelings, people in recovery don't reject me; when I tell the worst about myself, they listen and laugh. I love the laughter in meetings; it reminds me of how lucky we are to be alive again.

Today, it's safe for me to risk getting close to other human beings by sharing honestly.

53

The total person sings, not just the vocal chords.
ESTHER BRONER

Newcomer
Last night, I dreamed I had a slip. There I was, sneaking my addictive substance, in such a small quantity that it didn't seem to matter. When I realized that I'd have to face people at a meeting, I thought, "I just won't tell them; they'll never know." I woke up with my heart pounding. It seemed so real that at first I wasn't sure it had been a dream.

Sponsor
Most of us have had dreams or fantasies of using, especially in early recovery. They're useful as a source of information,

like a letter from one part of the mind to another. They remind us of who we are: underneath conscious awareness is someone who wouldn't mind going back to using and being sneaky and dishonest, who wouldn't care if we died in the process. The good news is that this *was* a dream, that you woke up in recovery, and that you chose to share your discomfort. Acknowledging our negative thoughts robs them of their power over us. Dreaming of a relapse, and talking about it, may help keep us from having one.

Today, I am not in denial.
Awareness of my addictive self strengthens my recovery.

54

Earth's the right place for love.
ROBERT FROST

Newcomer

I have to get up early in the morning, so I don't like hanging around after evening meetings. I always thank the speaker, but then I leave pretty quickly, so that I won't get caught in one of those long, drawn-out conversations, miss out on sleep, and feel tired the next day. I do feel a little funny leaving, though, almost as if I'm sneaking out.

Sponsor

I wonder if you're leaving early because you don't have a second to spare, or for some other reason. There's a happy medium, somewhere between a long, drawn-out conversation and sneaking out. Saying hello, sharing some hugs or handshakes, exchanging phone numbers with someone we'd like to talk to later, or briefly joining the crew that's putting away chairs are some of the simple ways of feeling more like a part of things.

For me, making genuine contact with my peers in recovery is essential. When I was in early recovery, I called myself "shy" or "too busy" when in truth I was wary of people, even somewhat frightened. I chose to sit at the edge of things, then blamed others for my belief that I was an outsider. Becoming willing to set limits, to say no confidently when I needed to, freed me to enjoy getting to know others.

To be at ease in a group of people doesn't always come naturally, but it's one of the most important areas of recovery.

Today, I make good use of time by reaching out to people.

~ *55* ~

Your misery can always be refunded.
SAYING HEARD AT MEETINGS

Newcomer
I heard someone say, "Recovery ruins your drinking." What does that mean?

Sponsor
From our first day in recovery, we know that there is an alternative to our suffering. We may choose to ignore that knowledge, but we can't entirely erase it. We can't convince ourselves that we can safely go back to what we've done in the past. The recovering part of us just won't buy it.

We've changed many things about our lives. We go to meetings, call sponsors, show up for work and for situations involving others. We read literature we hadn't even heard of a short time ago, and we talk openly to people who, until recently, were complete strangers to us. We're examining our lives, challenging every belief and value we previously held.

All this change is knowledge. If we return to an addictive substance or behavior after a period of recovery, we do so knowing that we're acting out our addiction. We can't sustain our denial; we know that we're risking our lives and hurting others. And we know that there are people sitting in meetings, giving each other mutual support, facing the same addiction. It's hard to pretend that acting on the addiction instead of treating it gives us lasting pleasure or security.

Today, I'm living in the solution, not in the problem.

56

Things are in the saddle,
And ride mankind.
RALPH WALDO EMERSON

Newcomer
I have a life, not just this program. Work deadlines, family obligations, bills, things I have to get done. I have a lot of responsibility, and it isn't going to go away just because I'm in recovery. And now I have all these new things I'm supposed to do: meetings, phone calls, literature, Steps. I desperately need some time off to catch up with my real life.

Sponsor

When I was active in my disease, time was my enemy. Sometimes I let obligations slide until a situation felt desperate. Sometimes I threw myself into my duties, worked without stopping, then burned out. Recovery offers me a simple way to deal with responsibilities: one day at a time.

Maintaining recovery by attending a meeting, making a call, and reading literature—things we do to stay sober today—takes less time than the hours we spent pursuing our addictions, indulging in them, being slowed down or stopped by them. Working on things consistently, even just a little each day, produces results in all areas of life. I no longer resent time for recovery, any more than I resent the need for food and sleep. When we take time to recharge our batteries, we renew energy for the chores of our lives, become more focused and productive. In this way, surprisingly, our recovery actually *gives* us time.

Nothing's so urgent that I can't sit through a meeting, talk to my sponsor, or take a moment to pray. As I nourish my recovering self, I have more to offer work and relationships. Today, time is on my side.

57

Freedom is nothing else but a chance to be better.
ALBERT CAMUS

Newcomer

This thing of having to go to meetings all the time—I feel as if I'm substituting a whole new addiction for the old one.

Sponsor

Like you, I depend on the tools of the program. I have habits (attending meetings, reading program literature, offering service, praying, meditating) that have replaced many habits of my actively addicted years. I wouldn't want to have to live without my new habits. By maintaining our healthy sobriety, we are treating a disease, not acquiring another one.

When we were using, we were far from free. Substances and behaviors that threatened our lives and serenity were in charge. Today, once we choose to take the simple steps that support recovery and healing, we have lives in which we can make independent and worthy choices.

**Today, I know the difference between
healthful habits and addictions.**

58

Who may regret what was, since it has made himself himself?

JOHN FREEMAN

Newcomer

I'm tormented when I think of all the time I wasted, the wrong decisions I made. I'll never get back the missed opportunities. I feel as if I've procrastinated my life away.

Sponsor

It took years to get here; why should everything clear up overnight? The willingness that you are bringing to your recovery right now is a precious asset. Give yourself some pats on the back for the new life you are living today. Recovery challenges every former idea, habit, and value. Each time you say no to an addictive substance or behavior— each time you ask for help—you're building a new self.

In time, through taking the actions suggested by the Twelve Steps, you'll arrive at a place in which it will be less discouraging to look at the past. You'll begin to appreciate the strengths your past life has given you and see ways to clear the clogged channels. Meanwhile, here's a suggestion: make at least one of the meetings you go to regularly a Step meeting. It will familiarize you with the program and help you prepare to take the Steps when you're ready. In time, what seems impossible today will become possible.

I am grateful for this day, and for all the days that led me to it. I trust the process of recovery.

59

Delay is preferable to error.
THOMAS JEFFERSON

Newcomer

I don't trust my ability to stay with anything for a long time. I've been so inconsistent in the past. I have the feeling that eventually I'll get sick of all of my good new habits and go back to where I was before.

Sponsor

What happened to "One day at a time"? We're not required to deal with tomorrow's recovery right now. For the next twenty-four hours, any one of us can avoid picking up our drug of choice. That's all we have to do, and just by doing it, we're doing it perfectly.

Self-trust is a new habit that may not have put down deep roots in us yet. We're still close to the days when the only way we knew of taking care of ourselves was to use our addictions. It's important to remember that we are not the same people we used to be. We're in the process of forming new habits—meetings, literature, sharing, service—that are as powerful as the old ones. If we begin drifting a little from our new habits, we notice the difference in how we're feeling and can return to doing what worked. Every day in recovery adds to the store of sober experiences on which we can draw.

Today, I am the person I've always wanted to be.

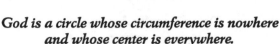

60

> *God is a circle whose circumference is nowhere*
> *and whose center is everywhere.*
> NICOLAUS CUSANUS

Newcomer

How can I believe that a Power greater than myself can restore me to sanity? I used to pray a lot, but it didn't work. Look what happened to me!

Sponsor

Yes, it's an excellent idea to look at what did happen to us. There was a progression of events, inner or outer, that led to greater and greater discomfort. At last, living in active addiction became intolerable. Something within us wanted to surrender—and now, however long it took us, we are in recovery. Something in us must have wanted to choose life, not death.

In recovery, we can embrace and nurture the part of ourselves that is aligned with Spirit. The sanity we're rediscovering in ourselves includes acceptance of our human limitations, letting go of results we can't control. We can let go of praying for things to happen exactly as we want, on our timetable. We can begin to be open to the miracles all around us.

My life was given to me as a gift, and now I've been given that gift all over again. I have a choice of what to do with it. Should I blame my Higher Power for the fact that it took me so long to get here? Or should I greet the Spirit within me and say, "Welcome! I've been waiting. I'm glad you finally came home."

Whatever happens today offers me opportunities to
deepen my relationship with my soul.

Anyone can get sober....
The trick is to stay and to live sober.
LIVING SOBER

Newcomer

At one meeting someone mentioned having had a slip. He had been back in recovery for three days. No one criticized him; in fact, everyone applauded. To be honest, it makes me think about seeing what it would be like to have a few drinks or a drug again, just for a day or a weekend.

Sponsor

Over the years, I've watched people come and go in recovery. I've been grateful to the people who relapsed and were lucky enough to come back and share their experience. They taught me a lot by talking about how their disease had continued progressing even when they weren't active in it, and about how much more quickly their misery had returned this time. I'm grateful to them for having had the slip for me; now I don't have to risk it. There's a danger in going back out to experiment with controlled using; few who leave ever make it back. This is a life-threatening disease. People like us, who depend on using an addictive substance, can die from it. We understand the seriousness of our addictions and have no need to test recovery by trying to use "safely."

Today, I want life—all of it. I embrace my recovery;
I stick close to those who know how to stay stopped.

62

My way is to begin with the beginning.
GEORGE GORDON, LORD BYRON

Newcomer

Things have been going badly for me ever since I got up. This has been one of my worst days in recovery.

Sponsor

Recovery shows us that we're free to start the day over any time we like, morning, noon, or night. Sometimes I say to myself, "I've gotten through the past twenty-four hours without acting on my addiction. This moment I'm beginning a new twenty-four-hour period. I'm starting my day right now."

Then, no matter where I happen to be, I take a few minutes to do some of the things that usually help me. I pray for the willingness to do whatever is necessary to stay in recovery. If possible, I read a page of program literature or make a phone call, and plan to attend a meeting as soon as there's one I can get to. I take several slow, deep breaths. I treat myself with gentleness.

Whatever we're able to do today is enough. If we haven't picked up our addictions, we've participated in a miracle.

With the help of my Higher Power, I'm getting through whatever this day brings.

63

*I've been inside institutions,
my family. . . .*
SUSAN GRIFFIN

Newcomer

There are some people at meetings who start their sharing by saying, "Hello, Family." It sounds phony to me—do they really mean it? I don't think I'll ever really be a part of this community. It certainly doesn't feel like a family to me.

Sponsor

I can understand your shying away from the word "family." Our first addictive responses may have occurred when we were living with our family of origin. Some of us are angry at the kind of nurturing we received. Some of us wish we could help family members who need recovery; we feel disturbed at our inability to make that happen. Resentment, fear, shame, powerlessness, and a host of other feelings may surface in connection with our families.

We may not yet be willing to call others in recovery our "family." We're not required to. But we do need each other's stories, service, and recovery. In time, our mistrust lessens, if we keep showing up and working the program. We may even begin to sense that we are members of a community.

Today, I depend on a group of people in recovery
to keep coming back and sharing. I depend on myself,
too, to participate in this process with others.

Someone else's legs do you no good in traveling.
NIGERIAN PROVERB

Newcomer

I went over to offer help to someone at a meeting; she'd been sharing about a problem I thought I knew something about. She was chilly and asked me not to intrude. I felt pretty hurt.

Sponsor

Many of us drank or drugged in a controlled, calculated fashion. The desire to maintain the illusion of control over the uncontrollable may have come with us into recovery. We may be "people-pleasers," overly helpful or compliant, trying to take care of others, attempting to manipulate them to like and take care of us. Eager to come to the rescue, we may have trouble minding our own business. We may want to have the answer to other people's problems—it's a great distraction from our own. We may be quick to offer unasked-for advice, rather than sit with the feelings that another person's pain has awakened in us.

Today, I listen to my own and other people's feelings. I don't try to fix anyone, even myself.

*The place I really have to reach
is where I must already be.*
LUDWIG WITTGENSTEIN

Newcomer

I heard someone share that she'd always thought of smoking marijuana as her big, secret problem. Once she stopped smoking pot, it didn't take long for her to recognize that alcohol was another problem, in fact the major one. Now, in addition to AA, she goes to meetings for overeaters, and she says she also has problems with codependency. What should I make of all this? I think I may have more than one addiction; should I be going to another program, too? Am I going to spend the rest of my life just going from meeting to meeting?

Sponsor

I don't blame you for feeling upset at the thought of a lifetime of nothing but program-hopping. Who wouldn't? Many of us do have multiple addictions. Everyone's story is different. Some cross-addicted people find the tools and principles of one primary program sufficient for dealing with whatever addiction issues come up for them. Others gratefully avail themselves of the abundance of specialized programs of recovery.

Whichever we decide, most of us need a solid foundation in sobriety before considering a second program. Today, you're right where you should be, establishing a sober routine. That's a big change in itself, and it's bringing about still more changes. For now, why not keep your focus on staying with what you've begun so well. In time, more will be revealed.

> Today, I take the time I need to strengthen
> the roots of my recovery. I choose to branch out
> in new directions when it is clearly appropriate.

66

The difficulty in life is the choice.
GEORGE MOORE

Newcomer
I'm confused. Should I spend the evening with my old friends? I haven't told them I'm in this program yet; I'm afraid that they won't understand. They may tell me that I don't really have a problem. I don't want to have to cut off my ties to all my friends just because they're not in this program.

Sponsor
Decisions, decisions—what freedom! What adventure! When I was active in my addiction, I didn't have the luxury of making up my mind; my addiction was in charge. Today, how do I reconcile the suggestion to avoid people, places, and things that once led to using with the fact that I have some old friends who genuinely care for me and with whom I want to stay in touch? In trying to make a hard decision, I first ask myself honestly whether my choice will take me closer to my addiction or further from it. If I elect to spend time with nonprogram people, I feel free to excuse myself to use the phone, to check in with my sponsor or a recovering friend. I make sure that I have my own

transportation, and I leave when I'm ready. When you've had more experience and are more sure of your recovery, you may decide to share some of your recovery story with old friends—or you may not! The choice is always yours.

Whatever else I do, I stay close to meetings and recovering people. I choose nonaddictive ways to celebrate being alive.

67

Chance everywhere has power.
OVID

Newcomer
I heard someone say the other day that "coincidence is God's way of remaining anonymous." Am I really supposed to believe that God is involved in every insignificant piece of luck I have? It's a bit much for me to believe that my Higher Power is interested in whether or not I get a good parking space. And what about the days when everything *isn't* going my way?

Sponsor
Some people experience coincidence as evidence that our lives are in the hands of a loving God, and some see good or bad luck simply as part of the randomness of events. Maintaining good recovery doesn't require that we take a stand on this subject!

There's another way of thinking about seemingly chance happenings: Wherever they come from, whatever else they are, coincidences are sober opportunities. When I bump into someone I've been thinking about making amends to, I have an opportunity to do it on the spot, and I don't pass it up.

When I've been avoiding taking one particular Step and find myself at a meeting where that very Step is being discussed, I have a chance to let go of my resistance then and there.

What we call coincidence involves a meeting of events with our own awakened spirit. In recovery, we often see openings for taking action and for feeling gratitude—opportunities that we would have missed if we were still active in our addictions.

> Today, I am awake and alive to opportunities
> for sober action.

68

**Anything *done with focus, awareness,
or mindfulness is a meditation.***
DAVID HARP

Newcomer
I hear people talk about meditating, but I don't seem to know how. When I try sitting still, my mind wanders, or I fall asleep. I just don't get it.

Sponsor
Even in recovery, we have an endless capacity for being confused. There are literally dozens of different approaches to meditation and many books and classes that teach them. Some forms of meditation come out of ancient traditions, some are religious, and some are just methods of relaxation. You can practice meditation alone or with others, in silence or chanting, sitting or walking. Even cleaning house can be a form of meditation!

Over time, I've found a simple approach to meditation that feels natural and right for me. If you'd like to try it, here's how: Take three to five minutes for time out to sit quietly, without distractions. Scan your body and mind, and let go of any tensions you notice. Breathe naturally, and pay attention to what that feels like. Whatever thoughts or sensations arise, don't make yourself wrong for having them. Afterward, you may notice that you feel calm and refreshed.

**Whatever I choose to do today, I practice doing it
with ease and pleasure. I keep it simple.
I don't judge my progress.**

69

The door must either be shut or be open.
OLIVER GOLDSMITH

Newcomer
Step Three begins with the words "Made a decision . . ." Sometimes I wonder whether I did make a decision to come here. I felt desperate; there really wasn't any choice.

Sponsor
Many of us have felt the desperation you speak of and saw this program as our last chance. Some of us came here to placate another person, to help a friend we thought needed recovery, or because a court of law required us to. Some of us came here with willingness and eager curiosity; we sensed that we were "home" right from the beginning. Others were reluctant and skeptical. Though each of us had to make a conscious decision to come to a meeting, it may feel as if something more than our own intentions got us here.

Now that we're here, we still have to make the decision to stay sober. We can elect to embrace recovery, or we can reject it and turn ourselves back over to addiction. We pray each day for the courage to remain in recovery. No one can force us to choose life and love, but it's here, if we have the willingness to choose it.

Today, it's easy and natural
to make decisions that support my recovery.

 **70**

What loneliness is more lonely than distrust?
GEORGE ELIOT

Newcomer

When I hear, in Step Three, "turn our will and our lives over to the care of God," my hackles go up. I want to lead a free, independent life. I don't want to give up my ability to think and to make my own decisions.

Sponsor

Step Three doesn't ask us to give up our ability to think or to make choices, but rather to trust in the existence of love and caring. When we were active in our addictions, we tried to care for ourselves with a substance or behavior that may have helped us at first, but eventually failed us. What seemed to feed us, in time starved us. In recovery, we become open to choosing more dependable ways of loving and caring for ourselves. To prepare for Step Three, it's useful to make a list of some of the many things that support and nurture us each day.

We find love and nourishment in helping and accepting help from other recovering addicts, in the dependability of meetings and program principles, in the people we meet on our path who put more light in our day. Music, exercise, creativity, laughter, meditation, prayer, tuning in to nature's rhythms, noticing the miracle of our own breathing and our bodies' capacity to heal—there is food for our spirits everywhere, if we are willing to be fed. In recovery, we come to know ourselves as whole human beings, better able to think for ourselves and make our own decisions, while sensing the loving support of something greater than our separate selves.

Today, I am willing to open myself to the abundance of love and care that recovery offers me.

71

A beginning, even the smallest, is all that is needed.
TWELVE STEPS AND TWELVE TRADITIONS

Newcomer
I don't have much faith in anything. How can I possibly take Step Three, turn my will and my life over to the care of God—even "God *as we understood Him*"—when I'm having so much difficulty believing and trusting? Where do you people get your faith? Is it for real?

Sponsor
You're not alone in thinking you lack faith; many of us entered recovery feeling that way. But, in fact, we do have faith, even if we ourselves can't see it yet: faith that this program can help us with the problem of our addictions.

Our willingness to try recovery is a significant beginning. By showing up, we've begun to take Step Three. Whatever our creed, or our refusal to embrace one, we do have the willingness to try this program. What eventually may come from this beginning is not something we have to worry about. The actions we take today are all we need concern ourselves with. In the present, our willingness to follow the program frees us from having to depend on an addiction.

Today, I begin to act out of faith that this program works.

72

It is improper for us to stoop in order to please.
JEAN PAUL SARTRE

Newcomer
I used to be arrogant about everything. I always had to be right. I constantly feared that people were trying to take advantage of me. Now I listen to others, take suggestions, and try to be helpful. I'm constantly being guided by other people—I guess I've turned my will over.

Sponsor
Turning our will and our lives over to the care of another human being may not be such a good idea. Sponsors, therapists, doctors, teachers, people practicing Twelve Step recovery—any of them may give us useful guidance, but they are all human. We can listen to what they have to say, keeping an open mind. But people in recovery don't automatically get wisdom or sainthood conferred on them. People

aren't perfect, and they couldn't possibly all know what's best for us; otherwise they'd all agree.

As we accumulate sober experience, we get better at trusting our own instincts, something that may have been a source of danger when we were active in our addictions. We learn from experience what's good for us, what nourishes us and brings us peace and joy.

It's not a spiritually sound practice to turn people, even those we respect and love, into our Higher Power. "Turning it over" includes trusting our inner guidance, acting responsibly, and accepting that we can't control outcomes.

Today, I look within and trust my truth.

73

We should pray as if everything depended upon God, and act as if everything depended upon us.
ABRAHAM JOSHUA HESCHEL

Newcomer
I hear so much about "letting go." But there are serious situations going on in my life that I can't ignore. Am I supposed to assume that things will get better on their own if I just let go?

Sponsor
The phrase "letting go," as it's used in the program, doesn't mean ignoring problematic situations, reneging on commitments, or repressing feelings. On the contrary, recovery makes it possible for us to take the responsible actions we feared and avoided when we were active in our addictions.

"Letting go" challenges our illusion that we're in control of the universe, but it doesn't suggest that we do nothing. There's a difference between acting responsibly and thinking we're in charge of how things turn out. We're responsible only for the actions we choose to take, not the outcomes. When we take an action that we know to be right, we change *ourselves* in the process. The effect on others is out of our hands. We don't have power to change other people. Nor can we change the past. Letting go means accepting our human limitations. It's a great relief to know that we're neither the cause nor the cure for most problems.

Today, I let go and let God.

74

I am years gone from my family, and miles away.
JERROLD MUNDIS

Newcomer
I keep hearing that recovery is a bridge back to life, but I don't think that I'll ever have a decent relationship with my family. I called a family member on the phone last night and said that I was in recovery. I got such a skeptical response. It's always the same story: no matter what I do, I can't please these people.

Sponsor
It takes time to build a feeling of centeredness and self-worth. In the early days of my recovery, my sense of self was easily shattered by a word or look that confirmed my

old belief that I didn't deserve much. I had to practice "Easy does it," especially with family members. I decided to keep family interactions light, for the time being. I made program calls just before and just after any call I made to my family. In time, I had enough self-esteem to face emotionally charged situations without threatening my recovery.

We have the responsibility to protect our new recovery by keeping some distance between ourselves and the people, places, and things that we drank or drugged or acted out over. And we have the opportunity to build self-esteem by participating in meetings. We can start simply: show up, help make coffee, set up chairs, empty ashtrays. We can listen, raise our hands to share, thank the speaker, say hello to another newcomer. Giving service, no matter how small the action, builds feelings of usefulness and self-respect.

Today, my thoughts and energy go into self-esteem, not self-rejection. I show up for my life. I deserve to surround myself with the love that is in the program.

75

Falling in love . . . is as much a drug as any that people swallow, snort, smoke, or shoot.
ANDREW WEIL

Newcomer

I'm attracted to another newcomer who goes to some of the meetings I go to. I can't help it; I just can't get this person out of my mind. My heart pounds when we're in the same room, and I can barely concentrate.

Sponsor

More than once in early recovery, I became intensely pre-occupied with thoughts of another person. In each case it was someone I didn't know well, but felt attracted to. Like you, I could hardly think about anything else. Though I was certainly distracted, I stayed sober. I went to lots of meetings—not always for the best reasons! These intense romantic preoccupations were something I have since learned to call obsession. Obsession doesn't have much in common with the process of getting to know others and letting them get to know me.

We can learn something about ourselves by paying attention when an obsession starts taking over our mental space. Is some feeling—anger, fear, or sadness, for example—making us uncomfortable? Obsession can function to keep us "safe" from the present reality. Our addictions served the same function when we were active.

Today, I practice staying in the moment. I reach out to other newcomers in the spirit of friendship.

76

The easiest kind of relationship for me is with ten thousand people. The hardest is with one.

JOAN BAEZ

Newcomer

Where were you yesterday? I called you at nine in the morning and eleven at night; both times I got your answering machine and left a message. I know you're a busy person, but I thought that people in this program would at least have the courtesy to return my calls.

Sponsor

I did have a busy day yesterday; I missed talking with you. This is going to happen once in a while, so I'm glad that you have other phone numbers and a meeting list.

When I was newly recovering, my motto was "I want what I want when I want it!" Sometimes my sponsor wasn't available instantly and had to call me back later; sometimes she said things I didn't want to hear at all. When my response was to withdraw—to stop calling, or miss meetings so I wouldn't have to see her—I closed the door to healing. But when I could summon the courage to say, "I feel hurt, I feel angry, I'm afraid to trust you!" we could talk about what was going on and reason things out together.

Thank you for letting me hear how upset you were that our routine was disrupted; it's an important part of the work you are doing in recovery. I won't always be able to give you what you want when you want it, but I do respect your feelings.

Today, I have the courage to call my sponsor, even though I may have thoughts or feelings I'd prefer to ignore. I keep the lines of communication open.

77

For a girl without a self, I was pretty stubborn.
ELEANOR ANTIN

Newcomer

I feel good today. Thank God I've got my willpower back again. I've seen the light: I just have to be strong and stay away from addictive substances.

Sponsor

I prefer the word "willingness" to "willpower." For me, willpower means forcing myself to do something disagreeable and self-depriving because someone else thinks I should. The trouble with relying on willpower—for me—is that I'm still a rebel in my heart of hearts. Give me something to rebel against, and, in time, I will. Though I may feel guilty when I break the rules, my rebelling somehow comforts me: It's familiar. It lets me feel like my old self. It lets me say, "This is me, whether *they* like it or not!"

Willingness, on the other hand, means making a free, open choice to let in the message of recovery. It doesn't mean always having to be strong. It doesn't mean having to have all the answers. If we have willingness, we can show up at meetings, listen, and feel supported by the presence of other recovering people and by the laughter in the room. We can grow in recovery through practicing the program and participating in the fellowship.

For today, I don't try to be strong. I go easy on myself by attending a meeting where I can relax and be myself. I enjoy listening to others share their experience.

 *78*

I still have my days when I have trouble, and I have to sit down and think about how far I've come.
WOMAN IN RECOVERY

Newcomer

I'm overwhelmed again. There's so much that I should get done today, so much ahead that scares me. I feel sick and indecisive. I've heard the slogan "First things first," but I don't know where to begin.

Sponsor

First, I suggest that you give yourself some credit for what you've already accomplished today. Yes, you *have* accomplished something. Here you are, awake: you've started another day of your new life in recovery. You know that no matter what happens today, you don't have to use an addictive substance. You're identifying some feelings and reaching out for help. All this is significantly different from old patterns of behavior.

"First things first" is a reminder that we can set priorities. The first priority for every single one of us in recovery is not picking up an addictive substance. Without recovery, none of the other things in our lives will have much chance to come to fruition. We have to save our lives first. If we need meetings, phone calls, or prayer to keep from losing recovery, we put those needs at the top of our list. Then we can sort out the rest and list things in order of importance.

Today, I celebrate how far I've come. I set priorities and keep recovery at the top of my list. I take small actions that get me closer to my goals.

79

The flower must drink the nature of the soil
Before it can put forth its blossoming.
JOHN KEATS

Newcomer

I've had to cut back on meetings lately, because my life is so full. There's so much to do, so much lost time to make up for. And the meetings are repetitive; I feel as if I can predict in advance what's going to happen there.

Sponsor

It's natural to experience fluctuations in our enthusiasm for sober routines; there are ups and downs in any relationship. At times, meetings seem like something "they" are requiring me to do, rather than something I've chosen. When I'm sitting there, I don't always pay close attention. I may feel irritated by a personality, bored hearing something I think I already know, or too distracted by my thoughts to focus on principles. But I keep going anyway, and the meetings—as if by magic—get better. Suddenly, I hear exactly what I need to hear. I suspect that the problem isn't so much with meetings as with my attitude.

By attending meetings and making calls *consistently*—not just when we feel desperate—we keep the lines of communication open. That way we maintain a basis of support for ourselves and others; we can count on its being there when we need it most.

I have a life now, and I am responsible for it.
Today, the decision I make to maintain my recovery
is my own decision. Establishing a sober routine
and sticking to it is a tool for maintaining that life.

80

We feel and know that we are eternal.
BARUCH SPINOZA

Newcomer

I'm feeling anxious and overwhelmed. My mind is tormenting me. I could hardly sit still at the meeting I went to. How am I going to get through the rest of the day?

Sponsor

When I'm anxious, I seem to forget to breathe properly, so let's bring our attention to our breathing, and inhale and exhale gently but deeply. Let's breathe in a way that feels natural, not holding our breath at any point, so that the inhalation continues naturally into the exhalation. Let's visualize bringing breath into the belly, as if we were breathing in and out through the navel.

As thoughts and distractions come into the mind, we notice that they're there, but we don't worry about them. We let them keep flowing out gently and easily, like the breath.

For these moments, there is nowhere else we have to be, nothing at all that we have to do. The past no longer exists. The future hasn't been born yet. We are here in this moment. Our bodies are breathing for us. Body and mind are one. There is only the present moment.

After our brief meditation, we feel centered and energized. We can use this technique to lower our stress levels whenever we wish.

**Today, I gently bring myself into the present moment.
I remember to breathe.**

81

Put some gratitude in your attitude.
SAYING HEARD AT MEETINGS

Newcomer

Often I hear someone say, "I'm so grateful" or "I'm a grateful recovering (whatever they are)." I don't understand. How can a person be *grateful* for alcoholism, compulsive overeating, codependency, or whatever has ruined his or her life?

Sponsor

I could not have begun this process we call recovery before knowing and accepting the fact that I have a disease. Lots of people out there die without ever hearing how we can stop the behavior that's killing us. Others have to suffer even longer than I did. I'm grateful that I finally hit bottom and became willing to do something about it. I'm grateful that recovery has given me a way of life that brings me freedom and self-esteem. I'm grateful to be here, awake, showing up for my life. I'm grateful for so-called little things I rarely noticed or thought about when I was active in my addiction—a bird, a flower, a smile.

Gratitude is a spiritual tool. I can choose to pick it up; I can cultivate the habit of using it.

Today, I cultivate gratitude.

82

My giant goes with me wherever I go.
RALPH WALDO EMERSON

Newcomer

This town is full of memories I'd like to get away from. I haven't had a change of scenery for a long time, and I'm thinking about a move. The job situation is supposed to be a lot better on the other side of the country, and I think I'd like the climate better there, too.

Sponsor

Understandably, some of us yearn to make dramatic changes in our outer lives, now that we've made such a big inner change. We're living without substances we depended on for so long, and we may suddenly feel freer—we may want to change everything as fast as possible. In my early recovery, it scared me to think of facing problems my addiction had caused at work and home, especially in relationships with people. I dreamed of starting a new, problem-free life somewhere else—a "geographic cure." Luckily, I accepted the suggestion that we not make major changes during the first year of recovery.

There can be freedom in *not* making a change. Without the stress of an unnecessary move, or a major work or relationship change, I could jump into recovery with both feet. It helped me to get to know myself better, to get clear about my motives and readiness for change.

We can live rich, fulfilling lives; no one's stopping us. Giving ourselves time at first to concentrate on the basics of recovery provides us with a solid basis for moving on in our lives.

> Recovery is a bridge back to life;
> today, I work on making the foundations strong.

83

This is a simple program for complicated people.
SAYING HEARD AT MEETINGS

Newcomer

I heard a speaker with years in recovery share that she'd always done it her own way—that she met friends at bars if she felt like it, had never had a sponsor, and sometimes went for months without a meeting. I know newcomers who've done similar things. What's the big deal?

Sponsor

Some people in recovery cling to rebellion. While they don't want to return to the horrors of active addiction, they aren't willing to surrender what they think of as individualism. They "get away with" skipping Steps and ignoring suggestions. One helps out at meetings, but keeps booze in the house. One gives advice to newcomers, but goes unsponsored.

The program doesn't ask that we give up what truly makes each of us an individual. It offers us clear guidelines, and promises that if we follow them, we won't have to risk a relapse. The program works for us, if we work it. Testing our recovery by trying to see what we can "get away with" is like playing a game of Russian roulette.

Today, I feel safety and strength as I follow the principles of this program. I know that true individuality comes from the self-knowledge that recovery affords me.

84

Anticipate the good so that you may enjoy it.
ETHIOPIAN PROVERB

Newcomer

I'm getting closer to ninety days—I'm in the eighties now. I'm excited. It's a miracle that I've been able to stay in recovery without interruption for this long. But I feel worried, too—or maybe I'm scared. I don't know what I'm feeling!

Sponsor

"Anniversary anxiety" is something many of us experience in recovery. For the preceding days or weeks, we're aware of the upcoming anniversary and its implications. We may anticipate speaking at a meeting or celebrating with recovering friends. Will we measure up to their expectations? To our own?

Perhaps we've been sharing our day count and enjoying the applause. As we approach ninety days, we may be afraid we'll become "invisible" at meetings. Depending on local program and group customs, we may be eligible to chair meetings. Are we going to have to handle more responsibilities than we feel ready for? The day of the anniversary itself, and the days following it, may be a setup for feeling as if we've graduated or won an athletic event. We may be afraid that recovery will disappoint us, once the cheering dies down.

It helps to know that this phenomenon is a common one. If you're experiencing it, one of the best antidotes is to share your concerns, both at meetings and with a sponsor. We've been there.

Today, I use the same tools of recovery that worked
in the very beginning: meetings, sharing, reading
recovery literature, prayer. They work.

85

I think even lying on my bed I can still do something.
DOROTHEA DIX

Newcomer

I'm not doing well with meditation. I tried going to a class, and I got fidgety after ten or fifteen minutes. I tried paying attention to my breath, but my back hurt, I was nervous and distracted, and I kept thinking how badly I wanted to leave. Forget about doing it at home—I can sit for five minutes, then I have to get up. How do people endure all-day meditations?

Sponsor

You may not be ready for long sessions of sitting meditation. For a beginner, even fifteen minutes may be too long. If you sense that the form of meditation you have tried is the one you're best suited to, you might consider starting with very brief sessions, as little as three to five minutes. After a few weeks, you may want to try adding another minute or two. You can work up to fifteen minutes gradually, over a long period of time, and then see whether you wish to add a bit more or not. Surprisingly, the key is knowing when to stop.

When something makes me anxious, I limit the amount of time I do it. I may have the willingness to do something for a few minutes every day that would frighten me for half an hour once a week. Lengthening the time little by little, being sure that I don't exceed the time limit I've set for the day, allows me to increase my tolerance gradually.

If sitting continues to be daunting for you, you may

want to consider exploring forms of meditation that include walking or chanting.

> Today, I do not judge my rate of progress.
> I take one small step on my spiritual journey.

86

*Before a secret is told, one can often feel
the weight of it in the atmosphere.*
SUSAN GRIFFIN

Newcomer
When I had a wisdom tooth pulled a few days ago, the dentist gave me a medication that contains codeine. I've heard people at meetings say they take their doctors' prescriptions, so I knew it was okay to use it if necessary. As it turned out, I didn't need to take any—the pain wasn't that bad. I don't know why, but I kept the pills. They're still in my medicine cabinet. Codeine isn't something I ever took when I was active.

Sponsor
You're right in thinking that you are in a danger area here. I recommend that you throw out the medication right now, and I don't mean just tossing it into the wastebasket. Flush the pills down the toilet, or put them in a rubbish bag and take it out of your house; I'll wait here while you do it.

There are medical reasons to use some drugs *as prescribed*. It's when we prescribe for ourselves, or start imagining pains to justify unnecessary doses, that we're in trouble. We can let the doctor know that we have a history of abusing substances and that it may cause us problems to take home more pills than we're likely to need. Knowing this, he or she may prescribe nonaddictive medicines when there is a choice.

Even if our use of pain killers is legitimate, sharing with a sponsor or at a meeting the fact that we have prescribed medicines in our possession is a good idea. If it's not a secret, it may seem less compelling to us.

Today, I don't have to have secrets. I stay on the recovery path by sharing feelings and events that might otherwise threaten my serenity.

87

Bring the body, and the mind will follow.
SAYING HEARD IN MEETINGS

Newcomer

What do people in recovery mean when they say they have "smart feet"?

Sponsor

In recovery, we develop daily habits that we don't question: the habit of attending meetings, the habit of picking up the telephone to call a sponsor or to share with another recovering person, the habit of starting and ending the day with our preferred combination of prayer, literature, and meditation. We do these things whether we feel like doing them or not, and in time they become second nature to us, automatic as our addictive behavior was in the past. If we don't have to discuss these habits with ourselves, argue about whether or not they'll make us feel better, or question whether we've outgrown them, our burden is lighter.

Once we're at a meeting or sharing with another recovering person or with our Higher Power, the unexpected happens. We're lifted out of the tyranny of addictive thinking. "Smart feet" are feet that carry us to a place we need to be, whether we know it ahead of time or not.

Today, I'm grateful for simple habits
that open my heart and mind to recovery.

88

The best things in life are not things.
ANN LANDERS

Newcomer

Style has always mattered to me. When I was active, I felt scorn for people who had no taste or flair. I know there's arrogance in that, but some part of me still loves glamour and doesn't want to give it up.

Sponsor

I used to think my addiction had something to do with being cool. I thought my use of addictive substances and behaviors made me stylish and sophisticated. Meanwhile, I didn't know how to live my life.

Romanticizing addiction and its trappings is a form of denial many of us have to address. Certain drinks, drugs, or behaviors may have seemed to us like instant power or sophistication—less boring and regular than the alternatives. Some of the rituals and accoutrements of addiction continue to be glamorized by advertising, films, and popular images and myths. We may tell ourselves that creative people have always been involved with drugs. We may feel a pang: is recovery going to strip us of our originality, our flair for the unusual?

We're who we are in spite of, not because of, addictive substances and behaviors. The originality and flair that you associate with addiction come from a deeper part of you. We can be true originals in recovery, through coming to know ourselves.

Today, I let go of any illusions about my addiction.

89

Ukwenza kuya emuva kuye phambili.
The doing moves backward, then forward.
NDEBELE PROVERB

Newcomer
I thought I'd lost the desire to pick up my addiction. Now I'm on the verge of celebrating ninety days, and all I can think of is how much I'd like to go back to my old life.

Sponsor
Anniversaries can be times of intense expectation for people in recovery. Anxiety, sadness, and other feelings may be mixed with jubilation and pride. Some of us go into denial: "If I've made it this far without the drug, maybe I don't really have the problem." Or "I can do this on my own now—who needs all those damn meetings!" Some of us feel like frauds; we've been fooling everyone into thinking that we can stay away from our addictions successfully. Intense feel-

ings—even those of pride and pleasure—can put us in danger of picking up our addictive substances.

Anniversaries are times when it's especially important to stay in touch with the people who've been sharing our journey. They can help us to celebrate and also to keep the anniversary in perspective. It's encouraging to know that they'll continue to be there as we continue to stay away from addictive substances and behaviors—one day at a time.

Today, I stay close to the program.
When I go out, I take phone numbers,
coins for making calls, and a willingness to use them.

90

*. . . who share their experience, strength
and hope with each other . . .*
ALCOHOLICS ANONYMOUS PREAMBLE

Newcomer
Now that I have ninety days in recovery, am I really supposed to get up in front of the room and speak? It's hard enough to make myself raise my hand to share at a meeting! Without my drug of choice, I'm really a shy, private person. I don't like it when people look at me. I don't have a gift for public speaking. I don't know how to make people laugh. I don't think that I know enough about recovery to lead a meeting.

Sponsor
Speaking at a meeting is not the same as public speaking; it's a tool that we use to stay sober. We don't have to impress or save anyone when we speak at a meeting. We

don't have to spout principles or explain Steps we haven't taken yet. We just have to be willing to share what we know to be true for each of us. If we set aside our egos and the baggage of fear and pride, we can talk honestly about our own experiences.

We can't anticipate or control how our words are going to help another person. Before speaking, I say a simple prayer: "Help me to be of use." The results aren't up to me. One time, I was so nervous that I forgot everything I'd planned to say. There were long pauses between every sentence. Afterward, a woman came up to me and said, "You've given me courage. In three years, I've never had the guts to speak. Now that I've seen you go through your fear, I think I can do it, too." I'd thought I was a failure, but she thanked me!

Today, I do service without calculating the results.
My honesty helps me and others to deepen
the experience of recovery.

91

I want to change things. I want to see things happen. I don't want just to talk about them.
JOHN KENNETH GALBRAITH

Newcomer
I feel as if I should be doing so much more than just staying in recovery and going to meetings. And yet, when I have free time, I'm not accomplishing much these days. I go to a meeting and then to coffee—"the meeting after the meeting," I've heard it called—and I get home and feel too tired

to do any more. When I have a big block of time, I don't know how to use it. I feel confused and discouraged.

This point in recovery is a time to be especially gentle with ourselves. When we look back at how we were feeling and what we were doing just before we entered recovery, we can see that "just staying in recovery and going to meetings" is a major change. To be free from our addictive behavior, to keep a commitment to a program of recovery—this is nothing short of a total revolution in our lives. We have made a commitment to live, not to punish ourselves for not doing it faster and more perfectly.

"The meeting after the meeting" is not a waste of time. It's important to get to know our peers in recovery. We can learn from one another, support one another. The changes we're experiencing are mirrored back to us by others who are undergoing similar transformations. It gives us experience, too, at being with people without the "help" of our addictive substance or behavior.

We don't have to worry about wasting time in early recovery. It is a miracle that we can simply *be*.

Today, I let myself be.

92

To be alive at all is to have scars.
JOHN STEINBECK

Newcomer
At a recent meeting, I heard someone sharing as if she'd solved every problem she'd ever had. She was smiling the

whole time she spoke, talking about how great everything is. I don't know why, but I felt angry afterward. She
sounded so glib and self-satisfied and know-it-all. If that's
recovery, I don't know if I want it.

Sponsor

I can identify with your anger. I, too, sometimes find it
irritating to hear someone chattering about his or her happiness and success, especially when my own life seems to
be full of messy problems. But it may not be the contrast
between her situation and your own that got you upset.
Perhaps you intuited that she may not, in fact, "have it
all together." Few humans do. I love hearing people talk
about the ways this program has helped them, but recovery
doesn't make us perfect.

It won't help my own recovery if I judge the quality of
someone else's. I know, though, that when I hear people
sharing at meetings, I'm drawn far more deeply to some
sharing than to others. Oddly enough, I sometimes get
more spiritual sustenance from hearing someone who is
having to cope with immense difficulties than from someone who appears to have none at all.

Recovery doesn't require perfection. In fact, perfection
isn't possible.

Today, I have unconditional love for myself,
whatever my scars or difficulties.
I extend this unconditional love to all those around me.

When you get to the end of your rope,
tie a knot and hang on.
FRANKLIN DELANO ROOSEVELT

Newcomer

Initially, I was excited about recovery. I felt better for a while. I hate to say it, but now that I'm not at the beginning any more, everything seems worse. I feel more cynical than ever.

Sponsor

What you're experiencing is part of the process of recovery. Many of us go through a "honeymoon" phase in early recovery. Our craving may feel miraculously lifted. Change feels easy, and hope replaces despair.

Then, life feels difficult again. We may perceive ourselves as having gotten worse, but that's not accurate. What's really happening is that, though our addictive craving has been treated, we still have our old problems, habits, and states of mind. We may be getting through the day, showing up for our work responsibilities, attending meetings, but not having much fun. We may wonder if what we've heard is really true—that "our worst day in recovery is better than our best day of active addiction." We may wonder whether recovery really is the answer, after all.

Our doubt makes clear to us that we have to do something. Staying where we are is too uncomfortable. We can attend a Step meeting and read program literature to begin to familiarize ourselves with our next Step. For spirits in need of healing, Step work leads to the next phase of recovery.

Today, I have the courage to move forward
in my journey of recovery.

*Try this bracelet: if it fits you, wear it; but if it hurts you,
throw it away no matter how shiny.*

KENYAN PROVERB

Newcomer

I hear some people in meetings who talk about having
strict sponsors and doing everything "by the book." There
are others who say that they follow the suggestions more
loosely. I heard one person say that she "sort of got recovery
by osmosis"—she's only dimly aware that she's been applying a particular Step to a situation in her life. I don't know
if all this diversity is such a good thing.

Sponsor

Diversity is a fact of life in recovery. We come in many
shapes and sizes, and from many different backgrounds and
histories. It stands to reason that our paths in recovery
aren't going to be carbon copies of one another. We share
the desire for recovery and the willingness to work at it.
Though we do have *addiction* in common, methods of recovery may vary. One size definitely doesn't fit all.

Some of us crave a great deal of structure and feel insecure without it. Some feel safer being told exactly what
action to take, when, and how. Others rebel against overly
detailed directions, feeling safe only if we sense we're being
given room to make our own mistakes. We're intuitively
drawn to people who have what we want, whose paths
offer the combination of supportiveness and challenge that
feels appropriate to our own needs. If our preferred way

hasn't been working, we may need to try switching for a while to a stricter or looser approach.

Today, I trust my experience and gut feelings about what will strengthen my recovery most effectively.

 **95**

Through prayer we may lose some of our arrogance and resistance.
OH SHINNAH

Newcomer

I've struggled with this addiction for so long. I think I'm finally ready to defeat it. I really want to do it right this time.

Sponsor

The program saying "The war is over" comes to mind when I hear you talking about struggle and defeat. In my experience, addiction doesn't respond well to force. In fact, it counters force with a force of its own. Addiction is stubborn. When we approach it with "white-knuckle" discipline, confusing willfulness with strength of character, we may be setting ourselves up for eventual relapse.

The alternative is an attitude of surrender. I begin each day acknowledging that I have a disease. I ask for help in living with it, not acting on it. I use the tools of the program and the support of the fellowship, replacing old habits with new ones that help maintain recovery. I used to keep the paraphernalia of my addictive life around me; now I keep reminders of recovery around me. I approach recovery with enthusiasm, gratitude, joy. If I feel the urge to fight, I know it's time for a meeting. Recovery is a journey I pray to continue, with the help of my Higher Power—one day at a time.

Today, I humbly ask for recovery to be given to me.
I don't have to do it alone.

96

. . . and there was a new voice
which you slowly
recognized as your own.
MARY OLIVER

Newcomer
I'm royally confused. At one meeting I hear people say how important psychotherapy is; at another, I hear people say that it's bad—all you need is the Twelve Steps. A speaker I heard mentioned antidepressant drugs and how they've changed her life; meanwhile, the man next to me was muttering that that's not a sober thing to do. I'm wondering what I should do. Maybe I need more than just this program.

Sponsor
The program doesn't offer professional or scientific advice. Instead, we share our experiences: what got us here, how we've stayed clean and sober so far. Once we've established new habits in place of old ones, it's perfectly appropriate to assess our individual needs. Some of us have medical, financial, or legal problems. A few have severe emotional problems. Some of us choose to seek professional help. For me,

just plain recovery—staying away from substances one day at a time—had to come first; without it, I couldn't begin to address the ways I'd neglected my health and well-being. Surprisingly, some of the decisions I struggled hardest with eventually became clear and simple.

As your process of recovery continues, you'll gain confidence in your intuition and judgment. Many questions that are causing you to experience conflict today will resolve themselves easily in time.

> Today, I set controversial questions aside
> while I learn to stay sober.

97

Surrender sooner.
SAYING HEARD AT MEETINGS

Newcomer
I've been working so hard to do everything I'm supposed to, in recovery and in the "real" world. But something in me wants to slow down, cry, and scream, maybe even collapse. The timing couldn't be less convenient. I should have waited to come into recovery.

Sponsor
How much choice do we really have about timing, about when we enter recovery? Hitting bottom is a spiritual crisis; like any other crisis, we have to address it when it occurs. We don't get to negotiate the terms. Similarly, we don't get to choose the nature or timing of the emotions we experience. We can stop our tears, but not our grief. If

we don't try to resist or block feelings, they flow through us surprisingly quickly.

Falling down doesn't mean we'll never get up again. We may need to let some things fall apart before we can move on. Those of us who were brought up to believe that we should be able to manage several things simultaneously, ignore our personal needs, and come through every crisis with a smile may have trouble letting go of our old ideas. It's okay to be imperfect in our recovery process. The sooner we let go, the better.

Today, I accept my Higher Power's timetable for me.

98

Never take anything for granted.
BENJAMIN DISRAELI

Newcomer
What is a "dry drunk"?

Sponsor
This expression may have first sprung up in AA. It's used to describe one of us who is abstaining from the use of alcohol but isn't thinking or behaving in a way that is sober. If we're full of self-will, if we constantly blame and rage at others, if we're controlled by our fears and resentments, we are probably "on a dry drunk." This expression might also be used to describe those of us with addictions other than alcohol when our lives are not sober. Our addictions are a package deal: certain attitudes and behaviors come with the compulsion to numb ourselves with particular substances or acts.

A "dry drunk" sometimes focuses on others and their addictive problems. Gossip, blame, argument, manipulative behavior, obsessive worrying, neglect of responsibilities—these are some common "dry drunk" behaviors. We may not be abusing a substance, but our attitudes and behavior qualify us as "dry drunks."

Today, my participation in this program helps me to maintain physical, mental, and spiritual recovery.

99

Other people don't always dream your dream.
LINDA RONSTADT

Newcomer
When people at meetings use the words "control" and "controlling," the tone is always negative. What's so bad about control? I'm glad that I have more control over my life, now that I'm not active in my addiction. I grew up hearing about "self-control" all the time. I assumed it was a good thing.

Sponsor
There are different ways in which people in recovery use the word "control." One of them, in the phrase "controlled drinking" or "controlled drugging," describes a state that's neither drunk nor sober. It's an attempt to use an addictive substance or behavior only in carefully measured amounts—the "I can handle it" approach. Those who engage in it cheat themselves both of the oblivion of addictive behavior and the joy of recovery. I can't imagine a grimmer form of denial; it means never being free of obsession with a drug.

We also use the word "control" to name the illusion that we're responsible for all the outcomes of our actions. The Serenity Prayer makes a distinction between things we can and can't control. It helps me to remember that I have control over my actions, but not over those of others. I can control what I eat, but not how my body processes the food and what I weigh. I can choose my words, but not how people will respond to them. We may expend a lot of energy trying to manipulate others to feel and behave as we wish. It may even seem to work sometimes—but that's an illusion. I don't deliberately do things that I think may offend people or hurt their feelings; but what they feel, do, or say in reaction to me is not in the realm of my control.

Today, I accept my powerlessness over addictive substances and my powerlessness over other people's thoughts and feelings.

⟫⟪ 100 ⟫⟪

I think the one lesson I have learned is that there is no substitute for paying attention.
DIANE SAWYER

Newcomer
I'm embarrassed to admit this, but I often sit in a meeting just looking at everyone's shoes and trying to decide which ones I like. Or I may be sort of half listening while looking at what people are wearing or how their hair is cut, trying to figure out whether the same thing would look okay on me. I guess I sound pretty superficial.

Sponsor

Sometimes the intensity of recovery feels overwhelming. We drift, thinking there's something wrong with the meeting or with us. Our thoughts are elsewhere, racing a mile a minute, or else we fall asleep. The problem isn't that we're easily bored or unwilling to concentrate. More likely, we're trying to get some relief from feelings that are surfacing within us. A lot happens at meetings. Some people are sharing stories that remind us of our own, and some are sharing their experience of a new way of life that challenges beliefs and habits we've held for a long time. It sometimes feels like too much. The experience itself of sitting in a room with other people uses mental and emotional energy, and may raise anxieties for some of us. It takes getting used to. The good news is that in time we do find it easier to be fully present.

**Today, I gently let go of concerns
about my rate of progress, as I remain consistent about
attending meetings and working the program.**

 *101*

*Say what you mean and mean what you say,
but don't be mean when you say it.*
SAYING HEARD AT MEETINGS

Newcomer

At a meeting I went to, the chairman made comments every time someone shared. Isn't that what they call "cross talk"?

Sponsor

Certain customs vary from meeting to meeting. I've heard more than one definition of "cross talk" and seen some differences in whether or not it's considered permissible to respond when others are sharing.

At most meetings, it's not customary to respond directly to what another person shares by offering opinions or advice. It's fine, though, to identify with what's been said and to share our own experience on a related feeling or topic. At some meetings the speaker responds to sharing, but rarely interrupts, even with a brief, good-humored comment. At others, the speaker simply says "thank you"—or nothing at all. Limiting cross talk promotes the habit of tolerance and helps create an atmosphere in which it's safe to share openly and honestly.

Other customs, too, vary from fellowship to fellowship, from place to place throughout the country, even from meeting to meeting in the same city or town. Some meetings give out chips to mark anniversaries; some celebrate them with cakes and presentations. Some meetings sell raffle tickets; the prize is usually program literature. Some meetings prohibit smoking. Such policies may be dictated by local custom or decided at business meetings or "group conscience" meetings.

Recovery keeps offering us opportunities to become more flexible and tolerant.

> Today, I am open and flexible.
> I cultivate lightness as I look and listen.

> *Happiness is a way-station between*
> *too little and too much.*
> **CHANNING POLLOCK**

Newcomer

I'm in a bind. Someone asked me to attend an event, and I said yes. I think I should be doing more than just going to meetings. Now that the date's almost here, I wish I'd said no; I don't really want to go. But I don't think I should let people down at the last minute any more—I did that too much when I was active in my addiction.

Sponsor

When I was new in recovery, I had a serious case of what we call "people-pleasing." It's taken time to sort out my own needs and desires. I've found that I need to spend time with people and that I also need time for solitude and rest. Chances to try new things are among the gifts of recovery, but I don't have to do everything that comes along. It still takes effort to plan ahead for activities I care about and to leave room for spontaneity.

Making choices that please and nurture us is healthy. If we need to, we can change our minds and our plans—it's not the same thing as picking up our addictions. We need to be clear about our motives, however. If we find that we're consistently waiting until the last minute, then backing out of commitments, perhaps we're letting fear make our decisions. And sometimes, it's just plain easier to go ahead and keep a commitment we're less than thrilled about. If we've made a mistake, it's not the end of the world; our mistakes are our teachers. Through trial and error, we eventually learn how to choose good company and make appropriate commitments.

Today, I'm showing up for my life.

103

Creating intimacy is a skill.
LAUREL MELLIN

Newcomer

The so-called suggestion not to have relationships in the first year makes me angry. The rest of the world falls in love, and people get together. Why can't I?

Sponsor

Let's remember that there are many, many kinds of relationships, including friendships, professional relationships, and relationships like ours, the sponsor-sponsee relationship. All of them offer valuable experience and practice at something we addicts don't know much about: the gradual process, over time, of sharing ourselves with fellow human beings.

As a newly recovering person, you still have a lot to learn about yourself. Why rush the process? The person you are today and the person you will be after several months in recovery may not have much in common. You may quickly outgrow a romantic relationship that you enter into this early in your journey. Other newcomers, like you, are involved in a revolutionary process of growth and change. If you risk getting involved with a newcomer, you may find yourself unceremoniously dumped or vulnerable to the person's unreasonable demands or unthinking behavior. Instead, you can choose to allow yourself a luxury during these early months—that of creating a sensitive, loving relationship with yourself.

Today, I cherish my new, growing relationship with myself. I look and listen lovingly to my needs and wants.

Showing up for life. Being blessed with the rebirth
that recovery brings. One day at a time.
BETTY FORD

Newcomer

Chronologically, I'm a grown-up, but in some ways I'm far behind. It feels as if I'm growing up all over again.

Sponsor

Some people in the program say that our emotional development stopped at the point when we became active in our addictions: if we abused drugs beginning at age sixteen, then we've entered recovery with the emotional development of a sixteen-year-old.

That's an oversimplification, but it points the way to a truth. Most of us enter recovery inexperienced at whatever aspects of our lives we avoided through addiction. We may feel awkward in social contexts; we may have missed out on education; we may not have found appropriate, fulfilling work. Some of us still have to learn the basics of self-care; others have numerous adult-world accomplishments, but no dependable sense of self-esteem. At times we may feel as if we're part child, part adolescent, part mature person rolled into one.

We're not stupid or shallow. We're complex people, each with our own histories, strengths, and needs. We're capable of profound change. Happily, we're not alone in our struggles to mature and become integrated individuals.

Today, I have patience with myself
as I learn more about who I am and how to live.

The readiness is all.
WILLIAM SHAKESPEARE

Newcomer

I went to two different Step meetings this week, in different parts of town, and both of them were on the Fourth Step. I keep hearing that "there are no coincidences." Does this mean I'm supposed to start the Fourth Step now? How do I know if I'm ready?

Sponsor

First of all, I'm glad to hear that you're going to Step meetings, and I encourage you to keep it up. Your willingness has brought you a long way already, and it continues to be the key.

In approaching a new Step, I find it useful to ask myself if I've taken the Steps that precede it in a complete, wholehearted way.

I review Step One and remember why I'm on this path of recovery in the first place: addiction brought me to spiritual depths I don't want to sink to again.

Reviewing Step Two reminds me that I'm not alone, and that I have faith that I'll be given what I need to become a whole and free person again.

Step Three reminds me that I've made a decision. I'm willing to do what's necessary for recovery and to trust the process. I remember that I only have to do my part; my progress in recovery isn't entirely up to me. My Higher Power will do the rest. When I reach Step Four, I trust that

in the process of writing about the events of my addictive
life, I'll be taken care of.

Today, I bring willingness and an open mind to the next
step in my recovery. I relax and trust that I am not alone.

 *106*

Life can only be understood backwards;
but it must be lived forwards.
SÖREN KIERKEGAARD

Newcomer

When I look at Step Four, the phrase "the exact nature of
our wrongs" sounds so grim and old-fashioned. I don't
know if I can face my past that way.

Sponsor

We have a phrase—"the arrogant worm"—to express the
way some of us think of ourselves: one moment we're too
important to take the Steps; another moment we're the
worst things that ever walked the face of the earth. Both
are distortions. I'm a human being living among other
human beings. I'm not a saint, but I'm not a worm, either.
Words I've said or failed to say, and actions I've taken or
not taken have had an impact both on other people and
on myself. Chances are that the behavior I'd most like
to forget is the behavior most important to include in my
inventory,

The point of this Step isn't just to list our faults, nor is it to beat ourselves up for them. Nor is it to complain about the ways we've been victimized by people or circumstances. It is to look at where our addictions have taken us.

In recovery, I cherish my innate sense of right and wrong. Today, it leads me to take actions for which I esteem myself.

 *107*

Happy for us if the grace of God enables us to live so that we retain innocency and freshness of character down to old age.
MARY ANN WENDELL

Newcomer

I've always been down on myself—that's my problem. When I look at the Steps and see "searching and fearless moral inventory," "the exact nature of our wrongs," and "defects of character," the language seems so judgmental. It depresses me to think of myself in such negative terms.

Sponsor

Like you, I found certain phrases in the Steps off-putting at first. I changed them in my mind: for "wrongs," I substituted "things I would like to have done differently"; for "defects," I substituted "old habits and ways of reacting that I'd like to be free of." I needed the gentlest possible approach; I'd been beating myself up for as long as I could remember.

The Steps aren't asking us to blame or to punish ourselves. Many of us accept the idea that we inherited a predisposition for our addictions and that things that happened in our lives provided opportunities for addiction to take hold. Fortunately, recovery offers us the opportunity to see ourselves with clarity and compassion, to free ourselves to become the people we've always wanted to be. We can work the Twelve Steps with infinite gentleness and caring, for ourselves and for the truth.

Today, my compassion for myself
opens me to the gentleness of the program.

108

*Would you take a stick and punish your hand
because it lacked understanding?*
RABBI SHMELKE OF NIKOLSBURG

Newcomer
What is a "moral inventory," exactly?

Sponsor
There are many approaches to Step Four in program literature and in publications about recovery; at Step meetings you'll hear people describe still other methods suggested by their sponsors. All these methods involve writing—one of the most powerful tools we have in recovery.

Taking our moral inventory helps us get to know ourselves better by looking honestly at our behavior and its impact on ourselves and others. One simple, effective approach, as suggested in AA's Big Book, focuses on two key emotions: fear and resentment. We make as complete as possible a list of people and institutions we have feared and resented. We identify what it is in us that feels threatened by each individual on our list. The result is a portrait—not of others, but of ourselves and the feelings that have fueled our addictive lives.

Another approach is to list our assets and deficits, as we might do for a business. A balanced picture includes pluses as well as minuses, so for those of us who are experts at self-dislike, it's important to note not only our past mistakes, but also the progress we've made. How are we evolving into more honest, caring, responsible people? What are we doing better? What are our positive qualities, and how do they contribute to a strong recovery?

**Today, I think about writing a searching and fearless
moral inventory of myself. In the spirit of honesty,
I will record assets as well as deficits.**

 *109*

You can look at the past—but don't stare.
FRANCIS BRADY

Newcomer
From what I hear, many people don't write a Fourth Step inventory until a year or two after entering recovery. Some wait three, even four years. I've heard the expression "A Step a year." Should I wait?

Sponsor
In the early days of AA, newcomers were guided through the Steps within a few days or weeks of getting sober. Many people were helped to a new, sober life that way. Over time, a more gradual approach has proved just as effective for newcomers in AA and other Twelve Step programs.

Today, those who are committed to staying in recovery

have a great deal of fellowship support available. We have a proliferation of programs, many models of long-term experience in recovery, and large numbers of meetings to choose from. With all this support, some may choose to postpone Steps Four through Twelve, yet still manage to stay sober—though "a Step a year," if taken literally, could be a prescription for endlessly postponing the joy of recovery. Honest self-examination is a necessary part of the process that leads to the waking up of our spirits. Why delay it?

For us, gentleness is essential in doing the Fourth Step. Our purpose is not self-punishment or humiliation. It's letting go of the guilt and shame that led us to numb ourselves with addictive substances and behaviors. We can begin by keeping a Fourth Step file or index cards on which we list fears and resentments one or two at a time, as we remember them. Or we can use a gentle Step Four workbook. Because we trust that a Higher Power is part of our process, we don't have to put off Step Four or hurry through it.

Today, I look at my past with honesty and compassion.

⇌ *110* ⇌

*If you do not tell the truth about yourself
you cannot tell it about other people.*
VIRGINIA WOOLF

Newcomer
Why should I have to take the blame for everything? What about the things other people have done to me?

Sponsor

Taking Step Four isn't about blaming ourselves or others. It can help us with our anger at those we believe have harmed us. When we write a Fourth Step, we name all the people and institutions we fear and resent. By putting into writing the wrongs we believe each of them has committed, we see the array of fears and resentments that burden our minds and disturb our serenity.

It's human nature to fear or resent people we haven't treated well. If I neglect someone—lie to her, cheat her, or take something away from her that I know deep down is rightfully hers—I don't very much want to see or think about her. I tell myself, "It's all her fault." Guilt feels unpleasant; I may turn to my addiction to keep it at bay. Step Four asks me to take an honest look at the ways I myself contributed to or even caused the situation I'm so upset about.

But there may also be certain things we didn't cause. What if we're convinced that we're right? Instead of plotting revenge, we can understand that there are others who are mentally or spiritually ill. We can acknowledge what they have done, without having to cling to resentment. We can ask in our prayers that they be healed.

Today, I let faith replace my fears and resentments.

✎ *111* ✎

I climbed the ladder of success wrong by wrong.
PATRICIA BROOKS

Newcomer

I'd like to go back to the old days, just for a little while. It's so hard being sober every day, and in every situation. There were many things that using made easier.

Sometimes we look back on our days of active addiction with fondness. We miss the experiences that became available to us when we acted out. Depending on our history and drug of choice, we may remember times when we moved easily in social situations, talked or danced with greater ease, even entered relationships without a lot of fuss and agony. Or maybe we had a greater sense of power in work situations: we remember a time when we worked around the clock without feeling tired, triumphantly meeting a deadline. We may simply miss the drug itself, its familiar physical sensations or psychological effects.

It's better to acknowledge this sense of loss than to ignore it. If we're willing to go back, imaginatively, to what we think of as our days of freedom, then we can also remember what followed. Feelings of pleasure, expansiveness, or power eventually led to the very states we were attempting to anesthetize: exhaustion, dependency, self-dislike.

Today, I see the history of my addiction with clarity.

112

***A ship in port is safe,
but that is not what ships are built for.***
BENAZIR BHUTTO

Newcomer

I've been meaning to get started on the Fourth Step, but I just haven't had enough time to myself.

Problems having to do with time are often about something else. If we're procrastinating, usually it's because we fear something.

For me, this fear is almost always the mistaken belief that I'm not worthy. I think that I won't be able to do an adequate job or that others will devalue my efforts. And what if I'm a success? I may want success, but fear that I won't be able to live up to the new, higher standards I'll have set for myself.

If there's something we want to do, we can find the time to begin it. Length of time is far less critical than consistency. For example, ten or fifteen minutes of writing every morning can add up to hundreds of pages in the course of a year. Whatever the project, we'll probably find that we get more practiced and efficient as we go. As a result, the clarity of our vision and quality of our work will improve. Continuing our journey through the Steps will enhance the quality of our sober lives with greater freedom and self-esteem. We are worth it.

**Today, I begin something I've been putting off.
I commit to continuing, a little bit at a time.**

~ *113* ~

*The moment one definitely commits oneself,
then Providence moves too.*
JOHANN WOLFGANG VON GOETHE

Newcomer

I sat down last night and tried to begin writing my Fourth Step. So many feelings went swirling through me that I got completely blocked. My life is full of things I feel embarrassed and ashamed about. There are secrets I've never told anyone. Some of these things are just too personal. How am I ever going to share them with another human being?

Sponsor

No wonder you're anxious. It sounds as if you're trying to do Step Five before you've begun Step Four. Each Step involves taking a specific action and having the willingness and faith to complete that action. In Step Four, the action is to write, and to be fearless and thorough as we do so. The Step doesn't mention sharing what we write. It's premature to decide whom to share with, and it's counterproductive, in any case, to speculate about how someone is going to respond. Today, it's just you, putting words on paper—that is your focus in the present moment.

I'm glad that you've shared your fear of this task with me. When we speak out loud about a fear, it begins to lose its power over us. As we so often hear in meetings, the opposite of fear is faith. We can pray for courage as we begin this Step. We can continue to pray each time fear arises in the process of writing.

I promise that by the time you've completed your Fourth Step, the process will have moved you to a new place, one you can't really know or understand ahead of time. Only then will you be ready for the next Step.

Today, I stay focused on the present and on the task at hand. I let past and future go. I remember to breathe, as I replace fear with faith.

**There but for the grace of God go I.**
OLD SAYING, SOURCE OF A PROGRAM SLOGAN

Newcomer

I hear some people talk about the truly terrible depths they sank to when they were active in their addictions. That's not me, though. I've always had a roof over my head. The bills got paid. I always got to work on time and did what I was supposed to do. I feel sorry for anyone who's gone through such debasing experiences, but I don't really relate to them.

Sponsor

Those who have lost everything and then entered recovery are blessed with clarity. They don't have to entertain doubts about where addiction can bring us—any of us. If we persist in addiction, we will lose health, home, friends, reputation, work, purpose, and soul. I learn from listening to their stories what extremes my addiction is capable of taking me to if I go back to using.

Addiction is often called a disease of denial. No addict wants to admit to having an addiction. I clung to my excuses like a life raft. If I met certain minimum requirements of work and civilized behavior, I could rationalize away the thought that I had a problem. I functioned more or less adequately in spite of my addiction. This fact fed my denial and postponed my surrender.

Many of us carry our denial into recovery. Some days denial rears its head more insistently than others. The best medicine for denial is to listen with an open mind, to identify with others' feelings, and to share our own memories of active addiction.

Today, I honor my urge for healing. As I listen to others in recovery, I identify with the feelings they share.

Home, in one form or another, is the great object of life.
JOSIAH HOLLAND

Newcomer

I know this sounds trivial, but it's still bothering me. My house is a mess. It feels out of control. It's going to take forever to get it together. It's not the sort of thing I can ask someone to help me with; I'm ashamed to let anyone see it.

Sponsor

In early recovery, we may crave change, but feel too depressed to know how to go about it. We may be overwhelmed just thinking of all the work involved in clearing up the wreckage of the past, whether it involves a messy house, unpaid bills, back taxes, work commitments, or personal promises.

As with so many chores, we can approach cleaning house little by little. Instead of pulling everything out of all the closets, we can limit ourselves to fifteen minutes or half an hour to fill a trash bag with things we don't want in our lives any more. If we can't simply throw things away, we can start filling a carton for a charitable organization. Short periods of time once or twice a week eventually add up.

Recovery began with a single action. Taking the First

Step prepared us for the Second. There are times when we feel we're at a standstill, others when we progress rapidly. The overall length of time isn't the point; it's the quality of the ongoing process. We can begin it at any time.

One more thing: are we really so much worse than everyone around us that we can't ask for help? If we can't accept hands-on help, how about making phone calls before, during, and after tough chores?

Today, I take one step toward creating order.

116

The young man who has not wept is a savage,
and the old man who will not laugh is a fool.
GEORGE SANTAYANA

Newcomer

I feel close to tears today, for no good reason. Listening to someone talking about his children, I actually did start to cry, and later I came close to tears again just because someone asked me how I was feeling. Everything has been going so well, and now this! I don't want to be one of those people who are full of self-pity, and I don't want my boss or my friends to think that my emotions are out of control.

Sponsor

When I was active in my disease, I rarely laughed or cried from the heart. Whether I felt sad or happy, angry or afraid, any feeling made me uncomfortable; a strong emotion was a signal to medicate myself. In early recovery, even after we have gone through physical withdrawal, our tears may flow seemingly for no reason as our bodies and spirits cleanse themselves and restore inner balance. There is no such thing as a "wrong" feeling. Nowadays, though I don't need to cry as often, I can let others see my feelings without fear of being judged; my new willingness just to be myself helps others— it lets them see that they, too, are free to be themselves.

Today, I don't have to deny or judge
my feelings or the feelings of others.
Tears and laughter are both gifts of my recovery.

117

Do we not find freedom
along the guiding lines of discipline?
JONATHAN SWIFT

Newcomer
What does it mean when someone says, "I'm going to do a Fourth Step on this"? I thought Step Four was a thorough history of where my using took me. Do I have to write it again whenever a problem comes up?

Sponsor
Many people who are "searching and fearless" in taking the Fourth Step never feel the need to take another one. Others decide later in recovery to take another Fourth Step in light of what they've learned about themselves. It's a matter of personal preference and need. Step Ten suggests a way to keep the inventory process up to date by making a daily or on-the-spot review of our motives and actions.

We can learn from our experience of Step Four how to approach a specific problem in recovery. When people say, "I'm going to do a Fourth Step on it," they usually mean that they will go back to the method of Step Four and do some writing about a current problem, taking a close and thorough look at their motives and behavior. This is an example of what's meant by the phrase (from Step Twelve) "practicing these principles in all our affairs."

Today, I trust that the Twelve Steps can shed light on whether situations or problems arise in my day.

 *118*

Everything may happen.
SENECA

Newcomer
I was talking with someone in recovery about how to deal with a difficult situation I think may arise. The person said to me, "Stop projecting." I felt put down. This thing I'm worrying about is a real possibility, not something I'm making up; I think I should be prepared for it. What's so bad about "projecting"?

Sponsor
Some people in recovery call Steps Four through Nine a way to clear up the wreckage of the past. A friend says she knows that she's projecting when she's "worrying about the wreckage of the future"!

There's certainly nothing wrong with having goals and making plans, but we need to watch that we're not obsessing. When I was active in my addiction, making plans was always a problem. I would frequently commit myself to something in advance, then panic; there was a fifty-fifty chance that I'd cancel when the day arrived. Sometimes I was in complete denial about the future and avoided necessary scheduling.

In recovery, we can and should make realistic plans. We have to pack suitcases for a trip, set up work schedules that make it possible to keep our commitments, make social appointments that will bring fun into our lives. And we can learn to leave some breathing space so that we're not booked in advance for every day and every evening.

Today, I have goals and plans. I take appropriate actions and turn the results over to my Higher Power.

 *119*

*One must get **a thing before one can** forget **it**.*
OLIVER WENDELL HOLMES

Newcomer
I hear people talk about having the desire for their drug of choice lifted. I don't know if that's what's happening to me, exactly. I know I don't want to repeat the painful experiences of my past, and I'm not picking up. But that doesn't mean I never think about what it would be like to use again.

Sponsor
There's a difference between desire and compulsion. There are sober alcoholics who sometimes still experience a desire to drink, as do active alcoholics who've lost jobs, homes, or families through their disease. Those who respond to cravings with addictive substances and behaviors instead of the tools of recovery are compelled to keep using. We may continue to have the desire for certain things, but the difference is our willingness to come to meetings and treat our compulsion.

We still live with the disease, though many of us no longer experience addiction signals—we don't hear the old voices inside telling us that we want to pick up a drink, a drug, or an addictive behavior. The voice of recovery inside us is stronger. We don't make the mistake of thinking we've been cured. For most of us, the longer our recovery, the more aware we are of our vulnerability to addiction. If we think an addictive behavior all the way through, we remember the suffering that followed the momentary relief. The central importance of recovery in our lives becomes clearer as we accumulate time in the program.

Today, I'm grateful for reminders of my addiction; they strengthen my commitment to recovery.

 *120*

Relationships don't end; they change.
FRANCIS BRADY

Newcomer
There's another newcomer I've been spending a lot of time with. We go to meetings together, go to coffee afterward. We talk on the phone. We've gone to some events outside the fellowship, too, and I'm starting to wonder if it's okay to be getting this involved.

Sponsor
There's nothing wrong with making new friends! It's valuable to get to know some peers in recovery, people who got sober at about the same time that you did. Your peers are probably going through experiences similar to your own. Sharing together and offering mutual encouragement can

connect you to the fellowship and create a sense of community that is there for you over time. As you grow in recovery, there's nothing quite like knowing people who remember what you were like in the beginning and who have watched your progress as you have watched theirs.

If other issues related to this are coming up for you, you may need to take a further look. Each situation is different. If something feels "off," you can trust your gut reaction. Is it really your choice to spend a lot of time together, or do you feel you have to say yes whenever someone "needs" you? Are you sending a message that you're more available than you really are?

Or are you concerned that something romantic may be developing between you? It can seem wonderful, at first, to be in love and sharing a program of recovery. But a romantic relationship between two newcomers may keep both of you more involved with one another than with the program.

Today, I have a choice about the people I spend time with. I am rich in support from friends who share the values and experiences of recovery.

⇒ *121* ⇒

Always do one thing less than you think you can do.
BERNARD BARUCH

Newcomer

In my first few months of recovery, I gave most of my attention to this program. Since becoming able to function better, I've taken on more responsibilities in my work life. I'm trying to do what I can to clear up debts and make some financial progress. But I'm overwhelmed with all my responsibilities, and I feel tired much of the time.

I identify with your desire to try to make up for lost time. When I first entered recovery, I felt exhausted just thinking about how much I had to make up for and how little time there was to accomplish everything. It didn't occur to me that relaxation and creativity were equally as important and that, in fact, they were necessities of life.

You may need to reassess the responsibilities you've taken on. This is a good time for you to think about which of your responsibilities are essential, and which give you genuine pleasure. You may find that you can drop some activities to make time for others that lift your spirits instead of draining them. We didn't enter recovery to make ourselves miserable. Joy is not only possible; it's a requirement!

Today, I honor my need for joy.

 *122*

***One never notices what has been done;
one can only see what remains to be done.***
MARIE CURIE

Newcomer

You seem so tolerant, so easygoing. You're always telling me to relax. Shouldn't you be tougher on me?

Sponsor

Why are we so hard on ourselves, so impatient, so dissatisfied with the ongoing miracle of our recovery?

In our hearts, we don't believe in the effectiveness of going through a gradual process over time; that's not how we learned to do things in our lives of active addiction. Consuming an addictive substance or acting out a compulsion had an almost instantaneous effect. We grew accustomed to making things happen that fast, and today we may think that if things take time, we're somehow defective. Perhaps we've had little experience of practicing something on a regular basis, without forcing results. Work and effort; gentleness, relaxation, rest—all these are necessary parts of the same process.

Today, I'm satisfied with who I am, what I have, what I do.

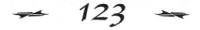

123

If you obey all the rules, you miss all the fun.
KATHARINE HEPBURN

Newcomer

I went to a wedding where it seemed as if everyone but me was celebrating in ways I used to love—overeating and getting drunk, among other things. Either they were consuming stuff right under my nose, or else they were talking about all their little addictive habits without questioning them, as if they hadn't a care in the world.

Sponsor

First, let me congratulate you for getting through a demanding social event without picking up. We go through a process in recovery that begins with feelings of loss and deprivation and progresses to a sense of freedom. It takes awhile.

In early recovery, I envied and resented nonaddicts. Everywhere I looked, people seemed to be bingeing in one way or another without negative consequences. It took time to accept that the things *they* could do without negative consequences—or believed they could do—were toxic for me. As my denial lifted, my attitude toward recovery became somewhat egotistical. For some time, I lived off a sense of superiority. *They* were in the dark, I thought. *They* were the ones who were deprived; I'd found a better way.

Over time, we stop being so concerned about others' lives. What other people do for fun is their business; we have our own path. It doesn't make us better or worse than anyone else, but it does make us different.

Today, I love being alive; I celebrate my recovery.

124

Nobuddy ever fergits where he buried a hatchet.
KIN HUBBARD

Newcomer
There's someone close to me who was always after me to quit my addictive behavior. Now that I'm in recovery, he's angry at me all the time. Is this what I deserve for recovering?

Sponsor
The people who were in our lives when we were active in our addictions had much to be angry about. The damage we did was real. We were present physically, but we weren't functioning fully. Many of us were self-centered and emotionally absent. Whether as partners or friends, parents or children, employees or employers, we couldn't be depended on.

People around us learned not to count on us in certain ways, and those who didn't reject us may have enabled our addictions by making excuses for us, rationalizing to themselves about our inadequacies, and shouldering more than their share of mutual responsibilities.

Now that we're safely in recovery, the truth of what they've had to put up with may be more painfully obvious to them than before. The anger and hurt they've been keeping inside all this time may come spilling out of them.

Understanding that our addictive behavior has had an impact on others is a crucial part of our recovery. They have their own healing process to go through. We can't hurry it or make it happen.

Today, I practice patience and compassion
for all those who have been affected by my addiction.

125

No one's career plans include becoming an addict....
JEFFREY SKINNER

Newcomer

I had a haircut today. The hairdresser had just come back from Holland, where certain drugs are legal, and he talked about "space cakes"—cakes filled with marijuana and hashish—that he'd eaten on the plane instead of drinking. I said that I didn't drink any more, and that the thought of flying made me anxious. He said, "Well, you can have a Valium, can't you?" I just nodded. For a moment, it seemed reasonable.

Sponsor

Watching people use, or listening to them refer casually to drugs or behavior that for us is poison, can be disturbing. We may envy these people. We may try to explain ourselves to them. We may mistakenly try to save them, even when they haven't shown any signs of identifying their behavior or substance use as a problem of addiction.

We can save ourselves a lot of trouble by not trying to diagnose other people's problems. We can share stories about encounters like yours in a meeting, where everyone will laugh with recognition. Above all, we can remember, as you did, that there is no room in a life of recovery for any sort of self-prescribed mood changer.

**Today, I live and let live. I respect my recovery
and don't have to explain or justify it to anyone.**

 *126*

Popularity is a Siren singing on a rock.
ANTHONY BURGESS

Newcomer

There's someone who's kind of a "star" at one of my regular meetings. Everyone seems to look up to him and love him. To me, he sounds stern and critical. Sometimes I don't raise my hand, thinking he'd disapprove of what I'd say.

Sponsor

"Principles before personalities" is a slogan that reminds me not to cultivate an attitude of worship toward any person in this fellowship. "Stars" are just other people in recovery, like us. No one person has all the answers. There are old-timers whose experience, love for the program, honesty, and humility are precious gifts. Newcomers, too, can add to what we learn about our addictions. We don't go to meetings to judge others, but to listen for what speaks to us and furthers our recovery.

Like you, I've sometimes fallen under the spell of a high-profile personality. Why invest one person with so much power? Why let one person's approval be so important here, of all places, where we can experience unconditional love? Why even assume that he or she has an opinion of us?

In recovery, we have the chance to get to know ourselves. Making a Higher Power out of another recovering person is an obstacle, not an aid, in this process.

Today, I focus on principles before personalities.

127

*Who says we're not living
in a time of war.*
ALI LIEBEGOTT

Newcomer
Sometimes people in meetings talk about suicide attempts they made when they were active in their addictions. Talking about it at a meeting seems unnecessarily heavy to me—it's not everyone's experience.

Sponsor
The disease that we have is a fatal one, if it's left untreated. Some of us made suicide attempts in the past. Some of us believe we were never that desperate. But aren't our active

addictions a form of suicide, too? What about the damaging effect on our health, over time, of the substances we consumed? What about the dangerous situations we got ourselves into through impaired judgment? What about the small deaths: the people we shut out through our addictions, the meaningful work or pleasure we denied ourselves, the dreams we deferred?

Each day we have the choice of adopting attitudes and taking actions that lead to recovery or to addiction—to life or to death.

Today, I'm entrusted with the precious gift of my life.

128

Speak boldly, and speak truly, shame the devil.
JOHN FLETCHER

Newcomer
Last time I shared at a meeting, I felt foolish. There were other people in the room whose troubles were so much more serious than mine. I hate the sound of whining. I don't want to be like that.

Sponsor
Sharing and listening to others share are the principal tools we have for staying in recovery. Though we may not get to share at every meeting we attend, it's necessary to share often, and from the heart. It relieves the pressure inside us that we might otherwise be tempted to relieve by picking up our drug of choice. It's wonderful that you're putting your hand up and talking honestly about your experience and feelings as recovery continues. It's required.

At meetings, I haven't heard much of what some call whining, though I've certainly heard people in pain. We may sometimes sound as if we're stuck in the same place for a while, but in time, we change. If we're following the path of recovery, growth is inevitable. Neither we nor anyone else can gain anything in recovery by judging a person's rate of growth or comparing one person's healing process with another.

> Today, I participate in restoring
> my own and others' health by sharing.

 **129**

*Falling in love with your doctor or nurse
or a fellow patient is an old romantic story.*
LIVING SOBER

Newcomer

A friend tells me that she's been experiencing feelings of attraction toward her sponsor. I've heard that this happens, even though most sponsors and sponsees follow the suggestion not to work together if a potential for attraction exists. What should be done about it?

Sponsor

I'm glad that you trust me—and yourself—enough to discuss this sensitive issue.

In most sponsor-sponsee relationships, both participants share a lot about themselves and let themselves be seen as they really are. The mutual respect and caring that can result is a blessing. However, in such a close relationship, feelings, thoughts, and wishes occasionally come up in the form of an attraction. In my own role as a sponsor, I've learned that certain intense feelings a sponsee may express, whether of attraction or anger, don't necessarily belong to me. This sort of emotional transference is common in therapy and other relationships in which the work is close and exposing.

Often, romantic feelings on the part of a sponsee pass quickly. Sometimes all that's needed is to share them. In my own opinion, it's good to give the problem some time—if it were to persist as a concern for either the sponsor or the sponsee, they'd want to reconsider the advisability of working together.

Today, I am grateful for boundaries, others' and my own, that make the fellowship a safe place.

 *130*

I'll agree to be your sponsor—if you'll agree to phone me every day and to call first if you think you're going to pick up.
MAN IN RECOVERY

Newcomer

I know I haven't called you for a while. You don't have to worry about me, though. I appreciate what you've done for me, but I just don't think I need to call you every single day. I've been able to stay away from my addictive substance without always talking about it.

Sponsor

No one can force you to do anything. Your life is your own. You are the one who's responsible for it. I can share my experiences and listen to yours, but I can't get another person drunk and I can't keep another person sober.

When I let others know what's really going on with me, I start feeling connected with them. That's not always comfortable. But I don't much like the work of attempting to control my disease in isolation, either. Consistent sharing with other recovering people is the core of recovery. It teaches us how to be honest.

I want to acknowledge your courage in saying no to me today. I trust that you'll say it a lot as you establish boundaries that let you feel safe with me and others. But if I'm going to sponsor you in your recovery, I need us to have an agreement about regular times to talk about the program and what's going on in your relationship to it. And I want to know that if you're tempted to act out your addiction, you'll call me first.

> Today, as relationships with people continue,
> I have the courage to identify my own needs.
> I set appropriate limits that allow me to stay
> connected with others and to keep my commitments.

131

Honesty is the best policy.
DAVID TUVILL

Newcomer

I've heard people talk about "firing" their sponsors, about sponsors "firing" their sponsees. I find that term disillusioning. I thought we were here to help one another.

Sponsor

Human relationships change, for all sorts of reasons, and there's nothing wrong with acknowledging that reality. Sponsors, like sponsees, are just people in recovery, growing and working the Steps; we don't always handle things perfectly. One sponsor may take on more than he or she is really prepared to handle; with phone calls coming day and night from an overload of sponsees, frequency or quality of communication may be inadequate. Another sponsor may enjoy being bossy and have trouble recognizing the difference between passing on program experience and trying to impose his or her will in areas where personal choice is appropriate. A sponsor may discover that a sponsee lacks the desire for recovery or has significant problems in an area in which the sponsor has no experience.

When differences are resolved by talking and listening, relationships grow and deepen. Are we avoiding necessary confrontation with ourselves or others? Or does growth, this time, mean that it's appropriate to separate? Honesty, courage, and love are qualities that help us make transitions in our relationships.

Today, my willingness to grow
enhances my relationships with others.

132

Joy delights in joy.
WILLIAM SHAKESPEARE

Newcomer

Our group is having an anniversary party, and I asked someone with a lot of time in the fellowship to go as my date. I really stuck my neck out: I let this person know that I felt attracted. Here's the answer I got: "I don't get involved with anyone with fewer than five years of recovery!" I wish I'd kept my mouth shut.

Sponsor

Don't make yourself wrong for asking for what you wanted. While there are kinder, more gracious ways of saying no, at least this person told the truth and didn't confuse you about what to expect in the future.

A date to go to a dance or a party can be just a date; it doesn't have to lead to deep involvement. You have the right to enjoy yourself and to have social companionship. It's good experience to attend some sober social events in our first year, especially with friends for whom recovery is as high a priority as it is for us.

The first parties I attended in recovery were truly scary to me—I hadn't had much experience enjoying other people's company without the "help" of my drug of choice. It may be more relaxing for you to lower the stakes by joining up with two or three recovery friends and attending the party in a group. Or you can sign up to contribute food or music or to help with decorating or cleaning up. Having a job to do is one way to feel part of things.

Today, I am grateful for the word "no."
I respect my own and others' honesty in saying it.
I feel joy in my recovery and say yes to celebration.

The art of life is to show your hand.
C. V. LUCAS

Newcomer

I've been thinking about talking to another sponsor. Not to replace you—our relationship is important to me, and I get a lot from it—but in addition to you.

Sponsor

We're lucky to have such an abundance of sober experience in this fellowship. There are many of us, and we can get to know people with various lengths of time in recovery, different experiences, different styles. Knowing others and having the willingness to let others know us is one of the keys to growing in recovery.

I support your wanting to enlarge your support system by taking on a second sponsor. There may be someone, for example, with whom you want to focus on spiritual matters.

Your expressing your desire for additional sponsorship gives us an opportunity to take a look at our own relationship. You may think that I won't be able to understand a particular issue that's troubling you. You may be worried about how much you've already shared with me—many of us in this fellowship are new to letting others get close, and we may feel anxious about it. Problems with relationships are often at the heart of problems of addiction. Whatever it is, I'm open to hearing about it, and I won't criticize your feelings or walk away. I've been there myself. Thank you for being willing to talk with me about your needs and plans.

**Today, I am willing to be honest and open
with a trusted person.**

The best elixir is a friend.
WILLIAM SOMERVILLE

Newcomer

How should I go about asking someone to hear my Fifth Step?

Sponsor

There are no rules about how to make a Fifth Step appointment. Some of us choose to take Step Five with a sponsor, some with a spiritual adviser or a therapist, some with a person we've heard share at meetings. People don't have to be in recovery to have some understanding of how this program works and to be good role models and listeners. More important is that they honor our commitment to recovery and our purpose in taking the Step.

Asking someone to perform this important role in our recovery involves discretion as well as trust. Do others have values and attitudes we respect? Is their relationship to the program a healthy one? As we do when approaching a potential sponsor, we ask, "Do we want what they have?" Are they genuinely willing?

Once we've made a choice, we can make a simple, direct request: "I'm ready to take Step Five and want to ask if you'd be willing to hear it." If we're turned down, we ask another appropriate person. We can trust our experience with other people.

Today, I trust my perceptions of others. I deserve to reach out to people whose quality of recovery I respect.

A certain amount of distrust is wholesome,
but not so much of others as of ourselves.
MADAME NECKER

Newcomer

I've always had a hard time asking people for things. Asking someone to hear my Fifth Step seems like placing such a burden on them.

Sponsor

Helping other members of this fellowship to achieve freedom from addiction is part of our primary purpose. Speaking and listening to other human beings whose journey resembles ours is one of the principal ways that we maintain our recovery. Being asked to hear a Fifth Step is usually regarded as a gift, not a burden.

Asking for help is a wonderful exercise in humility. It asks us to give up our idea that we're responsible for everything. It asks us to trust other adults to take care of themselves, to trust that if hearing the Step isn't feasible for them at this time, they'll say so. It asks us to give up our idea that we're unique and not capable of being understood, let alone forgiven, by anyone else. It asks us to let other people be close to us.

Step Five dissolves the sense of separation, both for the person sharing and for the person listening. Chances are that neither will ever forget the experience.

Today, a Power greater than myself
is with me in all my exchanges with others.

In the faces of men and women I see God.
WALT WHITMAN

Newcomer

I'm nervous about Step Five. It's already such a radical change for me to be honest with myself—which I guess is also a way of being honest with my Higher Power. Isn't that enough? Do I have to shame myself in front of another person?

Sponsor

No, we don't have to "shame" ourselves in front of another person; but yes, we do have to share our inventory with a human being. I'm glad that you experienced the presence of your Higher Power as you took stock of your life. Your Higher Power will also be present when you share your inventory with another person.

This exchange between two people is a sacred one. The Fifth Step requires one of us to share, the other to hear, details of a past in which self-centered fear and resentment took us places we don't want to return to. It's an experience of intimacy: both participants know each other and themselves better when they're through. The listener is going to hear about feelings and choices that are reminders of his or her own. A listener may respond by sharing some similar experiences with us or may simply indicate to us that we're not unique; this helps us to put our past into perspective.

Step Five is just a beginning, a beginning of self-love and self-trust, a beginning of feelings of connection with the rest of humanity. In time, as recovery continues, we'll be blessed by many opportunities to share ourselves honestly and deeply, whether at meetings or in conversations with trusted friends or loved ones.

**Today, I'm being healed by my honest sharing
and compassionate listening.**

 *137*

People tend to become what you tell them they are.
DOROTHY DeLAY

Newcomer
Someone I know keeps telling me what a great person I am. You'd think I'd love it, but it really upsets me. I don't like the attention, and I don't entirely believe it.

Sponsor
In early recovery, if someone expressed a high opinion of me, I felt as if I'd put something over on him or her; sooner or later, I thought, it would become clear what a fraud I was. Sometimes I had the opposite reaction: I ate up the praise and couldn't get enough. My ego went clear through the roof. It took both time in recovery and the hard work of getting to know myself to accept that other people's opinions were simply opinions, and I couldn't base my serenity on them. I want to please other people, and I still can't always accept compliments and criticisms without being briefly knocked off my center. If three people tell me the same thing about myself, I pay attention; there may be some useful information in the consistency of others' perceptions of me. But I don't put conditions on self-love or self-acceptance.

**Today, my love for myself and others
is unconditional love.**

Things do not change; we change.
HENRY DAVID THOREAU

Newcomer

Things look like they aren't going too badly, on the outside. But on the inside, I'm a mess. Sometimes I feel close to panic or despair. What's wrong with me?

Sponsor

Recovery allows us to get on with our lives. There's no prescribed schedule, and there's no rush. In time we find appropriate work, take care of health matters, become financially responsible. We create homes for ourselves and discover who our peers are and how we want to spend our time.

It's not unusual for our external lives to become repaired more quickly and easily than our internal ones. Some of the feelings we're experiencing are responses to things that happened some time ago. In recovery, we begin looking at the past through a different lens. We have spiritual tools that can help lift depression and anxiety. New experiences and outcomes become part of our memory bank. Our outlook changes. Comfort and joy become part of our emotional vocabulary.

Today, I experience myself as growing more comfortable in my own skin.

> *You know, a heart can be broken*
> *but it keeps on beating just the same.*
> FANNIE FLAGG

Newcomer

I hear people at meetings talking about depression as if it's a pretty serious thing. I wonder if I'm depressed; I feel down a lot of the time. But doesn't everyone get sad?

Sponsor

There's a big difference between sadness and depression. When we consistently block our tears, perhaps having been taught that they were wrong, perhaps not trusting that we'll be safe if we shed them, our sadness remains dammed up inside us and depression sets in. For some, it's not sadness that is being denied expression, but anger. Long-held anger, like unexpressed sorrow, acts like a toxic substance within us. Our connections to ourselves, other people, and our Higher Power are affected. There are chemical contributors to depression, too. Alcohol and other sedative drugs depress our physiological systems; antihistamine use can have a depressant effect, and so can excessive intake of the kinds of fats that clog our systems.

When we're depressed for long periods, it's hard for us to take initiative. Simple tasks seem like immense challenges. We feel emotionally flat. Our attitude toward others may be sullen. We didn't get sober to drift in the no-world of depression. As with other ailments, there is help for depression in recovery.

Today, I release my feelings
without self-censorship or shame.

Hell's rather out of date.
ALFRED SUTRO

Newcomer

What can I do about depression, short of getting professional help?

Sponsor

In recovery, we can begin addressing depression physically, mentally, and spiritually. We can exercise (aerobic activity, half an hour a day, five days a week, is a powerful and healthy mood changer). We can eat nourishing food and avoid depressants like alcohol and other sedatives. We can begin to understand and feel compassion for ourselves as we share at meetings and work the Twelve Steps in a committed and thorough way. We can let the program serve as a gateway to spiritual practice and connection.

Depression, if indeed that's our problem, is an illness that must be taken seriously and addressed accordingly. If we're suffering, there is absolutely nothing wrong with seeking professional help. Consulting a therapist doesn't have to mean taking antidepressant drugs. Sometimes, though, medication is clearly indicated; many people in recovery have been helped by it without compromising their recovery in any way. We don't get less sober by getting help.

Today, I take my mental, physical, and spiritual needs seriously; I reach out for help when I need it.

**Self pity is our worst enemy and if we yield to it,
we can never do anything wise in the world.**

HELEN KELLER

Newcomer

I'm feeling discouraged. I've always had health problems—backaches, allergies, and other physical problems. I've tried various remedies, taken vitamins on and off, and seen different kinds of practitioners. And, of course, I go to meetings. Sometimes I feel better for a few days; then suddenly things get worse. I'm miserable again today.

Sponsor

Our bodies have a way of getting our attention. There's an old story that asks, "How do you get a donkey to walk up a hill?" The answer is that first you hit him on the head with a two-by-four; then, when you've gotten his attention, you whisper in his ear—that way, you can get him to start walking up the hill. I think that we're sometimes a bit like donkeys, and that bodily pain is the two-by-four that finally gets our attention and gets us moving. From what you're telling me, I'd guess that something is wrong and is calling out for you to take an action.

It sounds as if up to now you've been trying a little of this and a little of that, taking half measures. That didn't work when you were active in your addiction; you had to overhaul your life and make a wholehearted commitment to recovery. Why should this be different? It may be time for you to look for a physician you're willing to trust, get a thorough checkup, and follow every one of his or her suggestions.

Recovery was the beginning of healing in your life. Having addressed your addiction and made some progress, you no longer find it acceptable to walk around in constant discomfort. That's a positive change.

**Today, I am willing to pay attention to my body
and to take whatever steps are needed for healing.**

 *142*

*Advice is seldom welcome,
and those who want it the most always like it the least.*
LORD CHESTERFIELD

Newcomer

This is going to sound strange, but sometimes I get fed up with all this kindness and caring. I talked a little at a meeting about a health problem I'm dealing with—I'd already seen a doctor—and at the break, people came over to talk to me, full of sympathy and concern. One told me to go to her doctor, another told me what kind of medicine I ought to be taking. I guess they meant well, but I hated it anyway.

Sponsor

Was it kindness and caring, or just people's need to give advice? In and out of meetings, we may find ourselves subjected to others' unsolicited opinions and advice. It's human to want to be helpful, but sometimes true helpfulness lies in simply acknowledging that we've heard the other person. It takes skill to be able to let someone know we care, without trying to take over. I can understand your irritation at being inundated with advice after you'd already sought a professional opinion and treatment for your problem; perhaps you felt as if your responsible, adult behavior was being ignored.

Even in matters of recovery, not everyone with time in the program has the right answer for us. When we share our own experience instead of preaching, others can hear us more easily. According to Twelve Step tradition, it's a program of attraction rather than promotion.

Today, I trust what my heart is telling me.

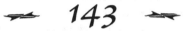

143

When angry, count four; when very angry, swear.
MARK TWAIN

Newcomer
I've just come from a meeting where every single person but me got to share. I had my hand up the whole time, and it was still up when it was time for the meeting to end. The person who led the meeting looked at his watch and said, "It's time to close." There weren't that many people at the meeting—I know he saw me. At times like this, I just want to forget this whole meeting thing.

Sponsor
I can understand your anger at feeling left out.

There are many meetings where the leader asks, a few moments before the closing, whether there's anyone in the room who has "a burning desire" to share, and others where the leader may say, "Please don't leave with a resentment; if you didn't get to share, please talk to one of us after the meeting." Sometimes the leader suggests that a person who didn't get the opportunity to share lead the group in the closing prayer. Any of these ways of acknowledging our presence can be helpful. But if we need to share and aren't given the opportunity, we can invite someone to join us for coffee, or we can call our sponsor.

With rare exceptions, Twelve Step program meetings begin and end precisely as scheduled. For me, it's comforting to be able to depend on that. In the old days, there wasn't much I could count on other than my addiction.

Today, I create opportunities for sharing.

144

This program is a little bit like ice cream: the basic substance is the same, but it comes in a variety of flavors.
WOMAN IN RECOVERY

Newcomer

I've been going to a meeting that, frankly, I just don't like. There's something dark and depressing about it. But I keep hearing people say that this disease is "cunning, baffling, and powerful." I wonder if maybe that's my problem. I could be fooling myself. Maybe I don't know what's good for me. Maybe I'm just lazy.

Sponsor

Let's take a practical look at your situation. This meeting you so dislike—do you have to make the best of it for now? Or is there one at another time or in another place that you can try out? It doesn't hurt to "change your seat" in recovery once in a while. I like to go to beginner's meetings, to meetings where there are people with long-term recovery, to anniversary meetings, to Step meetings, to large meetings where there's a feeling of high energy, to small meetings where I know I'll get the chance to share. We're lucky to have such variety available. Sometimes I travel a bit farther to get to meetings I particularly like. But I also have a home group, where I show up on a regular basis and let people get to know me. That way I can't hide.

You've sensed, rightly, that being consistent is good for us. But principles exist to guide us, not to punish ourselves with.

As I let the principles of the program guide me today, I use gentleness and common sense. I reason things out with my sponsor. I change my seat and take a fresh look at things.

145

Character is what you are in the dark.
DWIGHT MOODY

Newcomer
People in this program are always talking about not "isolating." Does that mean I'm supposed to be around people all the time? That doesn't sound very adult to me. I like spending time alone, when I can get it.

Sponsor
There's a big difference between solitude and isolation. Many of us do work that requires being alone, and many of us welcome opportunities to read, meditate, enjoy nature, listen to music, or whatever nourishes our spirit, in our own

company. When we are in tune with ourselves and our Higher Power, spending time alone doesn't have to mean loneliness. Like prayer, solitude can replenish us and give us a calmer, more centered self to bring back into the company of our fellow human beings.

There's another way of being alone, which is not beneficial. When we become preoccupied with an anxiety or obsession that keeps us from living in the present moment, when we're thirsting for understanding but scared or unwilling to open ourselves to anyone else, when we believe that we're hopelessly unique and not meant to be a part of the human family—these things foster a sense of isolation similar to that which we experienced when we were active in our addictions.

Getting to a daily meeting, talking with a sponsor, checking in with a good friend, letting someone know the truth of how we're doing—these are some of the ways to avoid becoming dangerously isolated.

Today, I make time for solitude and companionship.

146

Loneliness is the most terrible poverty.
MOTHER TERESA

Newcomer

When I was active, I was sometimes the life of the party, but often I sat on the edges of groups and just couldn't wait to get home and be alone with my drug of choice. Sometimes when I'm at a meeting, I feel the same way: I'm irritated with everyone in the room, antsy, anxious to leave. Then it's over and I get to be alone, but I still feel rotten.

Sponsor

If relating to other people was hard for us in the past, it makes sense that we haven't learned to like or trust people overnight. Depending on our histories, openness to people comes more easily and naturally to some of us than to others. If our past relationships were based on addictive substances or compulsive behaviors, we may not be aware that there are people who like us as we are and who don't intend to exploit or manipulate us.

This is an area in which "acting as if" can help us to have new experiences and eventually change our perspective. Sitting in the circle instead of on the edge; raising our hand to share when we least feel like it; forcing ourselves to speak even very briefly to at least one or two people at every meeting; making a daily call to our sponsor and to other recovering people—any one of these may be more difficult for us than reading the literature, working the Steps, or even staying away from our drug of choice. But it's our spiritual homework. The more we practice, the easier it gets.

Today, I take an action to counter any tendency to isolate with my disease.

⇒ *147* ⇒

All experience is an arch, to build upon.
HENRY ADAMS

Newcomer

I don't know exactly what I expected from recovery, but I guess I wanted more. Somehow, I thought I'd be happier.

Sponsor

I identify with your disappointment. When I was a couple of months sober, I could see that recovery had given me back my life, but I wasn't very happy with it yet. I no longer used addictive substances or behaviors to keep me from facing reality, but reality wasn't especially pleasant or easy. I'd neglected work, financial, and family problems. I lacked experience and skill at maintaining healthy human relationships. I didn't like what I saw when I looked in the mirror.

It was easy for me to turn around and blame the program of recovery for my dissatisfaction with myself and my circumstances. Over time, I'd come to depend on particular substances to "fix" my feelings instantly, and now I wanted a similar "quick fix" from the program. I didn't have much experience with gradual processes, so I didn't understand that real change—deep change—takes place over time.

Consistent, daily efforts to maintain our recovery eventually reveal more to us about who we are and what being alive offers. Though you may not feel happy all the time, happiness will be something you'll feel more deeply and steadily than in your "active" days. When we stay with recovery, we find in time that no matter what we're facing in the present moment, we're grateful to be free of addiction.

Today, I celebrate the miracle that I'm alive.
I keep returning to this program as a source of
sober living, confident that in time its promises
will be fulfilled for me.

*The trick is, knowing how to tip ourselves over
and let the beautiful stuff out.*
RAY BRADBURY

Newcomer

At a meeting, someone asked me how I was, and I started crying. I don't know what was the matter with me. I couldn't help it—the tears kept coming. The person I was talking to said, "You're so lucky you aren't embarrassed to cry; I wish I could do that." Later, I found myself laughing.

Sponsor

It's not surprising that laughter followed your tears. One of the best ways to heal the grief we're holding inside is to weep. There's no virtue in controlling our tears, as some people have mistakenly thought. Tears are not a sign of weakness, and recovery is not about learning to be stoics. We're meant to cry. Scientists have found that our tears contain toxic substances: when we weep, we are literally cleansing our bodies of poisons.

If you think you can't cry, don't worry. Tears of healing can't be forced; they well up when they're ready to flow. One thing is for sure: if you keep showing up for recovery, you will change. Feelings flow through us with greater ease as we keep surrendering to the process of recovery.

Today, my tears and laughter restore my health.

Don't pick up before the miracle.
SAYING HEARD IN MEETINGS

Newcomer
I feel miserable so much of the time now. My life is full of obligations I don't have any stomach for. It seems as if my inner demons are always after me, except for the hour or so a day I spend at a meeting. Sometimes I tell myself that if I picked up my addiction again, I could escape all this.

Sponsor
Thank you for your honesty. Your willingness to share your pain can help to counteract that voice that's telling you you'd be better off going back to your addiction.

We're dealing in reality without a filter, at the very same time that we're going through the pain of withdrawal from an addictive substance or behavior. In time, the externals will begin to seem a lot easier. The "demons," as you call them, are more troubling at first. They grow quieter in time and eventually leave, as we stay sober and learn how to face our problems rather than avoid them.

It's important to remember that depression, loneliness, and other negative emotions were not put there by our recovery. The old life we sometimes imagine going back to may not be as free and wonderful as we remember it; addiction blurred the feelings and sometimes kept the demons at bay, but only recovery will free us from them for good.

> **Today, I'm being changed into the person
> I've always wanted to become.**

I wish you a slow recovery.
SAYING HEARD IN MEETINGS

Newcomer

I feel as if I should be doing better than this by now.

Sponsor

I can identify with your belief that you should be doing better faster. I sometimes feel that about the pace of my own recovery, as if we recovering people are in some sort of race with time.

As active addicts, we had little experience with any long process. We believed in instant results, like the ones we were used to getting from our addictive substance or behavior. So we may not be qualified to judge what our rate of progress should be.

One antidote to my impatience is hearing about myself from people who saw me at meetings in the early days of my recovery. Paradoxically, I feel reassured when they laugh and make statements like, "I remember what you were like: you were bouncing off the walls!" Their perspective reminds me that I've come a distance on my journey.

What can best further your journey is leaving the timetable for recovery in your Higher Power's hands as you focus your whole being—all of your attention—on this present moment.

Today, I don't measure myself. I trust that I'm everything I should be in this moment.

151

There is a way to look at the past. Don't hide from it.
It will not catch you if you don't repeat it.
PEARL BAILEY

Newcomer

The speaker at a meeting I attended talked about his last days of active addiction. He had no friends, no possessions. He lived in a kind of extreme degradation, isolation, and poverty that I haven't experienced. If one person hadn't helped him, he'd never have made it to recovery. For some reason, he reached me on a deeper level than other speakers with whom I have much more in common.

Sponsor

Perhaps your story has more in common with extreme, rock-bottom misery than you know.

In early recovery, I accepted my need for a program of recovery, but thought there were many who were worse off than I was. It took time and willingness to face my past with excruciating honesty, to grasp the depths of my loneliness and despair at the end of active addiction.

A house, a job, a bank account, and even family and friends are no protection from where this disease can take us. Whether we've gone all the way downhill or stopped part way down, we sense that we were on a course of self-destruction more isolated and dangerous than we were willing to admit.

Today, I'm grateful for every story of addiction and recovery that I hear; there is something in each of them that illuminates my own path.

She who conceals her disease cannot expect to be cured.
ETHIOPIAN PROVERB

Newcomer

I finally took a formal Fifth Step. I'd been dreading it for a long time. It meant being honest in a way that I never had been before. I thought I wasn't going to survive the experience with a shred of self-esteem. But I was wrong.

Sponsor

Congratulations on your courage. Self-esteem, as you've discovered, won't come from concealing parts of ourselves we think will cause another person to reject us. When we hide in hope of receiving someone's approval, we cheat ourselves twice: we lose the freedom of being ourselves, and we discover the emptiness of mere approval.

A formal Fifth Step is a rare opportunity to be entirely ourselves in front of another human being and not suffer ill consequences. There's no wrong way to do it. In the company of someone whose recovery we respect and trust, we can safely reveal what we may not be ready to share even with a family member or an intimate friend. We won't be judged.

We may instead be reminded that a complete inventory is not simply a catalog of shortcomings or of things we wish we'd done differently, but of assets as well.

Today, my self-trust allows me to reach out to others.

Today I have grown taller from walking with the trees.
KARLE WILSON BAKER

Newcomer

The person who listened to my Fifth Step was tuned in to just how frightened I was. He said, "You think I have a poor opinion of you for what you've shared, don't you?" And he was right: I was full of shame.

I know that not everyone who hears Step Five works this way, but what he did really helped. He shared events from his life prior to recovery that matched what I'd told him. What he'd done in his past wasn't identical, but it was equally destructive. There was much more to him under the surface than I'd guessed.

To say I was relieved was an understatement. He didn't judge me; he didn't judge himself. I feel as if my entire life changed in the process of sharing this Step.

Sponsor

I can rejoice with you because I, too, have experienced the freedom that comes from knowing I'm no longer alone with my secrets. I'd been judge and jury for so many years. I never thought to give myself the compassion or forgiveness that I felt for other people. Though my sponsor didn't get into the details of her own history when she listened to my Fifth Step, she made it clear that my story was no worse—and no better—than others she'd heard. Nothing seemed to shock her or put her off—not even my worst. I thought, "So this is what it means to be human."

Today, I'm a member of the human family.

Dangers foreseen are the sooner prevented.
RICHARD FRANCK

Newcomer

Lately I keep feeling pulled by thoughts of a minor habit, something that was never important to me before. I keep thinking, "Where's the harm? It's not what brought me in here. It's not going to kill me."

Sponsor

In recovery, we may still hold on to the belief that something outside ourselves will fix us. We may have quit alcohol, marijuana, heroin, or compulsive gambling, but may think that pints of ice cream or hours of television pose no problem for us. Or perhaps we've stopped overeating compulsively and find ourselves craving a drink or a cigarette when we're under stress.

We're vulnerable to potentially addictive habits, and we may need to pay attention to our attraction to substances or activities that others can take or leave. Our use of anything compulsively may get worse; it may turn into a new dependency or even make us less careful about treating our primary addiction.

If we're having questions about a particular substance or behavior, we can ask ourselves *why* we want to use it. Are there feelings, positive or negative, that we're uncomfortable with? Are there things we have to do that we're avoiding? At times like this, it can be helpful to increase the number of meetings we're attending. Talking about our concerns with a sponsor or another person whose recovery we trust may also help take some of the pressure off.

Today, I stay connected to my feelings.

You've no idea what a poor opinion I have of myself,
and how little I deserve it.

W. S. GILBERT

Newcomer

I've been invited to speak at a meeting. It's not one I usually go to; it's out of my neighborhood, in an area where
I'm pretty sure many people have had far worse experiences than mine. I'm afraid that they won't take me seriously, and I'm nervous.

Sponsor

Let's assume that most of the people in the room sincerely
want recovery. Like you, they've learned that it's better to
identify than to compare. They'll be listening for feelings
similar to the ones they had when they were active in their
addictions; they'll be listening for the miracle—the choice
of recovery over addiction—and for the dignity and self-
esteem of a sober life. Like you, many of them will listen
for one thing to take away that is useful in their recovery.
There's no way we can know ahead of time what will strike
one of our listeners as helpful. And if what you say doesn't
keep anyone sober but yourself, that's one life saved.

The more willing we are to set ego considerations aside,
the more room there is for our Higher Power to flow
through us and others.

Today, I pray to be useful.

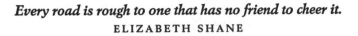

Every road is rough to one that has no friend to cheer it.
ELIZABETH SHANE

Newcomer

Good things are happening in my life now. But I still find myself uncomfortable a lot of the time and wishing I could run. I imagine leaving everyone and everything I'm connected to behind me.

Sponsor

Our disease wants us alone. When we're isolated from other recovering people, our own demons have their way with us. Even when we've experienced a success, we may be afraid that it can't happen again or that we may have to pay a penalty for so much good. Our minds start working overtime. We're haunted by our thoughts. Escape seems appealing. Our "fight-or-flight" mechanism, originally intended to help us survive, turns against us.

The antidote for craving escape is, surprisingly, bringing ourselves into contact with people. We can go to a meeting and, if possible, share what's going on with us. As addicts, we have a history of medicating our feelings—one way of running from them. If we allow ourselves to experience our feelings, accept them, and share them with others, they'll pass through us. Surrender is required.

Today, I surrender to happiness.

Nobody can be exactly like me.
Sometimes even I have trouble doing it.
TALLULAH BANKHEAD

Newcomer

I'm not so sure about this idea in Step Six of giving up all my so-called character defects. There are things about me that some people might not approve of but that don't really hurt anyone. They're what makes me unique and interesting. I wouldn't want to live in a totally bland world.

Sponsor

I identify with your fear, but I promise that Step Six is not intended to erase us. It's human nature to cling to the attitudes and behaviors we already know, even when they've brought us discomfort or isolated us from others.

There's something of the "dry drunk" in our desire to continue to act exactly as we did when we were active in our addictions. It's as if an alcoholic who admitted his or her powerlessness over alcohol agreed to stop drinking, but continued to spend all of his or her time in bars, insisting that nothing interesting could be happening anywhere else. What would happen if we let go? Who would we become? Perhaps we resist surrendering our old habits out of fear that underneath the armor of our character defects there isn't much to be proud of.

Each of us is created with a unique combination of qualities and talents. It's not our defects that make us special and fulfill our natures; they only stand in the way.

Today, I move forward to greet the self I don't know yet.

*True emancipation lies in the acceptance of the whole
past, in deriving strength from all my roots.*
PAULI MURRAY

Newcomer

Step Six asks us to be "entirely ready to have God remove
all these defects of character." I don't understand what action is involved, why it's a whole separate Step.

Sponsor

Once again, the Steps remind us that there are processes
in our experience of living, that one experience follows
another. The piano soloist doesn't arrive at the concert
hall planning to "wing it" in the most difficult passages
of the concerto. The ease of playing comes not merely
from talent, but from preparation.

Step Five was our preparation for Step Six. Sharing our
inventory with a trusted person, we saw clearly that much
of our previous lives had been shaped by our insatiable
craving for a drug. No longer sitting alone with our guilt
and shame, no longer fleeing into addictive behavior, we
aired what we thought were our worst secrets. We felt the
relief that comes from knowing we're connected with
other human beings. Change seemed like the only possible
direction; we didn't want to repeat our past.

Step Six asks us to be certain that we're prepared
for fundamental change. If we pass over this Step in a
perfunctory way, we won't have the inner certainty that
subsequent Steps will require of us.

**Today, I see the freedom that results from
willingness to surrender my defects.**

Such as I am, I am a precious gift.
ZORAH NEALE HURSTON

Newcomer

Sometimes I think I'm basically dishonest. I've fooled you and other people into thinking I'm capable of real change.

Sponsor

Sounds like you're having one of those moments of intense self-doubt we all go through in recovery. At times like this, we have no compassion for ourselves. Our regrets about the past and our fears about the future are all we can see right now. If other people show compassion for us, we think that we've put something over on them—or worse, that they, too, are the frauds we've judged ourselves to be.

After we've chosen recovery and experienced the hope it offers, the darkness we've carried inside seems to rise up and almost overwhelm us. With help, we can recognize it for what it is and step back from it. This isn't the moment to draw conclusions about our capacity for recovery. What we're experiencing today is part of a process that brings self-esteem and freedom.

I'm willing to trust those who refuse to endorse my harsh judgment of myself. Recovery holds more of the truth than I can see today.

Gossip is the opiate of the oppressed.
ERICA JONG

Newcomer

Someone I know in this fellowship announced to me that she's not a gossip, then proceeded to ask my advice about a personal situation involving another member of the fellowship. I jumped right into it; I know gossip is wrong, but I was flattered to be taken into her confidence. Now, whenever I see the person who was gossiped about, I think about what I heard.

Sponsor

Gossip and criticism of others is often described as harmless, but it is not. It harms everyone concerned: the gossiper, those who hear him or her, and the person gossiped about. It divides us from one another, fostering an "us against them" mentality that threatens the basis of recovery—threatens our acknowledgment of a common problem, our need for sharing and identification with others, our commitment to group unity and welfare. When we take other people's inventories, we lose sight of our own; it's not healthy for our recovery.

If we're not sure how to handle a people problem we're facing, we may need to reason things out with someone we trust. Crossing the boundary into gossip or character assassination, however, is something we can learn to live without.

Today, I respect the power of words.
I use them for healing, rather than harm.

Nothing so needs reforming as other people's habits.
MARK TWAIN

Newcomer

There's someone who comes to my favorite meeting, sits in the front, and always puts his hand up. When he gets called on, I groan inwardly. I think he's mentally ill. He tells wild, unbelievable tales of his past, an exaggerated mix of fame and glory, degradation and violence. This man ruins the meetings. I don't understand how other people put up with him or why they keep calling on him.

Sponsor

In the course of recovery, I've heard sharing I found obnoxious. I've taken others' inventories all through some meetings. This one doesn't belong, that one talks too much, another gives unsober advice. Worse, the chairperson won't cut these nuisances off. Shouldn't there be more rules?

In fact, we do have simple suggestions that we trust people to follow. Our most important suggestion is that members have a desire to stop drinking (or using food, drugs, codependency—whichever addictive substance or behavior is the focus of a particular fellowship). Another, from the guidelines of most groups, is that no one may disrupt a meeting.

If a meeting can continue without fanfare or judgment, then no one's thoughts are "disruptive." It's not up to us to say who qualifies to be in a room of recovery; we can decide that only about ourselves. Over time, I've become more tolerant of others' eccentricities. I'm grateful that my own differences, too, are accepted in this place of unconditional love.

Today, I keep the focus on myself and my recovery. I make a commitment to begin to know myself more intimately.

 *162*

I take a breath when I have to.
ETHEL MERMAN

Newcomer

There's someone in my life for whose welfare I'm responsible. I feel frustrated and angry. I'm doing what I'm supposed to do, but I'm not getting much cooperation. Today, I feel invisible.

Sponsor

Caregiving, whether of a new baby, an older child, a sick partner or friend, or an aging parent, is demanding work under any circumstances. Some of us have full-time jobs caring for others—we're parents, nurses, medical aides, social workers, therapists, pastors, teachers. Many of us have no choice but to continue in our roles as caregivers, even while we're going through the immense upheaval of early recovery.

If we find ourselves enjoying the taste of martyrdom, it's time to air out our egos. Part of our work in recovery is learning to have respect for our physical and emotional limitations, avoiding resentment and burnout. We may need to get to a meeting and let off some steam. We may need to take time for a walk, a swim, a nap, or something that nurtures us and recharges our batteries. We may need to let go of our perfectionism.

Today, there's only one thing I need to do perfectly, and that is to stay away from my drug of choice.

163

Above all, anger needs to be felt so it can be talked through, understood and integrated, rather than acted out. In this way, it cleanses the self.
TIAN DAYTON

Newcomer
Today I felt so angry at someone who was chattering on and on that I just wanted to smash something. I hardly even know this person, and I have no idea why I feel such fury or what to do about it.

Sponsor
Anger isn't necessarily logical. Sometimes a little thing, a seemingly harmless word or a look, ignites anger that is already inside us. In the early days of my recovery, this happened so frequently that I began to sense that I was constantly carrying a load of anger; it didn't take much to set it off. My sponsor said, "Of course you're angry—you can't have your addictive substance anymore!"

Wherever it comes from, we don't have to deny our anger or judge it. But going over and over it, feeding it, letting it turn into an obsession, can be painful. There are many safe ways to discharge anger without hurting ourselves or others: we can share it at a meeting or with a counselor; we can write about it, or we can get some good physical exercise, like running or vigorous walking, to release tension and keep things flowing through us.

**Whether or not my anger makes sense today,
I don't deny it and I don't whip it up. I acknowledge it,
and I find a safe setting in which to release it.**

 *164*

All deception is self-deception.
SHIRLEY ELIAS

Newcomer
I needed a day off so badly last week that I called in sick. Then I felt uncomfortable all day. It reminded me of the way I used to feel when I was active in my addiction. Was what I did so terrible?

Sponsor
Whatever we choose to do has an impact on ourselves and others, and being sober and clear, we're more aware of that impact. Telling a "harmless" lie in recovery may not affect other people or institutions in the long run as seriously as it affects us. When we lie in recovery, we ourselves suffer the consequences. We have feelings much like those we experienced when we were using. Fear, secrecy, guilt, and low self-esteem isolate us and may lead to our wanting to act out our addictions. Perhaps next time you need a "mental health day" away from work, you'll ask for a personal day or vacation day instead of setting yourself up for a slip by faking illness.

Honesty in small things as well as large can get to be a habit that simplifies our lives and enhances our recovery. It's freedom!

Today, my honesty gives me strength as I
take actions appropriate to a person in recovery.

 *165*

When I was six I made my mother a little hat—
out of her new blouse.
LILY DACHÉ

Newcomer

When I was active, I thought I only had a problem with one substance. I could stay away from it for weeks, or even months, at a time if I used another substance instead. I know now that these were two sides of the same addiction. Something similar may be happening in recovery. I have a strange feeling every time I comfort myself in one particular way. I have the sense that there's something "off" about it.

Sponsor

Those of us who are in search of oblivion are inventive about finding ways to achieve it, whether consciously or not. We know the difference between eating a serving of a sweet dessert and consuming a pint of it in the middle of the night, between watching a favorite TV sitcom and lying on the couch, channel-surfing for hours. Even reading can be turned into a compulsive act. It's not the activity itself, but our reasons for using it that tell us if we're having a problem.

Program tools for becoming conscious of our motives include increased meeting attendance, sponsor contact, honest sharing, and a Fourth Step focus on the problem. Sometimes, the seemingly harmless habit is even more serious than the one we're addressing in our current Twelve Step program. If so, the process of recovery will help us to sort out our priorities.

Today, I take addiction in all its forms seriously.

166

The net of Heaven has large meshes and yet nothing escapes it.

LAO-TZU

Newcomer

Step Six wants me to get rid of all my defects. I'm glad that I've quit using my drug of choice, but I don't know if I'll be able to get rid of *all* my defects.

Sponsor

Step Six, "Were entirely ready to have God remove all these defects of character," is often misunderstood.

This Step doesn't say that we ought to try to remove certain traits on our own. Instead, it requires willingness, the same willingness which brought us to recovery. Step Six asks us to surrender, to *allow* our Higher Power to remove our defects.

Does this mean that we say a prayer tonight, and tomorrow we will find that fear, resentment, grandiosity, low self-esteem, or whatever else we wish were different about ourselves has been lifted? It seems unreasonable that our resistance to such thorough change is going to evaporate overnight. In recovery, we've begun to experience what a gradual process is like. As long as we remain committed to recovery and willing to cooperate with opportunities for growth, we'll continue to undergo changes in our character.

Today, I trust that my spirit is capable of continuing to grow. I'm willing to cooperate with the process of change.

You never find yourself until you face the truth.
PEARL BAILEY

Newcomer
Step Six doesn't seem like anything I need to spend much time doing. I've always wanted to get over my shortcomings. I don't think much soul-searching is required.

Sponsor
There's a reason that Step Six includes the word "entirely" in "Were entirely ready to have God remove all these defects of character." Taking this Step requires a measure of thoroughness and honesty beyond even what we asked of ourselves in Steps Four and Five. We go deeper, not simply admitting the impact of our behavior. We try to determine whether certain undesirable behaviors have somehow served a *positive* function in our lives that make us reluctant to let go of them permanently. For example, an addictive substance or behavior may have made social life or work easier for us for a time. Though we don't want to return to

the addiction, we may be convinced that we can't relate successfully to others or accomplish anything worthwhile in the world without it.

Or perhaps there's something we've done repeatedly that makes us feel guilty and reinforces a sense of shame. Unpleasant as it feels, we're used to it; it makes us recognizable to ourselves and maintains the status quo in our relationships. We may fear that if we let go of it completely, the self we know and depend on will die. Taking time for Step Six can help us become willing to let go.

Today, I trust that I am whole without my old, unproductive attitudes and behaviors.

168

All human nature vigorously resists grace because grace changes us and the change is painful.
FLANNERY O'CONNOR

Newcomer
Is there a particular action involved in taking Step Six?

Sponsor
One of the gifts of Step Six is that it helps me to remember that I'm not recovering on my own. I've let go of the mistaken belief that I depend only on my own will and intellect. Step Six reminds me that a Power greater than myself can restore me to wholeness and health. As the process continues, I go within and find the willingness both to ask for guidance and to accept it.

The action of Step Six is the action of humility and of

faith. It requires that we come to terms with our inability to solve problems on our own. It parallels Step Two, another step of preparation: before we made the decision to turn our will and our lives over to the care of a Higher Power for restoration and healing, we had come to see and accept the possibility of that restoration. We trusted that wholeness was possible for us again, and that a Power greater than ourselves could accomplish it.

Today, I trust my Higher Power to be with me, wherever I am.

169

What are we doing here? We're reaching for the stars.
CHRISTA MCAULIFFE

Newcomer
There's so much I've failed at, so much I haven't done. I've missed out on certain opportunities forever. I know I have to make the best of what's left, but sometimes I think, "What's the use?"

Sponsor
Addictive episodes begin small: one drink, one compulsive bite, one unsecured debt. Recovery, too, begins with one simple act: walking into a meeting place, making a phone call, raising a hand. Single actions become habits and are part of the ongoing process of creating new selves.

We continue recovering a Step at a time, a day at a time. We don't succumb to fatalism or to the belief that if we give up on ourselves, all will be taken care of. It's no longer acceptable for us to drift; we have ideals and values to which we want to be true. The past is over, but not the opportunity for joy and fulfillment. We can continue to grow and develop at any age. Each of us has something of unique value to contribute, and it's not too late to make a beginning today.

> Today, I take one step in the direction of
> becoming the person I want to be.

≫≈ *170* ≈≫

All happiness depends on a leisurely breakfast.
JOHN GUNTHER

Newcomer

I'm trying to make up for my years of self-centeredness; I want to give service to others in this fellowship and find time for friends and family. But it's starting to feel as if I always have somewhere to go and something I've promised to do.

Sponsor

It doesn't sound like you're having much fun. While you may need to work on setting realistic goals and managing time, you've hit upon a deeper issue.

We don't have to function at burnout level in order to be good human beings. A smile, a kind word, or simply saying "Thanks for what you shared" can sometimes be of more use to other people than trying to come up with solutions to their problems.

For some of us, overwork and overresponsibility is a way

of numbing ourselves. If all you're doing is work, do you have the patience and spiritual energy to listen to what's being said at meetings? Can you hear your own inner voice? Can you feel joy?

**Today, I slow down and stop to look at the
beauty around me and within me.**

<hr>

171

*Healing is a matter of time,
but it is sometimes also a matter of opportunity.*
HIPPOCRATES

Newcomer
Hospital visits, funerals, and things like that have never been my favorites. They're even harder for me now that I don't have my addiction to help me through.

Sponsor
When I'm confronting a personal loss, whether it's my own or someone else's, I become aware of my feelings of grief. I still have a lot of grieving to go through.

When I felt loss and sadness in the past, I was overwhelmed. Inside, I was afraid my feelings would destroy me, and I turned to addictive substances and behaviors for protection. When I entered recovery, I gave up what had been, in effect, an anesthetic. At first, recovery itself made me feel almost euphoric—high. But when the excitement of early recovery wore off, I had to face losses I'd been denying for years. A deep sense of sadness from my past welled up in me. And now I had another loss to mourn, the loss of the addiction that I'd taken refuge in.

Whenever I experience a new loss, feelings about old ones rise to the surface. What helps, more than finding ways to avoid difficult feelings, is sitting with them and letting myself feel them. They won't destroy me. They pass and make room for other feelings—when I'm not trying to ward off difficult feelings, happiness, too, seems to flow more freely into my life.

> Today, I go through my feelings
> by letting them go through me.

━ *172* ━

Grief is itself a medicine.
WILLIAM COWPER

Newcomer

There were many things I did when I was active in my addiction—positive things, creative work—that have totally fallen apart. I don't know how to begin again. Recovery has become my entire life.

Sponsor

At the beginning of my own recovery, going to meetings was most of what I did for a while; I was grateful that they were there to fill my time and hold me together. I showed up for work, but I felt shaky. I was afraid that my former feelings of competence and energy were gone for good. In time, I became able to function far better. The wonderful parts of my old life weren't lost; they were more available to me than ever before.

Hearing you reminds me that recovery is still relatively

new to us, compared with our years of active addiction. There are days when we're not sure who we are any more. Our old lives may seem preferable to this discomfort and uncertainty.

It's necessary to grieve for the people we were. The grief that we experience is good recovery work. It's the beginning, not the end. Our true selves will emerge in recovery over time.

> Today, I trust that what I most cherish in life
> is alive within me.

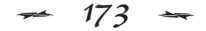

173

More of me comes out when I improvise.
EDWARD HOPPER

Newcomer

Lately, I've been wanting to try all kinds of things that I haven't done since I was a kid, or that I never did at all. I feel drawn to paint sets, puzzles, even some toys and stuffed animals. What's happening to me? Is recovery making me childish?

Sponsor

Leave it to us addicts to think that there's something wrong with us if we dare to feel happy. How delightful to feel drawn to childlike pleasures. We may be learning to take ourselves less seriously, at last.

There's a big difference between childish and child*like.* Play nourishes the life force. We never outgrow our need for it. In recovery, the sense that life is dark—nothing but problems, problems, problems—begins giving way to lightness. Our natural energy and curiosity come bubbling up from our spirits. What a change from the heaviness we felt when we first got here!

It's important for us to set aside some time to do things that aren't productive and goal-oriented. If we're interested in looking, we'll find peers in recovery who can help us dream up sober ways to lighten our hearts.

Play is food and exercise for the spirit. If we make time for play, we can approach the serious demands of our adult lives with rested, lively minds.

Today, the time I give to play makes work easier.

 *174*

Those who have known grief seldom seem sad.
BENJAMIN DISRAELI

Newcomer
I'm in limbo. My old life has ended—I know I can't be that person any more—and I don't really have a new life yet. I'm afraid that this program may turn me into someone that I won't be able to recognize.

Sponsor
We haven't lost ourselves; we've taken down the barrier to fulfilling our real natures. The addictive part of ourselves that we knew best, felt most at home with, is gone. We have feelings akin to those of a person mourning for a loved one, but we may not feel comfortable sharing about our loss. We may be especially reluctant to say anything that

might sound as if we miss our active addictive use or behavior. We may hide how we're feeling from ourselves as well as from others.

The loss of our addicted selves is, though necessary, nonetheless painful. We can't get beyond it without first taking time to grieve and to acknowledge what we've left behind. What did we love and depend on? What would we like to keep? What are we willing to bury? Sharing our grief out loud with someone we trust is optional, but it can be a powerful means of releasing the tears we need to shed.

Today, I say good-bye to my past life, with compassion for the person I used to be. Every experience of my past has made my life in recovery today possible.

175

Loneliness is a terrible blindness.
CHRISTINA STEAD

Newcomer
I'm not fighting the addiction itself any more. In a strange way, where I am right now feels more painful. The drama and some of the magic of early recovery are over. When I'm not actually at a meeting, I feel as if I'm sitting in a bare room, alone with my feelings and terribly lonely.

Sponsor
I remember the time you're talking about. We're no longer brand-new in the program; we're not shaking from withdrawal; we're not rebelling against suggestions. We're not sure what's left of our old self, and we don't know who our

new self will turn out to be, or even if we can count on one to emerge. We feel as if we're alone and facing a void. It may be reassuring to know that most of us have gone through this feeling of immense loneliness, and that it has left us. In time, our perception shifted. Our lives were filled with more abundance than we ever imagined.

For today, there are things we can do to alleviate loneliness. We can begin to nurture a relationship with our Higher Power through prayer and meditation. We can make a gratitude list to lift ourselves out of self-pity. We can reach out and begin the gradual process of getting to know people in recovery better: thanking the speaker, putting our hands up, taking phone numbers and using them, volunteering to speak to a group. We can stop believing that our happiness is entirely up to circumstance. We, too, are worth getting to know.

> Today, I let go of my fantasy of instant relationship
> and take a step in the long process
> of getting to know another person.

176

*Constant togetherness is fine—
but only for Siamese twins.*
VICTORIA BILLINGS

Newcomer

I heard someone in recovery say, "I don't have relationships, I take hostages." Everyone laughed, but it left me feeling insecure about how to evaluate my own relationships. How close is too close?

Sponsor

Though we may not feel comfortable with many other people when we first get here, perhaps there's one particular person we feel we can trust—a mate, an old friend who has remained loyal, a peer in recovery, a sponsor. We may have the desire to check everything with this other person, and we find ourselves spending hours on the phone or in his or her company.

Strong, healthy relationships are vital. They're a blessing, not a problem. Problems arise if we feel so dependent on another person's approval that we lose touch with our feelings and preferences; if we isolate as a pair, always protected from the joys and challenges of new friendships; or if our constant togetherness creates a pressure-cooker buildup of intensity. Recovery requires thoughtful self-examination and self-challenge. Though others can offer to witness, support, and love us, our recovery work is ours alone. It takes courage to allow ourselves and others autonomy within a relationship.

Today, as I include people in my life,
I leave myself and others room to be and to grow.

177

The creation of the world is not completed so long as we have not fulfilled our creative function in it.
MORDECAI KAPLAN

Newcomer

I'm interested in many different things, but I haven't focused on one yet. I feel as if I should know what I want to do with my life by now.

Sponsor

We have the ability, as long as we stay in recovery, to find our path and to fulfill our dreams. If many paths are beckoning, it will take time to explore and to have experiences that will show us where we most want to focus. Many tools, from the spiritual to the practical—including the Steps, prayer, and vocational counseling—are available to help us. In time, narrowing our options will give us the power that comes from concentrating our attention. For today, let's not rush to cross anything off the list.

Having been led to recovery and offered a second chance to live full lives, we don't have the right to thwart our Higher Power by giving up on ourselves. We're mistaken if we believe that we've outlived the possibility of being useful. We're mistaken if we believe that, having lost time in the past, we now have no right to a future. Patience with ourselves and the process is necessary.

> By staying in recovery today,
> I contribute toward the repair of the world.

 *178*

Friends are not so easily made as kept.
GEORGE SAVILLE

Newcomer

I stay near recovering people, as you've suggested. I speak with people at meetings and make phone calls, but I'm uncomfortable with so much sharing all the time. Sometimes I feel as if I can't face all these people, people, people.

Sponsor

At first, we may be overwhelmed by the array of personalities we encounter. We lack experience and skill at sober interactions; every encounter may feel intense and exhausting. Our sense of personal boundaries may be weak; we wonder how to deal with other people's needs and demands without obliterating ourselves. We crave intimacy, but fear that we're not ready for what it would require. Without our addictions to escape into, we sometimes feel like bolting. A solo trip across country may appeal to us more than a ten-minute coffee break at a meeting.

We can take the pressure off ourselves to get it right all at once. Group activities, like going to a coffee shop for "the meeting after the meeting," are a relaxed way to get used to being with others. Making friends is a gradual process. We have the right to take this process slowly and not rush into commitments—romantic or otherwise. We have choices. Over time, it becomes clear whether spending time with a particular person makes life better or worse. We learn how to satisfy our needs for both companionship and solitude.

Today, I practice "Easy does it"
in my developing relationships with others.

⇒ *179* ⇒

Housekeeping ain't no joke.
LOUISA MAY ALCOTT

Newcomer

I'm living in the same place where I hit bottom. I'm surrounded by reminders of my active life. I'd like to move or overhaul the place, but I don't have a choice right now. I don't have the money or the time.

As we continue caring for ourselves, the physical spaces we inhabit reflect our new self-esteem, clarity, and open-mindedness in recovery. It's a West Indian custom to buy a new broom for cleaning house after a move or major life change. I've tried it, and it worked; it inspired me to begin cleaning house! Of course, swept floors, made beds, and clear tabletops aren't everyone's idea of an orderly household; standards and personal needs and styles differ. What matters is maintaining our homes in a way that reflects our true selves and fosters our growing recovery.

Cleaning house is a state of mind. We need light and air in our surroundings, both literally and figuratively. Any time in recovery is a good time for sorting things out and letting go of what no longer fits us, whether it's an article of clothing or a relationship. It's something that we do periodically, throughout our lives. It may sometimes be painful, but it's necessary. It makes room for change.

Today, I let go of what no longer sustains me.

⇒ *180* ⇐

Life is not life at all without delight.
COVENTRY PATMORE

I'm tired of following the same routines week after week, month after month. I've been thinking about taking a trip for a few days. I know, I know—you warned me about "geographic changes." But I want to do something different.

Congratulations. I'm glad that you're planning to have some fun, and that you're not using program wisdom to beat yourself with.

Change is good for us. It can help wake up and refresh our spirits, show us things we haven't seen before, give us a new perspective on our ordinary lives. We can travel thousands of miles or stay close to home, as long as we take the principles and habits of recovery with us. Wherever we are, we can read a piece of program literature, pray for help staying in recovery, or phone our sponsors. The loving guidance of our Higher Power goes with us.

As we travel, it may be possible to attend meetings of our own Twelve Step fellowship or an open meeting of one of the many other Twelve Step programs. We can get listings ahead of time by making phone calls to our own program headquarters, and we can check local newspapers and phone directories when we arrive. Belonging to this fellowship is a little bit like having a membership in an international club; we can meet the "locals," wherever we go, by attending a meeting. The faces may be different, but the program is the same.

Today, I refresh my spirit by trying something unfamiliar.

They resemble us in more ways than they differ from us.
PEARL BUCK

Newcomer

I heard somebody complaining about "special-interest meetings." He said that we're here to solve our common problem, and that it isn't really program if we limit ourselves to homogeneous groups.

Sponsor

Those of us who live in sparsely populated areas don't have a wide choice of meetings; we attend what's available. If our community is ethnically or economically homogeneous, then so are our meetings—in which case, we're not all that different from those attending special-interest groups elsewhere. If we live in more densely populated areas, we may find meetings that appeal to specific constituencies: wheelchair-accessible meetings, meetings interpreted for the deaf, gay and lesbian meetings, Spanish-speaking meetings, young people's meetings, women's meetings, and others. For me, it's a privilege to attend both some special-interest meetings, where the similarity of my experiences with others' is comforting, and some very diverse meetings, where addiction and recovery are almost the only common denominators.

According to Twelve Step tradition, each group governs itself independently, refraining from decisions that would endanger other groups or our anonymous fellowship as a whole. A group can't formally affiliate itself with a political party, religion, or educational institution, for example, nor can it accept money from outside interests.

It's a blessing that this fellowship is large enough, in both numbers and spirit, to accommodate our variety.

Today, I appreciate both the differences
and the similarities between myself and others.

 *182*

It is not possible to step twice into the same river.
HERACLITUS

Newcomer

Suddenly, my life has become very full. Things I thought I had lost are coming back to me. Changes are taking place at work and in my personal life. Most of it is good, I guess, but I'm overwhelmed with feelings of fear. I don't know where I'm going; I wish things would stay still.

Sponsor

No one dislikes change as much as I do. When I was active in my addiction, I did everything I could to maintain the status quo. Things changed anyway—usually for the worse. Today, when good things come, I can feel just as scared of them as of bad things. I'm afraid that I won't know how to handle new challenges; I'm afraid people will find out how inadequate I feel. I remind myself that I'm not in charge of the way things turn out; I show up for life and do what I'm supposed to do. I'm responsible for the actions I take, not the results. I let myself take things slowly. I don't have to rush. And I don't have to face my fears alone: the more I talk about them, the easier things get.

As we go through periods of change or stress, it helps to imagine that we have a volume control knob; we can turn down the volume of our thoughts about the future and focus our attention on enjoying the present moment.

Today, I face change calmly. I enjoy the present moment and let the future take care of itself. The slower I go, the faster I'll get there.

 *183*

Great events make me quiet and calm;
it is only trifles that irritate my nerves.
QUEEN VICTORIA

Newcomer
A health insurance claim got rejected, and I have to submit it all over again; a plumbing job was left unfinished, and I'm going to have to keep calling my landlord; some equipment needs a minor adjustment, but I'll have to rebox the whole thing and get it to the repair place. . . . Life seems to be an endless succession of these little nightmares.

Sponsor
Two things seem wonderful to me about the complaints you have about your life today. The first is that you haven't picked up an addictive substance or behavior. In the old days, what set me off most was the little things. I've heard one person in recovery say, "I rarely drank or drugged over real tragedies. I did fine with the big things; it was when I broke a shoelace that I was in danger of losing my balance."

Today, your "broken shoelaces" didn't send you off the deep end.

The other blessing that strikes me, hearing these problems, is how full of life they are. We have places to live, running water, equipment to care for, and relationships with landlords and plumbers. We've been taking care of our health, and we have the ability to face filling out insurance forms. We can laugh more easily at glitches when we realize that they arise out of choices we've made to immerse ourselves in reality.

Today, my glass is no longer half empty, but half full.

184

One cannot collect all the beautiful shells on the beach.
ANNE MORROW LINDBERGH

Newcomer

I'm having trouble making decisions. There are big ones: Should I go back to school, or should I stay with my present job, where there's potential for advancement? And there's smaller stuff: Should I take advantage of special fares and use my vacation time now, or should I stay here and catch up with paperwork so I'll feel mentally free? I wish I could be two people at once; when I'm confused, all the options sound equal to me.

Sponsor

For some of us, addiction narrowed the options. When we were acting under a compulsion, we couldn't choose freely, let alone enjoy what we'd chosen. In recovery, we may lack experience recognizing our priorities and focusing our attention. Opportunities for making choices, instead of delighting us, may overwhelm us. Abundance may be driving us to distraction.

There is power and vision to be gained by narrowing our options, concentrating our energies. One test that works for me when I have a difficult choice between two alternatives is to ask myself, "If I only had two months to live, which of these things would I want to do?" When I listen closely for inner guidance, my own answers sometimes surprise me.

What if we make a mistake? We remind ourselves that we can do things differently next time. We don't have to punish ourselves for not knowing everything in advance. Human beings need to have experiences in order to find out what makes our lives better or worse.

Today, I don't let my decisions overwhelm me.
I'm open to what my inner wisdom tells me.

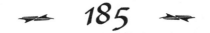

185

Whatever you can do or dream you can do, begin it.
JOHANN WOLFGANG VON GOETHE

Newcomer

I signed up to take a course in something I'm kind of interested in. I'm pretty anxious about it. I don't have the skills and experience that the other students have. I don't know if I can keep up with the work and still go to enough meetings. And even if I get through it, I doubt that I can afford to go further.

Sponsor

First, let me congratulate you for the courage and self-esteem it took for you to begin something new in recovery. Recovery is not an end in itself; as we frequently hear in meetings, it's a bridge back to life. Education is a path that beckons many recovering people. Taking just one step, like signing up for a course, furthers you on your journey.

At the same time, you'll want to take care to protect your recovery as you engage in new pursuits. Staying close to the program by going to regular and frequent meetings is still the top priority for anyone who doesn't want to relapse. The work we do to maintain our recovery is what makes everything else possible.

As for your doubts and fears, it's natural for them to come up. Instead of giving them too much attention, you can use this opportunity to calm and center yourself with meditation and to ask in prayer for help and courage in carrying out your Higher Power's will for you.

**Today, I take a small step forward on my journey,
without judging myself or my rate of progress.**

186

If you're going to be able to look back on something and laugh about it, you might as well laugh about it now.
MARIE OSMOND

Newcomer

I spoke to someone I work with about how I've been perceiving a particular situation between us, and disaster resulted. I tried hard to speak respectfully, to take responsibility for my own part and not blame the other person, but I wasn't heard at all. He attacked me and put me down; he really crossed the line. I was speechless at first, and then I yelled back; I had to defend myself. How do you fight fair when someone else is fighting dirty? The situation feels hopeless.

Sponsor

Perhaps you unwittingly touched a nerve, if the other person responded so explosively. His anger may have been waiting to erupt even before you spoke. He doesn't have the skill you've been trying to develop, of owning our own feelings without attacking. Perhaps attack is all he knows right now.

We don't have to assume that one unfortunate encounter is the end of a relationship. In a situation like the one you've described, we can remind ourselves that we're adults, dealing with someone who's behaving like a hurt or cornered child. We can be generous and compassionate to ourselves and the other person by detaching from the need to agree. Instead of trying to convince him or her to see things our way, we let go for now.

When we're ready, we may say something simple: "Sorry things got out of hand between us. Your opinion does matter to me." We can allow ourselves the freedom not to participate in arguments. Arguments require two participants.

**Today, I step back from argument,
with myself and with others.**

I could get through anything,
if only I didn't have to have my feelings!
WOMAN IN RECOVERY

Newcomer

Someone I counted as a friend has rejected me. I'm trying to be brave about it, but I've been on the verge of tears all day today. I'm embarrassed to be so needy.

Sponsor

"Trying to be brave" about a hurt sounds admirable, but is it really bravery?

Acknowledging and accepting our feelings is not a sign of weakness, but the opposite. True bravery, in my opinion, is not picking up a drink, a drug, a compulsive behavior. That takes courage, especially for someone who's been using addiction as a tool for survival.

I'm sorry that you've experienced a rejection, and I want you to know that your feelings about it don't lower my opinion of you. On the contrary, I admire your honesty and openness in speaking about what's happening. Your vulnerability is human and real. When you don't deny your feelings or dismiss yourself for having them, in time they will pass through you, and there will be room for new ones.

Today, I extend compassion to myself. My dedication to recovery reminds me that I have real courage.

I can live for two months on a good compliment.
MARK TWAIN

Newcomer

At a meeting I shared about a loss I've gone through, and the response was amazing. People expressed sympathy and understanding, and a number of them shared experiences of their own that were similar to mine. It surprised me. I'd told the same story at a different meeting, and people there didn't say a thing to me. I had left feeling like there was something wrong with me. I can't figure out what I did differently this time; maybe there was something about the way I shared.

Sponsor

My hunch is that the difference in response to your sharing from different groups of people had to do with things over which you had no control. There are many possible explanations for people's responses to us; we needn't assume we're responsible for what they do or don't do.

There's an Al-Anon slogan (nicknamed "The Three C's") that says, "I didn't cause it, I can't control it, and I can't cure it." For me, it's a helpful one to remember, especially when people in my life are active in an addiction or are on a "dry drunk." It's useful in situations with nonaddicts, too. Most human beings behave as they do for reasons that have little to do with us.

We're entitled to support and response from other human beings. When I find myself in a group where I experience a warm, engaged response from others, I make a point of returning. Support and validation from others quenches one of my deepest thirsts. But we can't rely on others to give us a sense of self-esteem. That comes from within; it grows as we do the work of recovery.

Today, I go where I find food for my spirit.

 *189*

Change in all things is sweet.
ARISTOTLE

Newcomer

I don't know why I'm still going through such emotional ups and downs at this point. I'm not in withdrawal, my body chemistry is no longer in chaos, and I know how to take better care of myself. I'm open to many new things, and I'm growing and changing faster than I ever expected. Why should I feel bad?

Sponsor

Each time I reach a new awareness, I have to go through a grieving process for the old me. Suddenly it feels as if I'm someone else, somewhere else. I'm not the person I was yesterday. Even if that person was less conscious and closer to active addiction, still, that person was the me I knew. Sometimes I miss that old familiar self. We'd spent a lot of time together.

Recovery awakens us to new possibilities. We have to change, experiment, take risks—even though we may think we detest change! Being alive and having joy sustains us. We may not have all the answers, but we want to ask the questions. Taking time for daily meditation helps us to find the peace and calm at our center. As recovery continues, the sense that everything is moving too quickly will slow down.

Today, though things may not be different, I am different.

 **190**

My favoured temple is a humble heart.
PHILIP JAMES BAILEY

Newcomer

What's with these people who are still coming to meetings after five, ten, even twenty years of recovery? If they don't have problems with addiction any more, why do they still spend so much of their free time here? And what about the ones who don't always sound so good? Hasn't the program worked for them?

Sponsor

Old-timers who are willing to keep coming and to let us see both their human vulnerability and their commitment to recovery are doing us—and themselves—a service. We have a saying here: "We don't graduate." There's no cure for my addiction, but there is healing.

For me, taking time to continue my relationship with meetings and to give service isn't a sacrifice. It helps me stay in touch with myself in ways that my day-to-day experience doesn't offer. Without meetings, it's too easy for us to start thinking that we're "cured" and that we might be able to handle just a little bit of our drug of choice again.

Most people who relapse start by drifting away from meetings. More stay out there than come back. Some of us die of our disease. I know that a few people manage to stay away from addiction on their own, but what's the virtue in proving that we can do something in isolation? It's easier, more heart-expanding, and more fun to be part of a fellowship.

And let's not forget gratitude. This program saved our lives. Like those whose example and help benefited us, we continue to "give it away in order to keep it."

**Today, I acknowledge the power of this addiction.
I don't take recovery for granted.**

191

"No" is a complete sentence.
SAYING HEARD AT MEETINGS

Newcomer

There's a member of a group I go to regularly who's been asking what my weekend plans are, then suggesting that we do various things together; this person has an idea for every evening or afternoon I have free! I sense that I'm being looked at as a possible romantic prospect, and I'm definitely not interested. I've been making excuses and not liking doing it. I don't want to hurt anyone's feelings, but I don't want to be dishonest, either.

Sponsor

We don't always want what others want; situations in which we have to say no keep arising in life. As you've discovered, making excuses or bending over backward to avoid people doesn't always alleviate our discomfort and may even intensify it. Most of us don't want to disappoint others, but indirectness sends the wrong message and only postpones disappointment.

I suspect that your power to hurt this person isn't as great as you think. Most of us have survived being said no to, especially if it's said in a way that allows us to keep our dignity. Communicating our truth sets an example of adult behavior in recovery; in the long run, our example may even prove helpful to the other person in a situation he or she has to face.

When we have something to say that is difficult for us, we can pray beforehand to be confident in our own feelings and to share them simply and clearly.

My honesty today is a gift to myself and others.

⇒ *192* ⇒

Good fences make good neighbors.
ROBERT FROST

Newcomer
I keep hearing people say things like "It's a selfish program." I don't like the sound of the word "selfish." I was too selfish when I was active in my addiction. You can't just want me to think of my own recovery. What about all the suffering in the world around me? What about social responsibility? Surely it's not wrong to try to help others.

Sponsor
I understand how that slogan may be misleading. I don't think that it's meant to encourage selfishness in the usual

sense of that word. I wouldn't characterize most people in recovery as selfish or ungenerous, would you? In fact, I think that the opposite is true.

The slogan is useful to remind us to have some humility. I can get pretty grandiose, thinking I ought to have all the answers for others. I'd rather be trying to figure out how to solve the world's problems than remembering that I need to do my work, make my dinner, and get enough rest.

There are lots of people around me with all sorts of needs. I don't like to disappoint people, so it's taken me awhile to accept that I can't be totally available to them all. It took time to develop some discrimination and to learn what boundaries felt comfortable to me. When someone asks something of us, we don't have to say yes automatically. We are honest with ourselves about our limitations and priorities, putting our recovery first. Remembering to keep the focus on ourselves as we go through recovery keeps us centered.

Today, I take my needs as a recovering person seriously.

 *193*

Worry, the interest paid by those who borrow trouble.
GEORGE WASHINGTON LYON

Newcomer
I took a test last week in a course I've signed up for at a local college. Immediately afterward, I started worrying about my grade. I had a feeling that the teacher had something against me, and that she might give me a C even though I really deserved a B. I was already planning what

I'd say to her. Then I got the test back—with an A on it. I'm having a good laugh about what I put myself through. I feel stupid for having worried so much.

Sponsor

First, congratulations on your hard work. In recovery, we can become more aware of our abilities and honor them. There's so much we can achieve, with patience and perseverance.

If I'm hearing you correctly, you underrated your ability, you assumed that someone both wished you ill and was going to behave unprofessionally, and you churned up your mind with worry about the future. The mental and emotional energy you put into expecting the worst from yourself and your teacher turned out to have nothing to do with reality. This is what people in Twelve Step programs refer to as "projection"—living in an imagined future instead of the present moment.

When I'm facing something new or difficult, I find that it calms me to pray to my Higher Power for the best possible outcome for all concerned. If we're not giving our attention to fear, mistrust, low self-esteem, or other negative feelings, we can concentrate on doing our best and turning over the results to a Power greater than ourselves. As with recovery, the rate at which we live all of our lives need only be one day at a time.

Today, I cherish the serenity that comes from cultivating a positive attitude toward myself and toward the eventual outcome of events.

Day is short as ever; time's as long as it has been.
GEECHEE PROVERB

Newcomer

A change in my work schedule means I can't go to my regular meeting anymore. By the time I'd be able to get there, only half an hour would be left. It's not worth it.

Sponsor

Once, when I was visiting another city, a friend and I drove all over in the rain looking for a meeting we'd heard about. We were in unfamiliar territory, and finding the street address took us over an hour. We talked, meanwhile, about our lives and our recovery; it was good sharing. At last we parked and found the meeting place. We realized that we'd walked in at the end, just as everyone was joining hands. We looked at one another and laughed, joined the circle, and said the Serenity Prayer with a roomful of recovering strangers. They seemed happy to let us join in. We'd all stayed sober for another day.

Yes, it's important to go to whole meetings; whole meetings are essential to recovery. But if, under special circumstances, the only meeting we can get to is part of a meeting, we do it. Skipping meetings where we can connect with other recovering people, especially those who've begun to get to know us, can compound feelings of isolation. It spells danger for our recovery.

In this day of recovery,
whatever I do, I do with all my attention.

Life is not an easy thing to embrace,
like trying to hug an elephant.
DIANE WAKOSKI

Newcomer

I sat through a meeting today in anger. It started when I walked in and saw who was up there speaking—someone I know and don't trust. She did everything her way, and I didn't hear much program, at least as I know it. I feel ashamed of having that reaction, especially at this point in recovery, but that's how I felt.

Sponsor

Thanks for your honesty. Most of us in recovery have strong feelings of resistance at one time or another. I've certainly experienced the kind you're talking about. Sometimes we all want what we want when we want it.

Recovery doesn't always come wrapped in the package I was hoping for. I blame my negative mood on other people in the room. I start taking inventory of others, and no one sounds sober enough for me.

As in any group of people, there are some we relate to with more ease, others with more difficulty. Over time, as we let go of criticism, our acceptance of others helps us to accept our whole selves.

Today, I see myself in others.
I look and listen with compassion.

*All things are connected like the blood which unites
one family. All things are connected.*
CHIEF SEATTLE

Newcomer

I was in such a foul mood at the last meeting I went to. I sat there gritting my teeth through the whole meeting, glaring at the speaker and at anyone who had the nerve to look at me. Here's the strange part: I felt better after the meeting anyway. I ate with a friend and laughed at myself a little. Today, everything looks different. Meetings look good to me again.

Sponsor

One of the greatest gifts of recovery is simply that meetings exist and that we go to them. We may be annoyed with everyone in the room, holding on to a foul mood for dear life, and at the same time experience deep healing.

The healing comes from a sense of belonging to a community of people in recovery. Even if I'm out of sync with everyone in the room on a given day, I'm still part of a process that includes them and that is larger than all of us. Whatever moods I go through, whatever resistance I let others see, no one will try to take away my seat in recovery. Often, when I'm expecting disapproval or rejection, I'm met with compassion or sympathetic laughter instead. It's what we mean by unconditional love. Even on the days when I can't see the love that's there, my sense that I'm somehow being held by this program is growing.

**Today, it strengthens me to know that I belong to a
community of people in recovery.**

Too much of a good thing can be wonderful.
MAE WEST

Newcomer

I've been asked to speak at a meeting I've never attended before. I know that speaking in this fellowship is a service, and that we're supposed to say yes when we're asked to do things in recovery. The problem is that the speaking engagement conflicts with my favorite regular meeting, the one where we all go out afterward; I hate missing it.

Sponsor

Decisions have often been a challenge for us. In active addiction, we may have been too ill to make a choice, or we made it by default: we forgot to show up, or we waited until the last minute and canceled because of some "unforeseen emergency" we invented to justify our excuse. We missed out on a lot of what life had to offer. In recovery, though we know how to show up for commitments, we often feel uncertain about what's the right thing to commit ourselves to. What if we make the wrong decision? If we choose plan A, what will we miss? If we choose plan B, we'll immediately regret not having chosen plan A.

Having choices is part of the abundance of our lives in recovery. Where two good options are concerned, there's no "wrong" decision. If we choose the unfamiliar, we can be open to meeting new people whose sharing will inspire us with a fresh point of view. Or we can nurture ourselves with the comfort of what's known.

All the choices I make today
have the potential to nourish me and my recovery.

She who tells the truth is not well liked.
BAMBARA PROVERB

Newcomer

An old friend of mine showed up at a meeting last week. He needs this program, and I was glad to see him. He told me how overjoyed he was to begin recovery. The next day, he showed up again. He was late, but he made more than half the meeting. He said he'd see me here again today, but he didn't show up or call. I'm going to phone him and try to find out what happened.

Sponsor

"Easy does it" may apply here. I'd be cautious about saying more than "I missed seeing you at the meeting." More might make your friend feel guilty. No one's ever stayed in recovery out of a sense of guilt, as far as I know.

Our friends know where to find meetings. We're not their sponsors or their only source of information and help. We—and they—may have no doubt that they *need* recovery. Whether they *want* it is another matter. Our simply being here indicates to friends and family members that recovery is possible for people like them, but to serve as examples, we have to maintain our own recovery.

I'm not suggesting that we never do anything for others. Far from it. But we can't force anyone to recover. Where friends or relatives are concerned, our intense interest may, paradoxically, make it more difficult for us to be helpful. A light touch is required.

Today, as I share my love for recovery, I have a light touch. I trust that each of us is in the care of a Higher Power.

Truth burns up error.
SOJOURNER TRUTH

Newcomer

Lately, I've been preoccupied with thoughts about a member of the group who's been pursuing me. So much mental energy goes into trying to figure out ways of warding off this person's attentions that I miss a lot of what's being said at meetings.

Today, I finally spoke up. I'd planned to say something like "Feeling comfortable at meetings is really important to me, so I want to be clear that I'm not willing to date friends from the group. I have to put my recovery first." What actually came out of my mouth didn't sound much like that! I hemmed and hawed, but I must have gotten it across, because the person acknowledged what I'd said and was sorry to have made me uncomfortable.

Sponsor

Congratulations. That's freedom. When we're finally able to say something that we've been holding back, it's an immense relief. Relationships—not just romantic ones, but those involving friends, family members, or people at work—sometimes require saying things we find difficult. The kind of appropriate, respectful sharing you did clears the air and makes closeness feel safer.

We can state the truth of our own feelings clearly and gently, without attacking or blaming the other person and putting him or her on the defensive. Instead of "Why did you . . ." or "You're making me feel . . .," we can say something like "I feel angry (hurt, happy, confused, etc.) when . . ." Instead of hurting others' feelings or inviting argument, we open the door to mutual honesty and understanding.

Today, I have the courage and humility to be truthful.

200

As a body everyone is single, as a soul never.
HERMAN HESSE

Newcomer

I've been to so many meetings. Sometimes I feel as if I'm hearing the same things over and over again. When someone starts to speak, I feel tired in advance. I think, "Oh, no—now I've got to hear that war story again."

Sponsor

At times, I've had similar feelings. I like to think of myself as a caring person, but the truth is that sometimes I feel as if I can't stand being reminded of the suffering of others. Where's my compassion?

I have a hunch that what's going on for me at such times is that, as I hear about other people's pain, I'm being reminded of my own. I don't want to dwell on my history. I want to be unique, not like all those others. I want to reject my addictive past. I don't want to hear reminders of what's inside of me. And I can't be patient and tender toward others if I'm not willing to be patient and tender toward myself.

But it's healing to listen to others. When I open my awareness and begin to accept the truth of my own and others' past suffering, my heart grows.

Today, I am aware of the presence of a Higher Power when I am in the presence of another person.

*God is not some kind of divine bellhop, to be summoned
to the service of our desires or needs.*
ABRAHAM JOSHUA HESCHEL

Newcomer

At a meeting about the Seventh Step, I heard the word "humility" over and over. I'm uncomfortable at the thought of people humiliating themselves; haven't we been through enough? I'm proud of my time in recovery, and I'm learning to be proud of myself.

Sponsor

I'm glad to hear that you've become skeptical about humiliation: degradation, disgrace, and shame have no place in our sober lives. Humility, though some of us have confused it with humiliation, is something else entirely. For me, humility is the simple recognition that we're not our own Higher Power. We don't always know what's best for us or for others. We can't order our Higher Power around, then despair when we don't get what we want when we want it.

Step Seven suggests that we continue cultivating the attitude of surrender that we assumed in Steps One, Two, and Three. It reminds us that we don't do everything by ourselves. We are willing to accept help from others and from the Spirit within that wants us to heal.

In Step Seven, we ask that characteristics and behaviors that stand in the way of our sobriety be removed. We don't demand instantaneous healing, but we do invite the process of change to begin by acknowledging our desire for it and our need for help.

**Today, I'm strong enough in recovery
to be willing to ask for help.**

Mistakes are a fact of life.
It is the response to error that counts.
NIKKI GIOVANNI

Newcomer

I was served something at a party that contained ingredients I wouldn't intentionally consume; they aren't a part of my life in recovery. I realized my mistake and stopped right away, but I felt betrayed and miserable. I've been so careful in social situations in recovery; it just hadn't occurred to me this time that I was in any danger. Do you consider this a slip?

Sponsor

I suspect that this is an experience you'll never forget. Happily, you were able to stop once you realized that you were dealing with a substance that, for you, is addictive. This wasn't a relapse, but it was a wake-up call. Instead of berating yourself for having made an honest mistake, I suggest that you share about the experience at meetings. Sharing helps us to see our experiences more clearly and to let them go. It's also a reminder that we can't just assume other people are looking out for our recovery. Avoiding unwanted substances or behaviors sometimes means asking questions or making special efforts. Staying away from our drug of choice is our own responsibility.

Today, I take full responsibility for my own recovery.

Home wasn't built in a day.
JANE ACE

Newcomer

I'm a lot better than when I was active in my addiction. But parts of my life still feel beyond my control. I don't mean earthquakes or floods. I mean getting to the dentist, repairing the car, doing the laundry, eating well. There are a lot of things I'm not taking care of the way I think I should.

Sponsor

Part of applying Steps Six and Seven to our lives is to take a look at simple behaviors that are keeping us uncomfortable and unbalanced in our recovery. Though we're not using addictive substances or behaviors, we may still be putting off the dentist, living on fast food, neglecting personal appearance, having no time for home or car maintenance, or letting bills pile up. The problems may seem minor—such things as always arriving ten minutes late to work, routinely losing keys or eyeglasses, never finding time for exercise—but they point to where we're stuck in our process of recovery. Over time, they pose risks to, rather than support of, our health and serenity.

We don't expect overnight cures, and we don't demand perfection of ourselves. We begin with awareness of what isn't working well for us. Then, each day, we take a small step toward change.

Today, I acknowledge a habit that stands between me and my serenity. I'm willing to take one small step toward changing it.

*The creative thinker is flexible and adaptable and
prepared to rearrange his thinking.*

A. J. CROPLEY

Newcomer

I'm in a crisis. I got myself into it; there's no one else to blame. I'm not sure what I'm going to do about it yet; I'm going back and forth over the alternatives. I can't think about anything else right now.

Sponsor

Your word "alternatives" is a helpful one. In most situations, we have more options to choose from than we can see at first. There usually is a "Plan B," if we're willing to open ourselves to it.

When I was active in my addiction—and for a period of time in recovery as well—I frequently found myself in the middle of a crisis. The sense of always being in crisis comes from a refusal to see that we have choices. For example, we may leave on time for an appointment but find ourselves in a traffic jam caused by an accident. If lateness is the inevitable result, we can choose to punish ourselves with whatever lateness represents to us, or we can say to ourselves, "I guess the schedule I had in mind for today has been changed; I may as well accept it." Without the additional burden of self-punishment, we can see things in perspective. Whatever happens, we don't pick up our addictive substance or behavior. We can turn to our Higher Power in prayer and meditation to help us regain a sense of balance.

**Today, I'm open to choosing among alternatives, as I
substitute the word "situation" for the word "problem."**

*I think of my illness as a school,
and finally I've graduated.*
GILDA RADNER

Newcomer

Things were going okay for a while, but now, suddenly, I have to drop everything and deal with a crisis. It feels so unfair—this wasn't supposed to happen in recovery.

Sponsor

We're not promised a problem-free life as a reward for maintaining recovery. Like all human beings, we experience things beyond our control. Disasters may occur in spite of how "good" we've been, how hard we've tried, how faithfully we've showed up for life. It may seem unfair, but it's reality.

We can take care of ourselves in a crisis by not assigning blame, not fantasizing about rescue, not refusing help, not escalating the problem through unsober behavior. We use whatever program tools we can—meetings, phone calls, prayer. We give our bodies the best nourishment, exercise, rest, and care we can. By maintaining our mental, spiritual, and physical health in these ways, we are better equipped to cope with crisis situations.

Today, I live in reality. I'm not a victim. I'm not alone.

Our most memorable days are marked by
an absence of control.
PATRICIA SMITH

Newcomer

My financial situation has unexpectedly changed, and I might have to rethink certain plans. Even though I intend to follow the principles of the program—owning up to my responsibilities honestly and promptly—I can't help feeling scared. I'm afraid to face certain people I have to change my arrangements with.

Sponsor

Though reliance on our Higher Power isn't something we reserve just for emergencies, there's nothing like a financial situation for the chance to exercise our faith.

When I was active in my addiction, the thought of powerlessness filled me with fear. I often lived as if I'd been cast in a melodrama whose inevitable outcome was shame and disgrace. Today, situations don't have to assume the proportions of a crisis. I can go to a meeting and share, talk things over with trustworthy persons, and remember that I am more than my problem. If debt is involved, whether of money or time, I can own it honestly and set realistic goals to resolve it. Self-esteem and a sense of perspective make it possible to handle situations more calmly. I don't pick up the old attitudes of my active life, any more than I would pick up an addictive substance.

We can face difficult situations with the sober confidence that comes from faith in our Higher Power and in the process of recovery. Today, I have the serenity that comes from living in faith, not fear.

To love what you do and feel that it matters—
how could anything be more fun?
KATHARINE GRAHAM

Newcomer

I've been asked to fill in for someone who usually makes coffee at my regular meeting. I said, "Yes, sure," without giving it a second thought. Now I've got to do it, and I'm feeling resentful. I'm ashamed to admit to such a petty resentment.

Sponsor

There have been many occasions when I've said yes to a request without paying attention to a hesitation I felt within myself. Sometimes my response comes out of the desire to be good; it's one of the forms of people-pleasing. Later, though I may keep the commitment I've made, I don't enjoy it; I feel somehow put upon.

In recovery, yes and no are both options, but it may take you some time to know what your heart is telling you. You may be confused by "I should" or "I have to" or by someone else's needs. If you feel conflicted and are not sure what you really want to do, whether it's a question of making coffee or attending a family wedding, you can give yourself some time to figure it out. You're not required to discuss your conflict with the person who's made the request, or to give an elaborate explanation for your decision once you make it.

Once we understand that we're making a free choice, we may even get pleasure out of doing something we previously resisted. If we give ourselves permission to say no, then saying yes can be a joy instead of a duty.

> Today, I honor my need to make genuine choices;
> I allow myself time to decide.

208

You cannot shake hands with a clenched fist.
INDIRA GANDHI

Newcomer

I attended a meeting outside of my neighborhood and had a surprising experience. As I looked around the room, I didn't see anyone who looked or dressed the way I do. I assumed I wouldn't connect with anyone here, but thought I'd at least hear enough of the program to get me through another day. I began by saying, "You don't know me; I'm a stranger to this meeting, but . . ."

When I finished sharing, the chairperson looked at me, addressed me by name, and said, "We do know you; all of us have had the feelings you're talking about. Welcome; we're glad you're here." I was shaken by her sincerity and warmth. It was humbling, after I'd blithely assumed that no one in the room would be able to relate to me. I seem to have to keep learning this lesson: I belong here.

Sponsor

I keep learning this lesson, too. Whether we wear black leather jackets or beige cardigans; live in trailers, farmhouses, or high-rises; however we speak, vote, or pray, we share the common problem of addiction and the bond of our commitment to recovery. If we listen well to others, we hear ourselves. If we share honestly, others hear us.

Your willingness to see yourself in those who appear different from you is an attitude that can also help you accept the diverse parts of yourself.

> Today, I don't make myself an outsider.
> I see what connects me to others and to myself.

 *209*

Love is or it ain't. Thin love ain't love at all.
TONI MORRISON

Newcomer

There's a friend in recovery who I've started to realize responds to me the way some members of my family did. It feels almost abusive. At first, we had frequent conversations, and she was willing to listen to whatever I was going through. She talked about herself, too, at great length. Now, when I tell her how I'm feeling, she puts me down. She doesn't come out and say, "Quit pitying yourself," but that's essentially the message. Her sudden mood changes are confusing, because sometimes she seems sympathetic.

Sponsor

Whatever else is happening, it sounds as if you're receiving some mixed signals. Your friend is somehow conveying, through tone or indirect remarks, some feelings she's not able to be direct about.

Real friendship in recovery is a blessing; we can give and accept support, share what works for us, laugh and celebrate together. Relationships that are based only on "dumping" our troubles or "getting dumped on" aren't very full or satisfying. An atmosphere of mutual complaining may help preserve the status quo, rather than support growth.

As we learn from discomfort and move on in our process of recovery, we become more discriminating about the people we spend time with. We deserve friends who are on our wavelength and who are sensitive to us—not people who subtly abuse us for having problems to work through or who can't decide whether or not they want our friendship.

Today, I have friends who nurture and delight me.

210

Remember if people talk behind your back,
it only means you are two steps ahead!
FANNIE FLAGG

Newcomer
In the beginning, I wanted to spread the amazing news and tell everyone that I was in recovery. Now I'm not sure it was such a good idea.

Sponsor

We don't have to give in to regrets about the past—including our recent past in recovery. But we can learn from it and base current decisions on what our experience has been teaching us.

Like you, I wanted to tell the world about my new-found recovery; it was too good to keep secret. I guess I thought that I had the answer for everyone; I imagined that I could save a few hundred souls by spreading the word. Good friends were genuinely delighted for me. One person at work said that I looked a lot more relaxed and happy, and asked me where these meetings were; eventually she did enter recovery. Another friend told me disapprovingly that he thought I should keep quiet about my addiction and recovery.

These days, I have less of a need to share unasked-for information indiscriminately. I make decisions based on my sense of a particular person or situation, rather than acting on impulse. When it feels right, I don't hesitate to share my recovery.

Today, I have the right to privacy.

Why do birds sing in the morning?
It's the triumphant shout:
"We got through another night."
ENID BAGNOLD

Newcomer

I've heard the expression "The person who got up first this morning is the most sober person in the room." But doesn't time in recovery count for anything?

Sponsor

I have great respect, as most of us do, for the experience of those who've been in recovery for long periods; I'm always interested in their perspective on things. I figure that they must have been doing something right, if they've lived for a significant length of time without returning to addictive substances or behavior

But emphasis on seniority might foster the mistaken belief that we can expect to finish our process of recovery some day. The tools that helped me to stay sober at the beginning are helping me to stay sober today. I need to live in the present moment. A focus on today is a gift that recovery both offers and depends on.

A slogan like the one you've quoted reminds me of that. So does the way some people refer to their length of time in recovery by saying that they've been here for "a few twenty-four hours" rather than a specific number of years. It's an act of humility.

I live and recover one day at a time.

*I always believed that if you set out to be successful,
then you already were.*
KATHERINE DUNHAM

Newcomer

I recently spent some time with a friend's family. They're not addicted to anything and never have been; they're just fine, upstanding people. Their home and work lives are stable. They contribute to their community. I couldn't help comparing myself with them and thinking that they wouldn't want to have much to do with me if they knew the real me.

Sponsor

Our practice of comparing our insides with other people's outsides makes us forget that we don't usually get to hear all the details of other people's past difficulties. We can't assume that there are large numbers of adult human beings outside of this program who never have to face challenges, fears, and situations that resemble our own.

And what about you? You've faced your problems courageously; you're committed to doing whatever it takes to stay away from addictive substances and behavior; you're a contributing participant in this community of recovering people.

Our self-esteem may require care and nurturing in recovery. Over time, shame leaves us and allows us to appreciate more fully the value of what we have to contribute. Our past suffering doesn't diminish us. It makes us more compassionate and more useful to our fellow human beings.

Today, I'm a person worth knowing. I respect my own unique combination of gifts; no one else is exactly like me.

The truth cannot always be told openly,
but somehow it does come out.
SIGMUND FREUD

Newcomer

Some days I don't feel as if I can share how difficult my problems are. I've been in recovery long enough to know that what's bothering me will eventually subside. I've heard "This, too, shall pass" often enough. Why complain about problems that are going to go away anyway? Why bother anyone?

Sponsor

The slogan "This, too, shall pass" is meant to give comfort, not to make stoics and martyrs of us. There's nothing wrong with letting others see what's going on with us and airing our feelings, whatever they happen to be. In fact, it's necessary for recovery.

My addictive behavior in the past was often triggered by a belief that my needs and feelings were somehow excessive, that no one would tolerate hearing about them. When feelings of unworthiness and shame kept me from speaking, the result was more of the same: low self-esteem and a sense of separation and difference from others.

We're not required to share everything that's going on in our lives whenever we put a hand up at a meeting. But we need to make sure that we don't carry things all by ourselves. We have plenty of options. Sharing at meetings is a good one. Others include making program calls, sitting down for coffee with a recovering friend, or scheduling a therapy or counseling session. And then there's talking regularly with a sponsor. It's an excellent way to begin letting go of the old habit of keeping quiet.

Today, I lighten my load by sharing with others.

⇌ *214* ⇋

As one goes through life one learns that if you don't paddle your own canoe, you don't move.
KATHARINE HEPBURN

Newcomer
I appreciate the fact that you remain friendly and even-tempered even though I don't always follow your advice.

Sponsor
Friends can disagree without having to end their relationship. I might have trouble sponsoring someone who never attends meetings, someone who has frequent relapses, or someone who complains about his or her problems without ever being willing to attempt the Steps. But occasional disagreements are a part of life.

A sponsor's suggestions aren't commands, any more than the Twelve Steps are. As a sponsor, I only make suggestions; even though they're based on my experience, I'm not always right about what will work for another person. And I may misjudge what another person's timetable is. I'm not infallible. I try not to let my ego get in the way, to feel hurt or angry when you need to try something on your own. Learning to make your own decisions is necessary to growth.

Each of us makes his or her own way through the

process of recovery. We learn more from our own experiences, good and bad, than from anything we read in a book or hear at a meeting.

Today, I learn from my experience.

 *215*

I wish I hadn't done a lot of things,
but on the other hand, if I hadn't, I wouldn't be here.
MADONNA

Newcomer
I know we're not supposed to have regrets any more, but I have them. Sometimes I'm afraid that I've been damaged beyond repair.

Sponsor
We have a longing for wholeness and the capacity to achieve it. Human beings aren't like pieces of machinery that are too broken or rusty to be of use. Our tissues regenerate in seemingly miraculous ways. Our minds and spirits are also capable of regeneration and renewal. Every day of our lives, we have opportunities to begin or further the process of healing.

When we're overcome with regret, the work we do in Steps Eight and Nine, acknowledging those we've harmed and attempting to make amends to them, is especially helpful. We don't just bury the past and try to forget it. We look at it honestly and without self-pity; we make whatever repairs are actually possible. We go through the process of grieving our losses. We integrate our past experiences into a

larger, more compassionate understanding of ourselves—
one that includes the protection and loving presence of the
Spirit within us.

Our past experience equips us to be especially helpful
to others who suffer. There is a use for everything that has
ever happened to us.

**Today, I put my past to use as I reach out
to others who suffer.**

 *216*

*To gain that which is worth having,
it may be necessary to lose everything else.*
BERNADETTE DEVLIN

Newcomer
When I listen to people at Step meetings, the word "humility" always seems to come up, no matter which Step is
being discussed. I still have resistance to that word.

Sponsor
Like many people in recovery, I've experienced some resistance to each Step as I've come to it; by letting myself feel
this resistance, then moving through it, I've learned some
things about myself. I think that our objections to each
Step add up to a portrait of our disease. Whether a particular Step addresses our relationship with a substance or a behavior, with ourselves, with other people, or with a Higher
Power, it asks us to see ourselves as part of something larger
than our own will. There has been arrogance and willfulness in our insistence on doing things our way, rejecting

help, trying to stand alone in the universe, and feeling unlovable and unforgivable.

Humility is simply a recognition that we have limitations. Paradoxically, accepting our limitations gives us the freedom to become part of something limitless.

Today, I have the courage to let go of resistance.

217

My memories are anything but a dispassionate chronicle.
ILYA EHRENBURG

Newcomer

I'm nervous about taking Step Eight. I can't help thinking ahead to Step Nine, actually talking to the people I owe amends to.

Sponsor

Remembering to stay in the present is one of the greatest challenges of living in recovery. If we're focusing on a future Step, letting the fear of it take over, we can't engage fully and wholeheartedly in the Step we're doing today.

When taking the first part of Step Eight, we make as complete a list of those we've harmed as memory allows. If we dimly remember an event but can't remember a name, we briefly describe the person. If we think that there's no hope of ever locating someone again, we still add him or her to the list. We may think that we've done less harm to some people than they've done to us. Still, we add their names to the list: this Step is about what we did, not about what others deserve.

By making this list we begin to see the extent of the harm we've done as the result of our addictive behavior, and to see how deeply interconnected our lives are with the lives of others. We realize that we're not alone in the world, and never have been.

Today, I look at my past without fear.
I have faith that my human relationships are being healed.

 *218*

*He who accounts all things easy
will have many difficulties.*
LAO-TZU

Newcomer
Is there any special way I should go about making an amends list? I think it's going to be a long one, and I don't know if I can trust my memory.

Sponsor
There are many ways to make an Eighth Step list. One is to look at the Fourth Step inventory we wrote and review the names of those we feared or resented. Or we can make a list by starting with friends, work associates, and family members in our present lives, then working backward in time.

We make an effort to remember every person we've harmed, but if we've forgotten some, we don't worry. As we continue to recover, memories return, often triggered by other people's sharing: we can add those names as they come to us.

Some recovering people choose to use index cards for

the amends list. The idea is to write the person's name (we can add his or her address and phone number, if we have them) at the top of the card, then write a phrase or a sentence about exactly what sort of harm we caused. We then turn the card over and note which of our characteristics or feelings lay behind the harm that we caused (for example, fear or low self-esteem). If we then arrange our stack of index cards according to the characteristics we've named on the reverse side, we may see clusters of attitudes and habits that reveal more to us about our underlying beliefs.

> **Today, I acknowledge that
> my thoughts and actions affect others.**

219

What is not recorded is not remembered.
BENAZIR BHUTTO

Newcomer
What if I don't think that I've harmed many people or that the harm was significant?

Sponsor
There's a program saying that when a train is wrecked, it's not just the engineer who gets hurt. We're not alone; none of us live in total isolation from others.

Perhaps we haven't stolen money, attacked anyone with our fists, demolished someone's character, or been sexually irresponsible. But if we've been angry, impatient, and critical, those around us have suffered from our lack of understanding and appreciation. Or have we been smothering and overresponsible, enabling others to neglect their own responsibilities? It simply isn't possible for someone whose life has been affected by an addiction not to have caused some damage, whether the damage has been mental, physical, or spiritual.

Taking this Step gently but thoroughly, neither overstating nor ignoring the impact we've had on others, can liberate us from the incorrect belief that we have no effect in the world.

> Today, I'm open to the healing that begins with
> making a list of everyone whom I have harmed.

⇒ *220* ⇒

The same heart beats in every human breast.
MATTHEW ARNOLD

Newcomer

Why do I hear some people say that they've put themselves on their own Eighth Step list? I thought that this Step was about the harm we did to other people.

Sponsor

The harm we did to other people also harmed us. All harm is also self-harm, just as all deception is also self-deception.

Take lying, for example. When I told a lie, I damaged my own relationship to the truth, to my Higher Power, and to others. One consequence of telling a lie was to feel guilty; unable to tolerate the feeling of guilt, I turned to my addiction to numb myself. The people to whom I lied may have been misled, but my lies affected me by damaging my self-esteem and blocking my connection with my spirit. After we've made an Eighth Step list of people we've harmed, we may also want to add a note, in each case, of the ways we harmed ourselves in the process. It will then be clear whether or not we should add our own names to the list of people to whom we owe amends.

Today, I become willing to make amends to myself.

221

I don't think of all the misery,
but of all the beauty that still remains.
ANNE FRANK

Newcomer
How can I forgive my parents and other people who shaped my childhood? If I'd gotten what I needed when I was young, I wouldn't have to go through all this stuff I'm facing now.

Sponsor
In the process of looking back at our past, we see the circumstances of our childhood in a clear light. We see how we reacted to situations that weren't of our making. We see that we did whatever we could to survive intact; we developed our own particular strategies and strengths. Today, we may feel as if all we can do is to assign blame to others and feel anger and resentment. We may not be ready to forgive people who harmed us. If this is the case, we can acknowledge it by saying, "Today, I'm not able to forgive ____." Forgiveness can't be forced. However, we needn't assume that we will never feel it.

Once we've looked honestly at our past, we can accept that we have survived it, and that we can take the actions necessary to be restored to wholeness. One such action is to become willing to forgive ourselves, whether or not we're ready to forgive others. We can forgive ourselves for everything we wish we had done differently and for whatever qualities in ourselves we've ignored or rejected. Forgiving ourselves is a necessity.

Today, I am grateful for my life
and for my capacity to heal.

222

Nursing her wrath to keep it warm . . .
ROBERT BURNS

Newcomer
A friend of mine treated me badly in the past. I feel uncomfortable whenever I think of her. Do I have to forgive her? Does she belong on my amends list?

Sponsor
Anger is a common human feeling; we can discharge it in a variety of ways that don't hurt us or anyone else, then move on. But grudges long and deeply held are something else. Obsession with what others have done poses a threat to our recovery.

Suppose we've taken an honest look at our own role and know that we ourselves did no harm. We may even have reviewed the conflict with a sponsor, therapist, or spiritual adviser, and are convinced that we're not deluding ourselves. We don't make amends to those we haven't harmed.

Relief comes only if we understand and accept that there are sick and suffering people, both in and out of recovery. We don't have to tolerate further harm, but we can choose not to pursue revenge or confrontation with those who are deluded, spiritually ill, or undeveloped. We can pray for their healing, as well as our own.

Today, I entrust the healing of all forms of sickness to my Higher Power.

 *223*

"I can forgive, but I cannot forget"
is only another way of saying, "I cannot forgive."
HENRY WARD BEECHER

Newcomer
Won't forgiving those who've done real harm make me a weaker person? I don't want to deny the real evils that exist.

Sponsor
The best of us are flawed; the worst of us have some redeeming features. Getting to know ourselves involves the willingness to face all aspects of our character—our generosity and selfishness, courage and fear, open and closed places.

If we can see ourselves with objectivity, then we're better equipped to see others, too, as they really are. We can imaginatively experience another person's pain or fear, and sense intuitively what he or she is trying to protect. We may be able to stop taking another's behavior toward us so personally, once we understand it as part of a defense system that was in place long before we entered the picture.

The word "compassion" means "feeling with"—sharing in another's suffering. Compassion doesn't diminish us. Exactly the opposite: it expands our hearts. When we can feel compassion, both for ourselves and for others, we experience just how powerful the action of forgiveness is.

Today, I clean the house of my spirit.
I no longer have to carry the weight of others' wrongs.

224

The more we know, the better we forgive.
MADAME DE STAËL

Newcomer
I can see some of the ways I harmed myself when I was active in my addiction, and I've added my own name to my amends list. How do I go about apologizing to myself? It seems absurd.

Sponsor
When it comes to making amends, "apologizing" isn't the whole story. When we apologize, we express regret for what we've done, sometimes offering an excuse or an explanation. "Amends" comes from a Latin word that means "to free from faults." When we make amends, we acknowledge what we did and then find a way to compensate or make up for it. In taking responsibility for our behavior, we change; we're free to move forward without the terrible burden of guilt.

We can begin to feel compassion for the person we were when we were active in our addiction, once we understand that we were trying to take care of ourselves in the only way we could at the time. In a sense, we began making amends to ourselves the day we entered recovery. For many of us, giving up our addictive substance or behavior is the hardest thing we've done in our lives, and the most freeing.

No one can give us the feelings of worthiness and self-esteem that are part of complete recovery; we must experience them ourselves. Forgiving ourselves is essential to our healing process. If we can't forgive ourselves today, we can pray for willingness, trusting that we'll grow in generosity and tenderness toward ourselves, as well as toward others.

Today, I grow in love and compassion for myself.

 *225*

In the course of time, we grow to love things we once hated and hate the things we once loved.
ROBERT LOUIS STEVENSON

Newcomer
What does "Be good to yourself" really mean? Sometimes when I'm supposed to be working, I want to lie around in bed and do nothing, or sit in front of the TV eating pints of ice cream. "Be good to yourself" comes into my head, so I let myself goof off; then I feel guilty.

Sponsor
There's nothing wrong with relaxing; in fact, many of us in recovery have had a lot to learn about having fun and not

treating ourselves like machines. Recovery is not about deprivation.

But being good to ourselves doesn't mean substituting new addictive substances or behaviors for the old ones. Eating a whole pint of ice cream a day, watching hours of TV, sleeping when we have things to do—these are forms of anesthesia. In that respect, they're no different from drinking alcohol or using heroin. They're ways of making feelings disappear, cutting off our connection with ourselves.

Being good to ourselves might mean taking a walk, listening to music, buying ourselves flowers, making plans with a friend—whatever genuinely nurtures us. It doesn't mean doing what we know through our experience or intuition is only going to deaden our spirits.

Today, I know how to nurture myself.

 **226**

The same stream of life that runs through my veins night and day, runs through the world and dances in rhythmic measure.
RABINDRANATH TAGORE

Newcomer
I love nature, but I just haven't been able to make the time or find the money to get away and enjoy it.

Sponsor
We don't have to travel in order to experience ourselves as part of the natural world. If we aren't able to have a garden, we can plant seeds in a windowsill container or put out a

bird feeder. We can tune in to natural rhythms by allowing ourselves quiet time when we first wake up in the morning instead of automatically turning on a news broadcast. When we eat, we can stop to smell the food, think about the earth it came from, and chew slowly enough to experience its taste. We can walk outdoors for a short time every day, experiencing the rhythm of our moving bodies and the sensation of sunlight, rain, or snow on our skin. We ourselves are a part of nature; we can quiet ourselves by observing the rhythm of our breathing in meditation. Instead of watching TV as we lie in bed at night, we can listen to birds, wind, or rustling leaves. If all we can hear outside our windows is the sound of cars or fire engines, we can listen to a tape of natural sounds.

Nature relieves our fatigue, tension, and stress. Becoming aware of nature, bringing ourselves into harmony with its rhythms, heals us.

**Today, I alternate activity with rest,
taking time to appreciate some part of the natural world.**

227

So do we put our life into every act.
RALPH WALDO EMERSON

Newcomer

There are many people I've shortchanged in my life. While making a list of those I've harmed, I realize I haven't been very good to myself, either. For as long as I can remember, I've wanted to do some creative work. It's something that I never used to think I could succeed at, but I've always wanted to try. Somehow, I've never had the time.

Shortchanging others and shortchanging ourselves—I think you're right to see a relationship between the two. If we are less than honest with someone else, if we don't keep our commitments to others, then we're doing these very same things to ourselves as well.

You've brought up your desire to acknowledge your creativity, something you've always wanted but have put off. Why has it been such a low priority, when it's clearly so important to you? Your creativity isn't self-indulgent. It's something that's very important to your spirit, important as a path of connection to yourself and to your Higher Power.

As you clear the channels between yourself and others, you're becoming more present for yourself. This clearing is an essential part of the path to creative expression and fulfillment.

Today, I honor my need for creative expression.

228

The more I learn of others' problems, the more my own problems automatically dissolve.
TARTHANG TULKU RINPOCHE

Newcomer

The second part of Step Eight says, "became willing to make amends to them all." I have to admit that this is a lot harder for me than simply recognizing that I've caused harm. I don't know if I'm ready to talk to certain people.

Sponsor

The willingness to make amends to everyone we've harmed, even those who may have harmed us, is something that we don't have to force or strive for. We become willing as part of yet another gradual process in recovery. We have begun to recognize that everything is interrelated, that whatever we've done to others, we've also done in some measure to ourselves. This is true not only of any harm that we've done, but also of the compassion that we've begun to feel. As we come to understand the impact of addiction on our lives, as we release our secrets and are met with gentleness and understanding, as we participate in the healing laughter at meetings, we replace old feelings of shame with compassion. Our new capacity to feel compassion for ourselves restores and revitalizes our understanding and care for others.

We become willing to make amends when we realize that in doing so, we are healing ourselves.

**Today, I cultivate openness and compassion
toward others.**

꘏ **229** ꘏

*Duty is what one expects from others—
it is not what one does oneself.*
OSCAR WILDE

Newcomer

I do intend to make amends to everyone I've harmed, but I still feel scared when I start to think about it.

Sponsor

The prospect of facing someone to whom we owe amends may bring up unnecessary fear if we cling to our old notion that we do everything alone.

We can plan to telephone a sponsor or program friend both before and after making the amend. We can ask for help from our Higher Power, praying for the willingness to make the amend, for the ability to speak our truth simply and clearly, and for the serenity that comes from understanding that another person's response is not in the realm of things we can control. Tools work, when we're willing to use them. As always, faith is the antidote to fear. If we feel that our faith is insufficient, we can listen to others in recovery sharing about their experience of the loving presence of a Higher Power—we can borrow from others' reserves of faith, when our own are low.

> Today, I'm not alone. I allow myself to
> ask for and accept the support I need and deserve.

230

Pray for the bastard.
SAYING HEARD AT MEETINGS

Newcomer

You've told me I should pray for someone who's been causing me all sorts of problems. But that's not going to change him, is it?

Sponsor

I've heard various descriptions of how prayer works. Some say God listens; some say our thoughts affect the energy of the universe and create change; some say that we're conditioning ourselves to transform our own attitudes, and that attitudes, good and bad, are contagious. It's a mystery—but it does work.

Someone I worked with seemed so disrespectful and unpleasant that I dreaded encounters with her. I began saying a daily prayer for her health and complete happiness. Before gatherings that included her, I prayed that communication between us would be easy and smooth and that each person's highest good in that situation would be realized. The effects were dramatic. I experienced relief from my fear of facing her and began to see her as a whole human being. I genuinely began to want her well-being. My body language and facial expressions probably changed; perhaps I stopped sending messages of dislike and rejection when I saw her. For whatever reason, she stopped turning her back on me and sometimes actually smiled.

I'm not suggesting that we try to manipulate others to behave as we wish. Specific results and timetables aren't in our hands. But I do know that our prayers are always effective in furthering our own and others' processes of healing.

> **Today, I pray for others, placing them in my Higher Power's hands.**

231

Thank God, guilt was never a rational thing.
EDMUND BURKE

Newcomer
Several days ago, I sent a check through the mail to pay my rent, but the landlord still hasn't received it. I spoke to him

on the phone, and he said he'd be willing to wait and see if it reached him in the coming week. He didn't even hint that he didn't believe me, but that's what I imagined.

Sponsor

I once heard this story from a friend:

Before Atlas (one of the gods in early Greek mythology) got the job of holding the world on his shoulders, someone else was supporting it. He said to Atlas, "There's something I have to do; please hold this for a moment," and walked away. For a moment, no one at all was holding up the world. Atlas stepped underneath and took the burden; he's been carrying the world ever since. But in that moment when no one at all had the world on his or her shoulders, nothing happened.

It takes a lot of energy to assume responsibility for something we can't control. A situation like the one you're describing is valuable; it can show us how willing we are to shoulder the burden of guilt, even when no harm has been done. Having an alternative plan—such as stopping payment on the first check, sending a replacement, or finding another way to get it to its destination—is helpful; it can short-circuit the cycle of unnecessary guilt.

Today, if things don't work out as expected, I make alternate plans. I don't take on the weight of the world.

It is hard to be good.
DIOGENES LAERTIUS

Newcomer

I chair a meeting once a week now. It involves opening up, closing, getting a speaker, setting out literature and chairs, and making sure everything gets put away. Last night there were two or three people I'd have liked to talk with after the meeting, but they were already involved in conversations. By the time I finished the cleanup, they were gone.

Sponsor

One of the reasons that service is so strongly recommended to us in early recovery is that it gets us to a meeting and helps us connect with other recovering people. It sounds as if this service commitment has somehow backfired for you: you're feeling isolated at the meeting, perhaps a bit resentful. I have a few practical suggestions: you can ask at the break for volunteers to clean up and put things away, and you can postpone supervising or participating in the cleanup while you reach out to some people for conversation after the meeting. You might even consider letting the speaker know that you hope he or she will call on you; sharing is another way to combat feelings of invisibility. If we're taking care of ourselves, making sure that our own needs are being met, we can serve with ease and pleasure.

Today, I take my need for sharing and connection
seriously and place it high on my list of priorities.
I seek opportunities to connect with others,
rather than waiting for them to come to me.

*The advantage of the emotions
is that they lead us astray.*
OSCAR WILDE

Newcomer

I don't understand the slogan "Feelings aren't facts." I thought that we were supposed to pay more attention to our feelings in recovery. This slogan makes it sound like our feelings will lead us astray.

Sponsor

Acknowledging our feelings and letting them pass through us is different from clinging to them, assuming they'll never change, taking self-destructive actions based on them, or letting them lead us into self-pity, resentment, or despair. An amazing thing about feelings is that they change.

If we're aware of having feelings that we dislike or that might lead us back to our addictions—such as anger, fear, or sadness—we can safely discharge anger through physical activity or sharing; we can cry when we're moved to cry. In recovery, our feelings aren't so frightening. We've seen them come and go.

Many of us have the habit of reacting to present circumstances with an array of negative feelings we're still carrying from the past. In recovery, we recognize that there is more than one way to respond.

**Today, my repertoire of possible responses is large,
as I go through my day with lightness.**

*Every day is a god, each day is a god,
and holiness holds forth in time.*
ANNIE DILLARD

Newcomer

I still don't seem to have much control over certain feelings. I woke up this morning feeling afraid of things I have to do today. I know I just have to show up and do my part—the results are out of my hands—but I still have that old sinking feeling.

Sponsor

Old feelings and thoughts may continue for some time in recovery, but we don't have to give them the power they used to have. We're blessed with alternatives to our old addictive habits of thinking and behaving. When we wake in fearful anticipation of what the day will bring, it's time once again to take actions that have worked for us so far in recovery.

We begin by expressing gratitude for the new day and for all the days that have led us to it. We can read some literature that comforts and lifts our spirits. We can make a program call. We can take time to nourish our bodies with food.

These morning rituals help us put the day into perspective: we've survived, and we're not alone. This day will not be exactly like any other, before it or after it. What lies ahead is certain to hold surprises.

I greet this day with celebration. I am alive.

I am my own universe, I my own professor.
SYLVIA ASHTON-WARNER

Newcomer

I've been trying to meditate every day this week, closing my eyes and concentrating on my breathing. I was hoping that it would help me with the depression I've been feeling on and off. A strange thing has been happening, though. Instead of feeling relaxed and refreshed, I become oddly disconnected and I start to panic.

Sponsor

Obviously, something that causes panic isn't a good choice for us, no matter how highly it's been recommended.

Anyone experiencing depression is not advised to meditate with the eyes closed for more than fifteen minutes at a time. If meditating with eyes closed feels disorienting and upsetting, we can try another method; there are numerous alternatives. Meditating with open eyes, focusing our vision on a natural object such as a shell, flame, or flower, can bring a sense of inner peace. Meditating while walking or chanting a mantra aloud can also be good choices for those suffering from depression.

I'm glad that you're alert to the instinct that's telling you not to force situations.

Today, I trust my intuitive sense of what I need.

Use what language you will,
you can never say anything but what you are.
RALPH WALDO EMERSON

Newcomer

Since so many of us are cross-addicted, why are some meetings closed?

Sponsor

Though a meeting may be listed as "closed," it's open to anyone who has a desire to stop using the substance or compulsive behavior that is the focus of the meeting. For example, if I'm a recovering compulsive overeater who has begun to explore my relationship with alcohol or drugs, I may attend closed meetings of AA or NA. However, observers, journalists, spouses, and interested friends, all of whom are welcome at "open" meetings, may not attend closed meetings. The existence of closed meetings offers a greater sense of security to those who are especially concerned about their anonymity and to those who prefer to keep discussions focused on a specific addiction.

Rather than engage in controversy about this issue, we need to respect the collective conscience and guidelines of the particular groups we attend. We can make an effort to find meetings where we feel comfortable telling the truth about how we got here. If we're attending an open meeting merely as a visitor, we listen, but refrain from sharing. We respect the anonymity of those present and don't carry news of what we've heard or seen, even to members of another anonymous fellowship.

Today, there's a place that's right for me;
I go there and know that I'm at home.

It's a day like any other.
JAMES SCHUYLER

Newcomer

Over these last several months, I've done a number of things sober for the first time since I can remember. I've survived my first New Year's Eve, family reunion, birthday, and Fourth of July without acting out my addiction. I love having gotten through these days, but it wasn't easy. I'm not sure I can say I celebrated, or that I'm looking forward to next year.

Sponsor

Holidays may pose a challenge to those of us in early recovery. They may raise questions about our relationships with loved ones, put us in close proximity to people who are acting out our addictions, and confront us with memories of our own past behavior. We still need to avoid people, places, and things that might lead us back to addiction: we can make decisions about where we want to be and with whom, based on our own most pressing needs in recovery. We can volunteer to help others: serving holiday dinners in a homeless shelter, speaking at a correctional facility, or leading a meeting are some techniques for strengthening our own recovery and cultivating gratitude. As holidays in recovery return, they'll be opportunities for us to notice and appreciate how far we've come.

**I avoid dramatic highs and lows
as I celebrate another day in recovery.**

In search of my mother's garden I found my own.
ALICE WALKER

Newcomer

I heard someone say that no one is in our lives by mistake. But am I supposed to believe that my boss is the best of all possible bosses? That people who've hurt me somehow did the right thing? Should I avoid people who threaten my recovery, or shouldn't I?

Sponsor

When we say, "No one comes into our lives by mistake," we don't mean that we're at the mercy of whomever we happen to encounter, but rather that every situation involving another human being offers us an opportunity for getting to know ourselves better and for growing spiritually.

We can choose our friends and associates. We're not required to like or trust everyone. But as we look at those we spend time with and those we avoid, those we embrace and those we fear, we learn a great deal about who we are. What part of ourselves are we intolerant of when we encounter it in someone else? What part of ourselves are we willing to face and deal with? What part of ourselves are we prepared to love unconditionally?

People in our lives can become our teachers, if we let them.

Today, I take the opportunity for growth
that the presence of someone in my life offers me.

*Accept the place the divine providence has
found for you, the society of your contemporaries,
the connection of events.*

RALPH WALDO EMERSON

Newcomer

Every time I look down the list of Steps, I get scared. The Ninth Step scares me most of all. I can't imagine talking with certain people again, let alone admitting wrongdoing.

Sponsor

In the early days of my recovery I felt much the way that you do now; you're not alone in holding on to old, familiar fears and resentments. The Twelve Steps are a suggested process, arranged in an order that works, one Step at a time. If I'm afraid of a Step, I may need to go back to the Step before it. For today, you're exactly where you're supposed to be. You've stopped using addictive substances. You're going to meetings, listening with an open heart, and practicing the Steps. All the rest will follow in time.

There's no need to worry about what the future will bring. You're on a day-at-a-time journey that changes you as you go. You'll have whatever you need to cope with each new situation as it arises. Best of all, you won't have to do it alone; in recovery, you have the loving support of friends, a sponsor, and a fellowship.

For today, I am exactly where I need to be.
I trust the process of recovery unfolding in my life.
I ask for help as I move through it.

*It is not the weak but the strong who practice tolerance,
and the strong do not weaken their position
showing tolerance.*

DAG HAMMARSKJOLD

Newcomer
What if I can't forgive myself?

Sponsor
Many of us in recovery are harder on ourselves than we'd
be on anyone else. The spiritual awakening that occurs
through the process of taking the Twelve Steps can help us
to let go of the habits of self-blame and self-punishment.

Entering recovery was an action that took faith and
courage; for most of us, it was the most difficult thing we'd
done in our lives. Now that we've taken that step, can we
genuinely believe that growth and change are over and that
happiness and freedom are for others, but not for us? In
time, with the help of our Higher Power, our capacity for
forgiveness will grow to include ourselves.

If we think that we can't forgive ourselves, we can pray
to become willing to forgive ourselves. If we think that we
can't pray to become willing, we can simply say the words,
"For today, I'm not yet willing to forgive myself." Putting it
this way leaves the door open. We haven't ruled out future
change. We've left room for the possibility that there will
come a day when we will have the willingness. In time,
more will be revealed.

Today, I trust that my Higher Power
hasn't brought me this far only to abandon me.

Don't be humble: you're not that great.
GOLDA MEIR

Newcomer

I'm still confused about the issue of forgiveness. What if someone takes advantage of me, harms me, or cheats me? Do I just do nothing?

Sponsor

We're not required to be doormats. Self-esteem requires us to speak our truth, when doing so isn't harmful to ourselves and doesn't harm others. We're not really doing people or institutions any favors by not acknowledging problems.

Not long ago, I bought a piece of equipment for my home office that turned out to be defective. In my days of active addiction, I'd have yelled at the salesman, threatened to sue the company, created a huge drama and a lot of ill will. Or I might have done nothing at all—simply swallowed my anger and taken a loss, or had the equipment repaired at my own expense. Both of these paths are those of a person with low self-esteem. In recovery, I could be clear, firm, and persistent about my expectation of having the defective equipment picked up and replaced.

Today, I expect myself and others to keep promises. Asking a manufacturer to stand behind a product is a way to express my respect for truth. Had my efforts failed to get results, I'd still have felt successful: simply by speaking honestly, I'd have achieved something important.

**Today, I acknowledge my needs firmly and clearly,
to myself and to others.**

*If you don't remember history accurately,
how can you learn?*

MAYA LIN

Newcomer

Someone from my past called yesterday. He left the message that he'd be speaking with me soon. I haven't seen this person since I started recovery. I know he can't take my recovery away from me, but I feel threatened. All I can think of, when I imagine seeing him again, is how the two of us used to act out together.

Sponsor

People, places, and things from our past continue to be an issue even after the first few months of recovery. It takes time to accumulate enough sober experience for the habit of recovery to feel stronger than the habit of acting out our addictions. Even now that saying no and asking for help have begun to seem like second nature to us, we're not invulnerable. People with long-term recovery have been known to have relapses.

You're right: another person can't take recovery away from us. But why subject ourselves to stresses that endanger our serenity and our sense of connection to people in the program? Sentimental feelings about the past and hopes of leading others to recovery are better put on the shelf. Relationships based on mutual enabling and acting out have no place in our recovery.

Today, I have a healthy respect for my disease. I keep my serenity by avoiding people, places, and things related to my addiction and by staying close to the fellowship.

Advice is what we ask for when we
already know the answer but wish we didn't.
ERICA JONG

Newcomer

There's someone I tried to help, earlier in my recovery. She called me again recently and told me a long story about how hard it was for her to stay sober, how difficult her life was. I mentioned meetings again, and she promised to come to one, but then went on talking. I'm exhausted from staying up late listening to her.

Sponsor

Trying to reason with someone on a binge does neither them nor us any good. When we sense that we're letting someone who's active pull us around and around on his or her merry-go-round, it's probably the disease that's in charge of the conversation.

Some people are genuinely drawn to recovery, but just aren't ready to commit to it. No matter how good our intentions, there's nothing we can do to hurry their process. Some people use our desire to be helpful to manipulate us; if they can keep us listening, they don't have to change.

We stop engaging in this process by detaching from argument about their many objections. We put it simply: Recovery is now the center of change in our lives. They're always welcome to come to a meeting and try it out, if they want what we have.

Today, I don't cajole anyone to try recovery.
I'm available to people who want what I have.

244

God grant me the serenity
To accept the things I cannot change,
The courage to change the things I can,
And the wisdom to know the difference.

THE SERENITY PRAYER

Newcomer

What if the person to whom I'm trying to make amends is still too angry to accept my apology or doesn't want anything to do with me?

Sponsor

This is an important question. When we speak our amends aloud or write them in a letter, as long as we have acknowledged the harm we've done and are committed to doing things differently, then our amends are genuine and we've done our part.

One of the things over which we have no control is the way another person reacts to our amends. He or she may be understanding, even loving and generous, or may not be as ready to forgive us as we are to acknowledge harm we've done. Hearing from us may revive old anger or pain. Some may think we're trying to get off easy. Our recovery itself may cause resentment.

In time, friends' or relatives' attitudes may change—or they may not. We can't force other human beings to forgive us or to want us in their lives, and we can't make things happen on our timetable.

Today, I do my part by taking appropriate actions;
I turn over the results of those actions
to my Higher Power.

245

Action is eloquence.
WILLIAM SHAKESPEARE

Newcomer

I think I'm willing to make amends, but what if the person I'm making amends to doesn't let me? I have family and friends who are uncomfortable if I talk about feelings or about anything having to do with the past.

Sponsor

Some people in our lives may not be quick to believe that we've gone through significant changes. If they're not ready to rely on us, to trust that things will be different, it may be less painful for them not to hear us speak of how we've harmed them in the past. Accepting that we caused harm in the past as a result of our addictions may trigger feelings of guilt about their role in their relationship with us, and it may require that they look at the role of addiction in their own lives. It may be painful for people to remember how they've been hurt by you or me. Or, as you're suggesting, they may simply be people who are uncomfortable talking about or listening to feelings.

Making amends isn't just saying we're sorry. What "making amends" really means is changing. We can amend relationships with other people by taking sober actions, by not repeating the kind of behavior that caused harm in the past. In time, they may be able to see that we are dependable and consistent, and that our role in relationships has changed for the better.

Our sense of completion with Step Nine doesn't depend on the way others respond. The change is within us.

**Today, my self-esteem comes from
doing things differently.**

❦ *246* ❦

Friends, though absent, are still present.
CICERO

Newcomer
Some of the people on my list of amends have moved, and I have no idea how to locate them.

Sponsor
Our new willingness to take responsibility for our choices has begun a process of healing within us. If we've made sincere efforts to locate people on our amends list, but haven't succeeded perfectly, then it's time to let go. Step Nine begins "Made direct amends to such people *wherever possible*" (emphasis added). There are circumstances over which we have no control.

My own experience, like that of many people in Twelve Step fellowships, is that once we're in recovery, threads from the past begin to weave themselves back into our lives. Surprisingly often, unexpected opportunities to make amends present themselves.

If such opportunities haven't yet arisen, we can be calm and confident that we have done our part simply by recognizing that amends are called for and by having the willingness to make them. Knowing this, we can have a measure of serenity when we think of people who aren't part of our present lives.

Today, I have the willingness for healing in all of my relationships.

 *247*

Prayer needs no speech.
MOHANDAS GANDHI

Newcomer
How can I make amends to someone who has died?

Sponsor
Relationships are healed in the heart. Loving communication need not be limited by time or space. It's useful to remember that our purpose in taking Step Nine is to amend ourselves and our behavior toward others, to end the cycle of guilt and isolation that will lead us back to active addiction.

There are many ways of making amends to someone who has passed away. Those that I've personally experienced as beneficial and deeply healing include the following: (1) We can write a letter of amends and share it with a sponsor, spiritual adviser, or trusted friend in recovery. (2) We can speak to the person in our hearts, praying both before and after for a complete, healing communication. (3) We can use our imagination to create a simple ritual for an amends "visit." For example, to make amends to my mother, I prepared to spend an evening with her, cooked and ate food she used to enjoy, lit candles, and listened to a tape I was fortunate enough to have of her voice. Then I spoke aloud to her as if she were present, and made amends. I listened, in meditation, for a loving response. The power of this experience was far greater than I'd expected.

When we make amends, whether or not the person to whom we're making them is physically present, we must be willing to forgive ourselves for what we wish we'd done differently.

Today, I let go of all obstacles to making amends.

248

Boldness has genius, power, and magic in it.
JOHANN WOLFGANG VON GOETHE

Newcomer
How is making amends going to change me?

Sponsor
For me, the experience of making amends was—and is—profoundly life-changing. I'd been carrying a burden of guilt with me everywhere. Even when I didn't realize it, a large part of my mental and physical energy was being used to carry it. It was always with me, keeping me from feeling free. When I finally started to make amends, all that weight I was carrying disappeared.

An amend doesn't stop with apologizing or making restitution. It's a commitment to change. Having gone through the process of admitting that I'd done some damage, accepting that the work of restitution was mine, and making the required amends, I became morally awake. I began to understand the consequences of my behavior.

Not that I've become perfect; I still do things that harm others. But seeing and admitting my responsibility for what I do and say has become a habit. With old amends over and done with, we don't have to be afraid of whom we'll meet. We don't have to hide from ourselves or anyone else.

**Today, I'm free. I don't have to pick up my addiction.
I don't have to behave in old, familiar ways.**

249

They who forgive most, shall be most forgiven.
PHILIP JAMES BAILEY

Newcomer

Some of the people I owe amends to aren't very kind or forgiving. How is making amends to them going to change anything?

Sponsor

The amends are ours, no one else's. We have no control over their effect on another person. Making amends changes us, whether we're met with silence, anger, or love.

For me, taking Step Nine significantly improved my relationships with myself and with other people, but not because everyone understood or wanted to restore our former association. Rather, my action of asking other people to hear my apology was the beginning of deep healing for me.

One woman with whom I'd had a financial disagreement had been writing angry letters to me from a distance for over two years. When I wrote to her admitting that I'd had an addictive problem and finally gave her the information she needed, she simply said, "That explains a lot." It was enough. I no longer had to cringe when I went to the mailbox: that was freedom. The amends you make will change you, whatever the response of those to whom you make them.

Today, I trust myself enough to speak the simple truth.

250

To be positive: to be mistaken at the top of one's voice.
AMBROSE BIERCE

Newcomer

I have what I think is a spiritual problem. There's someone I had a major conflict with in my days of active addiction. He did something unforgivable to me, yet he blames me! He never made amends to me, and I'm sure he never will. I've heard that he still goes around bad-mouthing me to other people. I'm furious! How should I handle seeing him?

Sponsor

I'm glad that you see this as a spiritual issue that needs some resolution. It's important to find some way of dealing with the sense of being injured by an "enemy." Our days of gossip and criticism are over, and violent retaliation is not an option if we want to stay in recovery.

Even after we have done Steps Eight and Nine, there may be people whose presence in our lives makes us profoundly uncomfortable. We don't have to be friends with everyone, and not everyone wants to be friends with us.

You and this other person have shared a small piece of the past. It *is* the past, and it can stay there. When you see him, you can nod or say "hello" in acknowledgment of this mutual past, and move on; in all likelihood, he'll take the cue from you and move on, too. You might consider praying to refrain from further conflict with him, praying to heal the memories that disturb you, praying to live in the freedom of the present. You'll be surprised how much lighter your feelings will become.

Today, I take my Higher Power with me wherever I go, even into my past.

⤙ *251* ⤚

Things get better. You don't necessarily get things.
WOMAN IN RECOVERY

Newcomer

I heard a speaker bubbling about how recovery had miraculously given him his life back. He shared about how he'd finally gotten all these things he wanted: a house, a car, a relationship. I thought that wasn't the point of recovery at all—but I do have to admit that I felt envious of his charmed life.

There's a saying sometimes heard at AA meetings: "If you don't drink one day at a time, then you don't drink one day at a time." To some, this statement suggests that recovery is limited, promising nothing but a change in habits where our addictive substance or behavior is concerned. To others it suggests more: life is uncertain and unpredictable, but those of us who don't pick up are guaranteed sobriety and a new way of life. The AA Big Book goes further, promising that significant emotional peace and freedom always result from taking the Steps with care and thoroughness.

The measure of our growth in recovery is not the number and quality of possessions we've been able to accumulate, but whether we're comfortable in our own skin, at peace with ourselves and others, able to treat ourselves and our fellow human beings with respect and care.

**Today, I work to allow the promises of recovery
to materialize in my life.**

252

A good garden may have some weeds.
THOMAS FULLER

Newcomer
I've done a few things I'm not proud of, but isn't that part of being human? Other people aren't perfect, either.

Sponsor

Looking honestly and unflinchingly at our behavior, while at the same time having compassion for ourselves, is a powerful combination. Steps Four through Nine offer us a simple process for clearing up the wreckage of the past so that we can live without the burden of regret. In recovery, we have the opportunity to change for the better, not to demand perfection of ourselves or others.

My perfectionism sometimes makes me forget that I'm engaged in a process of change over time. It also lets me exaggerate both how "good" and "bad" I am. If I'm not "the greatest" in some situation, I decide, in my arrogance, that I must be "the worst." What a strange way of giving myself importance! One of the program sayings reminds me not to compare my insides with other people's outsides. I have my own unique gifts; accepting and nurturing these gifts brings me joy and allows me to contribute to the human community.

We're capable of feeling love and compassion for others who are far from perfect. In recovery, we can learn to extend that love and compassion to ourselves.

For today, I delete "perfect" from my vocabulary and practice using the word "better."

253

First things first.
PROGRAM SLOGAN

Newcomer

I have such a full life now. I don't even mind having to deal with problems that are coming up with other people—they make me feel alive. But still, I'm looking forward to not having to go to so many meetings.

Sponsor
It's good to hear how rich and diverse your experiences have become, and to see that there are people and activities that mean so much to you. We're living our lives today; that's the point of recovery. But as we become more engaged with life, we may forget the hold that our addictive craving formerly had over us, how we were driven to do whatever it asked of us. By continuing to come to meetings, we stay conscious of our powerlessness over addiction.

I need to remember what brought me here. If I become casual about my recovery, I may convince myself that I can try "just a little" of my drug of choice. If I do that, then, inevitably, my moderation will give way to active addiction. We're still powerless over this disease; that doesn't change. By putting recovery first, we can continue enjoying the rich life we have today.

What kept me sober in the early days of my recovery are the same things that keep me sober today.

⤚ 254 ⤜

I accept reality and dare not question it.
WALT WHITMAN

Newcomer
I keep hearing that acceptance is the key to being happy. I think I'm still a long way from accepting myself just the way I am.

Sponsor

In my own early recovery, I was able to *admit* pretty quickly that I was powerless over my addiction; *accepting* that fact was a different story, however. For people like us, acceptance isn't likely to come overnight. Even when we've begun to get a feel for it, we need to maintain it a day at a time.

Accepting that we are alcoholics, addicts, compulsive overeaters, debtors, gamblers—whatever our addictions or compulsions—involves more than simply becoming aware that a particular craving has been in charge of our lives. It means unreservedly accepting that we have a disease for which there is treatment and reprieve, but no cure. Our lives themselves, and our potential for serenity and freedom, depend on this acceptance.

Acceptance means that when I come home from work feeling tired and thinking I'd like to skip my usual meeting and watch TV instead, I eat my supper and head for the meeting. It means I don't take time off from recovery for good behavior. It means keeping recovery at the top of my list of priorities, continuing to make daily use of the tools and suggestions that have brought relief and serenity in the past.

Today, I accept my addiction as a basic reality.

I can find no serenity until I accept that person, place, thing, or situation as being exactly the way it is supposed to be at this moment.

ALCOHOLICS ANONYMOUS (THE AA BIG BOOK)

Newcomer

Nothing much seems to have changed for me lately. I still have the same problems and issues I had months ago.

Sponsor

The Serenity Prayer asks me "to accept the things I cannot change." I used to think that meant things were never going to change—and that I'd better accept it! Now I realize not only that everything is capable of being changed, but that change is a fact of reality and I can't stop it. What the phrase "to accept the things I cannot change" means to me today is that there are many things that only my Higher Power can change. That doesn't mean things *won't* change, only that I can't force them to. I have the courage to do my part; I have faith that change takes place in my Higher Power's time.

I can't be sure I'm going to be offered a particular job; but I can shower, dress appropriately, show up for the interview on time, and represent my capabilities with honesty and dignity. If I'm persistent in these efforts, the right job will come in time. Or perhaps I'd like my weight to change. I can't control the numbers on my scale, but if I exercise and eat moderately, over time a moderate body will show up.

Our Higher Power's timetable often differs from our own; accepting that is a source of serenity.

Today, I let my Higher Power work in my life.
I have the courage to have faith.

I wonder if this new reality is going to destroy me.
BARBARA GUEST

Newcomer

I got the promotion I've been praying for. Now I'm afraid I'm not up to doing the job well enough. What if I'm a failure at it?

Sponsor

First of all, congratulations! But remember, you'll never fully experience how positive this moment is if you move right into the next available negative emotion.

Like you, I'm used to maintaining my daily quotient of doubt and fear. Success, however I've defined that word for myself, throws me off balance. I can belittle the accomplishment itself, brush it off, pretend it doesn't mean much. Or I can belittle myself: "I was just lucky," or "They must have made a mistake." I can even put my recovery at risk, finding substitute addictions in an effort to numb my discomfort at having a success.

Successes, like disappointments, are opportunities for surrender. I've watched you work hard for this success; you deserve it. You deserve, too, to take it in fully, to share about it, to celebrate it. It's time to take a few deep breaths and really feel this moment.

Today, I celebrate a success, large or small.

All the stories have been told long ago.
Your job is retelling. Relighting.
PAM GEMS

Newcomer

I can't believe how nervous I was about speaking at a neighborhood meeting. I was thinking, "These people already know all about me; I've got nothing to share that they haven't heard before." But after the meeting, lots of people thanked me

Sponsor

Every meeting is somehow different. Perhaps some people have heard us before, but most likely they bring a new awareness each time they hear us. What we say, as long as it's honest, will touch and connect with what's on other people's minds. What others have to share at the meeting is as important as the speaker's contribution. As all of us listen, identify, and speak in our various ways, our experience, strength, and hope become the warp and woof of another meeting. If our speaking keeps any one of us from acting out our addictions today, it's a success.

Speaking is a tool for staying sober and a service to the rest of us who listen. Your presence, your willingness to show up and share, speaks volumes all on its own.

Today, I have the self-esteem and the humility
to share myself as I am.

When you forget the beginner's awe, you start decaying.
NOBUKO ALBERY

Newcomer

I'm surprised at something I've recently felt happening to me at meetings. It's a kind of serendipity: whatever the speaker's story, whatever the topic or the literature being read, it seems to apply perfectly to what's going on in my life.

Sponsor

Some of us have this experience at the first meeting we attend. We're ready to be shown a way to live without addiction, to hear the words that will help us to heal. The experience of that first meeting slakes a spiritual thirst even greater than we knew we had. Some of us are blessed to be able to listen with the same kind of active, focused attention throughout our recovery; some of us gradually grow in our ability to identify with others and to feel gratitude. Whenever we listen with the expectation of hearing something that will meet our needs, we hear it.

You're feeling a connection to other people's sharing, in part because of the willingness, empathy, and gratitude you bring to meetings. When we are open and receptive, we can almost always count on someone's saying words that seem to speak directly to us.

Today, I listen actively;
I hear words that are meant for me.

259

*Everyone is a moon and has a dark side
which he never shows to anybody.*

MARK TWAIN

Newcomer

There's something about myself that I still haven't told you. It's an old secret, and I still don't feel able to talk about it, even though I know you're open-minded.

Sponsor

I'm glad that you feel trusting enough to reveal that there's still more to know about you. Many of us feel shame about an event from the past; many of us live with a habit, a feeling, or an inadequacy that doesn't fit our image of who we think we should be. We've done a lot of work to deny or disown our pasts, presenting a "cleaned-up" self to the outside world that we think will keep us safe from rejection.

But we don't entirely succeed in erasing the part of ourselves that threatens our self-image. Shame and denial remain with us, no matter how much energy we're using to sustain the illusion of a self we believe is more acceptable than our real self. When we begin to test this belief by sharing something we've been holding inside, we become more real to ourselves and others. We experience relief and increased energy.

You may not feel entirely safe in discussing this matter with me at this time; you may prefer to talk with a spiritual adviser, therapist, or program friend whose experience is closer to your own. I respect your need to begin to take this courageous step in a way that feels as safe as possible to you.

**Today, I'm willing to bring into the light
a part of myself that I've disowned.**

Drugs were always around.
JAMES TAYLOR

Newcomer

I spent a weekend as the guest of a friend who doesn't have my particular addictive problem. I welcomed the opportunity for a change of scene. My friend was respectful of my commitment to recovery and didn't try to get me to compromise my recovery in any way. Still, I kept imagining that she thought less of me for my sobriety. I wonder if I'll ever be totally comfortable around nonaddicted people.

Sponsor

It's not always easy for me to spend time with people who can safely do something that, for me, is life-threatening—even when they're courteous enough not to do it directly in front of me. If I'm dependent on another person for companionship and a sense of security, even for a short visit, my old coping mechanisms may come into play. I may attribute my own conflicting or uncomfortable feelings to the other person, or apologize when I'm actually feeling angry.

I don't think that it's time to assume that relating to other people is not for you. This was just a beginning. I'm glad that you trusted yourself to explore a new environment and to spend time with another person. Getting to know ourselves better often goes hand in hand with getting to know others better, too. Life-enriching experiences abound for those who are open to trying new things.

Today, I reach out to other people with a sense of ease.
I don't judge my reactions or experience;
I accept them simply as what is happening today.

Chop wood, carry water.
ZEN BUDDHIST SAYING

Newcomer

In some ways, my life has totally changed. The differences are dramatic. I have different habits, different friends, a different set of values. Still, a lot has stayed the same. I have financial problems, uncertainties about the work I'm doing, and significant relationship issues.

Sponsor

Your decision to live a sober life and practice a spiritual program has been the basis of a great deal of growth already. There's no reason to assume that you won't continue to make progress as you work on the areas in which your recovery is coming along more slowly.

There's probably no one alive who has solved every problem and integrated all the aspects of his or her psyche. Like the rest of humanity, those of us who are in recovery are "works in progress." We continue, whether we've achieved enlightenment or not, to perform the same simple daily tasks. As we keep maintaining our spiritual selves, our conscious awareness of what needs changing in our lives becomes clearer. The path to more complete recovery continues to be revealed to us.

**I do the work in front of me with care today,
paying attention to the details.**

In the well there is a clear, cold spring
From which one can drink.
THE BOOK OF CHANGES

Newcomer

For a little while yesterday, I had an extraordinary experience of happiness. I felt as if I could just *be*, with no sense of pressure or hurry; everything seemed to happen just as it should. No experience that I had in my days of active addiction was better than this one. I'd like to feel this way all the time.

Sponsor

Though we can't always have peak experiences, the sense that all is well and as it should be is available to us, if we choose to go there. It's reality, not illusion. In the past, our drug of choice may have brought momentary feelings of peace or connection, but it soon robbed us of more than it gave. Now, having accumulated some time in recovery, we've begun to have a more solid sense of ourselves. We've dropped some of our burden of fear and pressure. Whether in a meeting, meditating, or simply going from one place to another in our day, we relax more easily. We trust that we'll be here again tomorrow, and that things will continue to improve. As our self-centered fear lifts, we see beauty in what is around us. We sense our connection to others and to the Spirit moving through all of us. The gift of a peak experience like the one you've described continues to nurture and transform us even after it has passed.

Today, I see myself, others, and the natural world
with the eyes of my soul.

Follow your bliss.
JOSEPH CAMPBELL

Newcomer

I want to make a significant change in a certain aspect of my life. There are people around me giving me encouragement, but something in me is still having doubts. Can I do it? Should I try? Will I succeed?

Sponsor

We didn't get sober merely to do the safe things, the things that we think others expect of us, even the things we previously expected of ourselves. In recovery, we don't have to let feelings of self-doubt or scarcity rule us. We don't have to have a guarantee of what the outcome will be, because we know that we will continue to have the capacity to find creative alternatives. We can move toward becoming the larger, freer people that, deep in our souls, we already know we are. If what we currently view as obstacles were removed, what would we really like to be doing?

I have an exercise to propose, one I've found helpful over the years: it makes use of the powerful tool of writing to explore our desires for change and accomplishment. Try making a list of five things that you'd like to accomplish in the next five years, then lists of five things you'd like to accomplish in the next year, month, and week. List not just what you think you *can* achieve, but what you'd *like* to achieve. Sign and date each of the lists of five goals. In doing this, you've made a start toward imagining change in your life.

Today, I acknowledge my dream.
I take one action that moves me closer to it.

Every morning touch the earth.
Every night praise the worms.
Listen.

CATHERINE RISINGFLAME MOIRAI

Newcomer

Sometimes I miss the "good times," before my addiction turned on me. But I also have to admit—although I'm ashamed to—that sometimes I miss the drama and the insanity, too!

Sponsor

Your honesty always gives me insights about my own feelings in recovery. It may be that the intensity of our cravings and the extreme measures we were willing to take in order to satisfy them made us into dramatic people. Or perhaps it was the other way around: our love of excitement led us to experimentation and excess. Whichever came first, most of us have scorned moderation, taken risks, and lived close to the edge. We've identified ourselves as rebels, misfits, or people whose paths were uniquely difficult. We were attached to those self-images, which went hand in hand with our attachment to our drug of choice. It made us feel special and alive. In recovery, life offers an abundance of situations that require vision and courage. We don't have to imagine or create unnecessary drama to make daily life interesting. Over time, we may even learn to love a more balanced, peaceful life.

Today, I acknowledge my addiction to intensity.
I keep a sense of balance in my day
by taking time to breathe, stop, reflect,
and tune into the rhythms of the natural world.

There is no love apart from the deeds of love; no potentiality of love but that which is manifested in loving.
JEAN-PAUL SARTRE

Newcomer

Sometimes I wonder if I can give or receive love. When I think about my past in active addiction, there was passion and drama, but not a lot of love. There hasn't been much of it in my recovery so far, either.

Sponsor

What exactly are we talking about when we talk about love? Many of us—and this was certainly true of me—have used this word primarily to describe a fantasy. We imagined that somewhere there was an ideal person who could meet all our needs and make us whole. Love meant rescue or a problem-free relationship. When we didn't find it, we bewailed our loneliness and bad luck.

Love is not something that is bestowed on us. We can create it, every day. It grows in each of us as we take actions that affirm our respect and caring for others and ourselves. Love is not limited to romantic encounters, but extends to our daily relationships with other people, including our friends and members of our communities. Love is not in scarce supply. Our acts of kindness and service and our practice of genuine tolerance renew love in the world and in our hearts.

Today, I add to the abundance of many kinds of love in my life.

New grief awakens the old.
THOMAS FULLER

Newcomer

I've just gotten the news that someone I used to know passed away. I feel a little guilty that I wasn't in closer touch, but beyond that, I'm not feeling much of anything right now. I guess I'm numb. That makes me uncomfortable; I don't like thinking of myself as heartless.

Sponsor

Numbness can temporarily follow the death of a person or a relationship, even of a job or some other part of our lives. It doesn't mean that we're hard-hearted, but rather that we're not ready to experience our feelings of loss. You've faced so much loss recently, beginning with the loss of your old relationship with your addiction.

My father died when I was in my twenties, a time when I was active in my various addictions. In spite of the outward motions of mourning, I felt shut down at his funeral and for a long time afterward. Many years later, eighteen months in recovery, I woke up one morning weeping, after a vivid dream about him. Once I had finally given in to the awareness of loss and had experienced the depths of my anger and sadness, it was as if I had finally come to life again myself. Though my relationship with him had been a conflicted one, I was free to cherish the positive things he had given me and to embrace that part of him in my life today.

The grieving process takes its own time; eventually, we come through it.

Today, I accept where I am in the process of grieving my losses. I don't deny death or refuse to grieve.

There is no such thing as pure pleasure;
some anxiety always goes with it.
OVID

Newcomer

I have a short trip to make, no more than a few days. I've
called ahead about meetings; I haven't forgotten that I can
use the tools of recovery whether I'm at home or not. But
something seems to fill me with dread whenever I have to
go anywhere. It's almost as if I expect to die whenever I
leave home overnight.

Sponsor

Some of us have emotional difficulty making any kind of
transition. Like you, I used to feel a need to leave my home
in what some call "dying condition": closets in order, legal
papers in view, no mess for anyone to deal with. A program
friend has similar difficulties with transitions, but for a different reason. His childhood was very unstable: the family
moved often, and no place was home for long. Today,
whether he's packing to leave for a vacation or to return
from one, he feels the kind of fear you've described. For
years, until he understood the source of his anxiety, he'd
somehow manage to involve his spouse in an argument just
before they left home. Anger and intensity created a kind of
emotional safety net; it let him forget his fear of the transition itself.

In time, you may have more insight into what's causing
the feelings you've described. Meanwhile, you needn't risk
numbing them with an addictive substance or behavior. In

times of transition, it's important to stick close to the program, as you have, locating meetings and making phone calls.

Today, I make transitions smoothly
by using the tools of the program.

 **268**

When one has not had a good father,
one must create one.
FRIEDRICH NIETZSCHE

Newcomer

I've just had a visit with my family. I knew it might be difficult, but I wanted to go; there was something happening that I wanted to be a part of. I knew that it wasn't going to threaten my recovery—no way was I going to pick up my drug of choice. But I was surprised to see how fast my new sense of myself fell apart when I was with them. As soon as I walked through the door, they were asking the old questions, saying what they always say. I felt like their kid again, and not a very happy kid at that.

Sponsor

It sounds as if this visit took a great deal of psychic energy. I'm glad that you were able to be watchful about your recovery. It also sounds as if you have a desire to stay in contact with family, though right now it involves a lot of effort. Over time, you'll probably notice further changes in yourself when you're in their company. Meanwhile, it sounds as if you're not being too hard on yourself, or on them. After a family visit, it's especially important to parent ourselves in nurturing, loving ways.

What we've received from our families may not support our separateness and uniqueness, may not bless us with understanding or unconditional love. Perhaps we've internalized a parent's criticism or withholding and are continuing to experience the effects in our relationships with others or ourselves. Recovery gives us opportunities to identify these patterns and let them go, as we give ourselves unconditional love.

Today, I'm a loving parent to myself.

 **269**

*i found god in myself and i loved her
i loved her fiercely.*
NTOZAKE SHANGE

Newcomer
I'm beginning to feel less afraid of people. I'm beginning to think that there's a place for me in this world.

Sponsor
Our journey through Steps Four through Nine makes clear to us that we've had a significant impact on the people we've encountered in our lives. Some of us view this information in its most negative light, focusing only on the need to acknowledge and amend any harm we've done. But there's a further way to experience this information. Our

ability to have an effect on others' lives means that we can have a positive effect as well.

For many of us in recovery, finding our own voice has been a lifelong issue. Who are we? What do we have to say? Does anything about us make a difference in the world? Active addiction, fear, low self-esteem, and paralyzing anger have kept us from actively exploring these questions.

Recovery gives us the opportunity to "stake a claim" in the world without the fear of being crushed. We're here. Something inside us has begun to feel solid and sure. We're entitled to be here, to have desires, to have a voice.

> **Today, I am willing to take up space in the world.
> I am willing to be seen and heard.**

270

It is . . . crucial to claim the good in our lives at an experiential feeling level so that we can become comfortable with it and feel drawn toward accepting and creating more good.

TIAN DAYTON

Newcomer

Someone at a meeting announced that today was her nine-month anniversary. People applauded. I thought that we only clapped for ninety days, or for one year or more.

Sponsor

In early recovery, I was uncomfortable with many group customs. I didn't understand some of them, and I felt a mixture of envy and resentment at being (as I saw it) left out. The problem was mine. I can feel upset by unpredictable behavior or small changes in routine, perhaps because I want to think that I have some control over what's happening in my life.

Customs vary from region to region, group to group, and may take some getting used to. Some groups mark many more milestones in recovery than others. Some hand out commemorative chips. Some present anniversary cakes and medallions, and invite the celebrant or a sponsor or program friend to speak. All of these customs are ways to share with each other the news that the miracle of continuing recovery is possible. Our applause celebrates all of us and our shared commitment.

How wonderful that this woman wanted to mark today as special. She deserves our congratulations and thanks. We don't reach anniversaries without each other's help.

**Today, I join in celebrating recovery,
my own and others'. We are all miracles!**

Everybody wants to be somebody;
nobody wants to grow.
JOHANN WOLFGANG VON GOETHE

Newcomer

I went to an anniversary meeting and heard people with five, ten, and even—I couldn't believe it—twenty-seven years in recovery. They all seemed so together and sure of themselves. I wish I had their secret for serenity. I wish I could put my hand up and say, "I have nine years today," instead of nine months.

Sponsor

I hope that I'll be sitting in the room when you raise your hand to announce nine years of recovery. Today, I want to congratulate you for your nine months: it's a significant length of time. Anyone who puts that kind of time together is acting "against the grain": it's more natural for an alcoholic to drink, an overeater to eat compulsively, or a gambler to gamble than for any of us to stay sober or abstinent.

I can guarantee that every one of those people celebrating an anniversary of several years was once at a place in recovery that closely resembles your own. All of us have come through fear, doubt, anger, and discouragement. All of us have grown in faith, trust, humor, and confidence. There's no "fast track"; there are no secret solutions. We don't come into this program already knowing how to live a sober life. Everything we have was given to us.

I have a future in recovery; it holds more
than I know or hope for today.

You have to give it away in order to keep it.
SAYING HEARD IN MEETINGS

Newcomer

One of the meetings I go to is relatively small. Apparently, the same people have been taking various service positions over and over; at every meeting there's a request for volunteers. I've been wondering if I ought to put my hand up and offer to do something.

Sponsor

Since this is a meeting you like going to, why hesitate to help? Offering to fill a service position not only helps guarantee that the meeting will take place, but also gives you a good reason for showing up at it.

Meetings are the core of our sober lives. At the beginning, we don't stop to wonder how the tasks get done: we depend on meetings to be there for us when and where they're supposed to. As we mature in recovery, we become aware that other people have cooperated to make the meeting what it is. Some have found the space and arranged for rental; some are responsible for the treasury and regular payment of the group's expenses. Still others set up the room, make coffee, contact speakers, chair meetings, or buy literature. Commitment to a service position is an important step in recovery. We also give something, of course, simply by showing up, sharing, and listening.

Today, I don't take meetings for granted.
I help ensure that they happen.

*We are going to know a new freedom and a new
happiness....We will comprehend the word serenity
and we will know peace.*

ALCOHOLICS ANONYMOUS (THE AA BIG BOOK)

Newcomer

I keep hearing people refer to "the Promises." What are
they, exactly?

Sponsor

"The Promises" is the name given to a paragraph that follows a discussion of Step Nine in *Alcoholics Anonymous*
(the AA Big Book). That paragraph affirms that several
freedoms will come to us without fail, "if we are painstak-
ing" about the process of making amends.

Taking Step Nine with thoroughness and care, the
Promises tell us, is the path to freedom from self-pity, self-
centeredness, fear, confusion, and a sense of separation
from our fellow human beings. One of my favorite sentences in that paragraph is "We will not regret the past nor
wish to shut the door on it." When I first read it, it seemed
unimaginable. My life was filled with regret. My addiction
had helped me to shut out memories of my past life, and
had given me still more to regret in the process. But this
promise has, in fact, come true for me. Over time in recovery, as you work the Steps, the Promises will come true in
your life.

**Today, I have the courage to take a step toward
mental and emotional freedom.**

I am the doubter and the doubt.
RALPH WALDO EMERSON

Newcomer

People at meetings sometimes sound so optimistic, as if all it takes is recovery to make life perfect. Do you really think that I'll ever feel secure financially or that I'll have great relationships?

Sponsor

Recovery promises us that our fear, both of others and of economic insecurity, will leave us. Our *fear* will leave us: that's different from guaranteeing that our incomes will go up. Our relationships and economic circumstances often do go through changes for the better in recovery, but that's not what we are promised. Instead, recovery promises mental and emotional freedom. Our serenity is independent of external circumstances. And what most enriches us spiritually is the knowledge that at last we are of use to others.

It's not that I never have a moment of doubt, fear, regret, or self-dislike. But these emotions don't have to rule my life any more. Where the past is concerned, my regrets have been replaced by compassion and understanding for the person I used to be. It's freedom.

Today, I replace fear with faith,
self-doubt with self-acceptance.

> *Man did not weave the web of life;*
> *he is merely a strand in it.*
> *Whatever he does to the web, he does to himself.*
> CHIEF SEATTLE

Newcomer

I've been looking at the Tenth Step, and I'm intimidated by the way it sounds. Isn't all this emphasis on being "wrong" a way of beating ourselves up?

Sponsor

I agree with you that gentleness with ourselves is a good policy in recovery. But we can be both gentle and honest at the same time: they're not opposites. We can't grow if we're not willing to look honestly at our actions and at their consequences.

Whether in professional or personal relationships, we ourselves don't like dealing with people who can't be depended on to do what they've promised. We don't like selfishness or dishonesty in others. Why, then, should we gloss over these traits in ourselves?

In recovery, we're in the process of developing deeper, more intimate relationships with ourselves. As in our relationships with other human beings, we need to be willing to see clearly and to acknowledge what isn't having a good effect on us or on others.

I step back and take an honest look
at how I'm living my life today.

Love has a passion for puzzles, for problem solving, is a grope in the direction of creativity.

ANATOLE BROYARD

Newcomer

I've met someone that I think I'd like to be friends with—perhaps even more than friends. I know I still have distance to go in recovery, and I don't want to act compulsively, against the suggestion of the program.

The trouble is, I'm afraid that I'll completely lose out on getting to know this person if I don't act now.

Sponsor

It sounds as if life's beginning to get a little bit exciting. This is one of those wonderful problems that we get to have when we're no longer fighting the addiction every day; it's about people.

To me, your desire not to rush headlong into anything sounds pretty sensible. It takes a long, long time to get to know another person. We're entitled to take that time. But what if our pace is a problem for the other person? One person wants to go slow; the other person wants to go fast. It stands to reason that if we're both interested in the relationship, we'll agree to the slower pace.

Whether it's friendship or love we're talking about, sensitivity to the other person is required; we have to honor his or her needs, as well as our own. At the beginning of a new relationship, if another person disrespects needs that we've made clear are important to us, then he or she isn't likely to respect them later on. Those who do respect our needs can contribute something necessary to the process of creating a healthy relationship.

> Today, I respect my own needs
> and am willing to share what they are.

 *277*

Fall down seven times, stand up eight.
JAPANESE PROVERB

Newcomer
Why is there a need for a Tenth Step, when we've already done "a searching and fearless inventory" in Step Four?

Sponsor
Accepting the need to live my life a day at a time isn't easy for me. I've always wanted to know what was going to happen for the rest of my life. But in life, things are always changing and unfolding.

The Fourth Step helped us to see our past behavior more clearly. But our lives aren't over. We need to continue to be conscious of our motives and of the impact our behavior has on ourselves and others.

We have a need for the Tenth Step because we're human and because we have addictions. People in recovery aren't infallible. Recovery has given us new options for dealing with difficult situations, but we don't always turn to them. There are times when, in pain or fear or confusion, we rely on an old habit instead of on the principles of the program. As with Step Four, Step Ten helps to keep us from using addiction to anesthetize our feelings over things we wish we'd done differently.

> Today, I scan through my past twenty-four hours.
> I give myself credit for a day of recovery.
> I don't hesitate to acknowledge any wrongs
> that I'm aware of having committed.

278

Do not look where you fell, but where you slipped.
VAI PROVERB

Newcomer

You'd think that after everything I've been through, I'd never want to repeat any of the mistakes I've made before, but I do keep repeating them. I don't pick up, but I don't always behave the way I want to.

Sponsor

At times, I revert to old ways of handling things. It's almost as if my personality sets little traps for me, and I fall into them. I find myself being selfish or dishonest in spite of myself. Or I fall into gossip or criticism, self-importance or self-hatred. The good news is that when I act in these ways in recovery, I'm uncomfortable; I know that something isn't quite right. I remember the painful lessons of the past.

As children, we depended on others for our survival, and we made whatever accommodations we had to in order to be taken care of. Some of the habits we developed came with us into adulthood, even though they no longer had a useful function in our lives. Similarly, in active addiction, we depended on certain behaviors to care for ourselves as best we could. These behaviors aren't necessary for survival or self-nurturing any longer; and, in fact, they threaten our recovery. Step Ten is a tool for staying away from addictive drugs and behavior, no matter what happens to us in recovery—including success.

Today, I thrive on actions that further my self-esteem.
If I've made a mistake, I say so without punishing myself.

~ 279 ~

Shame kills faster than disease.
BUCHI EMECHETA

Newcomer
I've really screwed something up badly. It's not the first time, either; I've done this sort of thing before. I should know better by now. I can't believe how stupid I've been.

Sponsor
When I'm working Step Ten, I need to practice exercising my *judgment*, instead of merely being *judgmental*. I listen to the dialogues in my head and hear how critical I'm capable of being. I look at my old habit of using words against myself. My lack of charity and compassion toward myself won't improve the situation I'm feeling upset about, nor will it further my ability to be accepting of my fellow

human beings. It will keep me in a holding pattern of negativity and criticism. It won't help to repair any error or damage that has taken place; instead, it may block me from thinking of and taking an appropriate action.

An alternative to self-criticism is simply standing back and noticing behavior, in the same way that we notice our thoughts with detachment during meditation: "Oh—I've done *that*," or "I see that I'm having *that* feeling again." In the process of changing old patterns, paying attention is more productive than rushing to condemn ourselves.

Today, I choose words with conscious care.
I expand my vocabulary, replacing the language of attack and insult with words of understanding.

 *280*

Similarity is not the same thing as identity.
IBO PROVERB

Newcomer

Today, I actually heard my story! I don't mean just that I identified with the speaker's feelings, but that many of the exact same things that happened in his life have happened in mine: the place we grew up, the work his parents did, the particular way we first learned to use addiction as escape. He talked about some key experiences that both of us have had. I listened as if I were in a trance. It was a very positive experience for me.

Sponsor

Hearing specific details that match those in our own stories is not a requirement for recovery, but it is a gift whenever it happens. About halfway through my first year, I had an experience much like the one you're describing. The way it worked for me was to dissolve the last vestiges of my denial. It was like looking into a mirror and seeing my addiction with perfect clarity.

Differences in gender, age, class, religion, sexual preference, work, language, style—all of these dissolve as I listen to where addiction brought others and how they work their program today. Whatever the specifics, I can identify emotionally and spiritually. But I have also made a special-interest meeting one of my home groups—a meeting whose members share a common interest and a common addiction. Close friends with whom I feel free to share my life in detail abound there; they are a rich part of my life in recovery.

Today, I am open to meaningful connections with others whose lives are centered in recovery, as mine is.

All passions exaggerate:
it is because they exaggerate that they are passions.
SEBASTIEN-ROCHE NICOLAS DE CHAMFORT

Newcomer

Things are terrible; I feel as if I'm in my first day of recovery all over again. Thank God for this program: the one thing I'm completely sure about is that I don't want to go back to using my drug of choice.

Sponsor

It's clear that whatever else happens today, your commitment to recovery is solid. Perhaps you need a day to fall apart, to feel the chaotic swirl of your feelings, to see that much you've thought of as permanent and well functioning is separated only by the thinnest of lines from sheer nothingness. It might be a great relief.

In recovery, many of us arrive at a place where we just want to run or quit—not quit recovery itself, but other aspects of our lives. We may feel as if we've been holding things together, showing up and taking on a lot of responsibility, for some time now. Perhaps we think that if we let go, our part in the world will come to an end.

Many things have a tendency to hold together, whether we attend to them or not. Venting our feelings can give us energy for a fresh start.

Today, I drop my shoulders, I loosen my grip,
I vent my feelings.

> *One cannot but be perturbed when*
> *fire breaks out in a neighbor's house.*
> INDIRA GANDHI

Newcomer

There's someone I've gotten to know recently who told me she'd tried the program for a few months last year but didn't like it. One day, she announced that she'd had a few beers the night before. She said it in a tone meant to suggest that it wasn't a problem for her. Now it's clear that her use of alcohol has escalated again; she refers to it in some fashion whenever I see her.

I understand now that I can't force recovery on anyone. But when she mentioned "cleaning up," I said to her, as lightly as I could, "I go to lots of meetings, so if you ever feel like trying one again and want some company, let me know." I hope I did the right thing.

Sponsor

You did exactly what I'd have done. Much as you may have wanted to say more, you made your offer kindly and left it at that. You haven't brought up the issue repeatedly. You haven't let her relationship with alcohol affect your social or emotional life. You haven't "covered" for her, lent her money, or focused on her problems instead of on your work and school responsibilities. You haven't let your concern for her become an obsession.

You can be certain that she heard you. If she ever becomes willing to come to a meeting, she knows that you're there.

Today, I admit my powerlessness over
other people's addictions.

You were born God's original.
Try not to become someone's copy.
MARIAN WRIGHT EDELMAN

Newcomer

I feel capable and competent today. It's such a satisfying feeling. I got a compliment from someone at work, and for a change, instead of reacting with embarrassment, I knew I agreed. I simply said, "Thank you."

Sponsor

It's wonderful to hear you acknowledging yourself and naming your gifts, learning not to minimize yourself. The real you has been here all along, and so have your talents; what's different in recovery is that there are fewer obstacles in the way of your seeing and accepting yourself.

We each came into the world with our own unique combination of qualities. There is no one else anywhere who is exactly like us. We've survived addiction. Our suffering has made us more compassionate, more capable of valuing our lives.

Our journey in recovery is one of getting to know and value ourselves, of accepting all of us, the good and the bad, of discovering what we were meant to do and who we were meant to be in this lifetime. Some of us go off in different directions from those we took initially; others continue on a previous path, this time with joy and gratitude.

Today, recovery is giving me the chance to be me.

Those who do not know how to weep with their whole heart don't know how to laugh either.

GOLDA MEIR

Newcomer

I've gotten closer to myself lately. I'm not as afraid to accept the truth of where I've been, and what I've lost. It hurts, though. As I clear up, I can see the wreckage of the past far more vividly than I did even as recently as a few months ago, but I still have a lot of grieving to do.

Sponsor

As I become more whole, I grieve for the lost soul I now see myself to have been. I grieve for the person who was so damaged. I've changed so much; I'm still connected to my previous self, but I'm no longer where I was. In a sense, that person has had to die in order for me to be here today, alive and grateful. My past experience is part of what brought me here, and I thank the person I used to be for letting me survive.

For those who are willing, recovery makes it possible to have an intimate, loving relationship with ourselves. Like intimacy with others, intimacy with ourselves opens us to a wide array of feelings. Sober, we risk a deeper experience of feelings we previously tried to avoid.

**Today, as I become whole,
I grieve for the person I used to be.**

It is better to protest than to accept injustice.
ROSA PARKS

Newcomer

I've started to realize that I'm not being paid adequately for my work. I don't know if it's possible to change that in my current position, but it's making me see that I've undervalued my abilities for a long time now, and that has led others to undervalue me as well. In the past, because of my low self-esteem, I always told myself that I was lucky to have any job and I couldn't afford to rock the boat. Now I'm beginning to see things differently.

Sponsor

We deserve to be appropriately compensated for the work we do. There are some fields and positions in which the degree of financial compensation is limited, but the other rewards are great; we may choose work that pays less than we'd like but that allows us an opportunity to do something we love. Each of us must determine our own priorities. We need to be honest with ourselves about whether we're being appreciated or simply exploited; whether we're accepting the reality that there's a current market value for what we do or are too timid to ask for what our work is worth. Change is always possible.

Today, I take an honest look at my relationship to work.
If I'm dissatisfied with the work itself or the way I'm being
compensated, I take a step in the direction of change.

One must fight for a life of action, not reaction.
RITA MAE BROWN

Newcomer

I spoke up at work about a situation that I'm starting to find unacceptable. A person in a position superior to mine speaks to me in a way that's disrespectful. I'm good at the work I do, but this person is always tearing me down. I told her that I wanted her to treat me differently, and she seemed surprised and then defensive. When I was talking to her, I felt calm, centered, and strong. When I got home, I was shaking. I feel as if I'm going to be punished.

Sponsor

Each time we represent ourselves as people whose needs deserve to be taken seriously, we're strengthened. In time, it becomes second nature. We're less likely to let unacceptable situations build up over a long period of time; we recognize and address them promptly.

At first, we may have experiences like the one you describe: we're able to assert ourselves, but then suffer a kind of emotional "backlash." Maybe we've always taken what others dished out and have accumulated reserves of anger, or maybe we unleashed rage beyond anything the current situation merited. In either case, we reacted inappropriately, inviting others to retaliate. As our self-esteem is strengthened by recovery, we're no longer able to participate silently in unacceptable situations. I want to congratulate you for having the dignity and the courage to speak your truth, and to do it in a calm, undramatic way. Eventu-

ally, you'll lose the need to inflict punishment on yourself
for speaking up.

**Today, I'm neither a victim nor an aggressor.
I'm proactive in my life.**

 ## 287

*The birds' song gets on my nerves.
I feel like trampling every worm.*
PAUL KLEE

Newcomer

I try to refrain from violence, even the violence of making
certain kinds of comments to other people. But it's tough.
My Higher Power seems to be putting a succession of
people in my path who go out of their way to be rude or
crude, to charge me extra, or to humiliate me in some way
or other. How can I love everybody?

Sponsor

It's fascinating to me to watch how the outer world always
seems to mirror my own mood. For me, it's the best way to
explain the fact that there are times when everyone I meet
in the course of my day seems pleasant, kind, and generous,
and other times when I find enemies everywhere.

Al-Anon's "Three C's" remind us that there are circumstances and behaviors that we didn't cause, can't control,
and can't cure. We're powerless over an active alcoholic's
rage, for example. We can't make traffic go at the speed we
think best or force others to conduct themselves as we'd
like.

But other things being equal, our state of mind has some power to affect people around us. Our facial expression, body language, tone, and words make our feelings apparent. Our moods are contagious. If we meet the world with anger, resentment, fear, or negativity, the world will usually respond in kind. A smile, a buoyant heart, and an optimistic outlook will usually evoke positive responses. And whatever is out there, we have a choice about where to direct our attention, whether to focus on what's sunny or dark in our environment.

Today, I'm mindful of how my words and attitudes affect others.

 *288*

Nobody can give you wiser advice than yourself.
CICERO

Newcomer
Sometimes, when I check something out with you or with another person whose experience I trust, the answer I get isn't all that different from what I've already thought of on my own. I wonder if by asking for an opinion, I've simply created another kind of dependency.

Sponsor
The willingness to ask for help is what got us here in the first place—that willingness is a gift. Once we reached out, the healing process inside us began. We were open to the nourishment that our spirits needed for repair and growth; we were humble enough to accept it.

As we continue in recovery, small hints, rather than lengthy sermons, are sufficient to guide us. We've begun to trust our own gut feelings and to honor our intuitive wisdom. We may still appreciate the validation of those we respect. We may want help reasoning things out when we're confused or undecided about a course of action. There's nothing childish or dependent about that; staying open to learning from others is part of maturing and becoming more secure within ourselves.

Today, I listen for inner guidance. I trust my own wisdom.

289

Trust in God: She will provide.
EMMELINE PANKHURST

Newcomer
I brought a friend to a meeting recently. I was nervous all through it, wondering if the speaker was saying things in a way that made sense to her, judging what other people shared, and wanting them to like my friend and reach out to her. I felt as if I were the host at a big party, worrying about whether everyone was having a good time or not.

Sponsor
The experience you've described has valuable information to offer. It says, among other things, how much you appreciate recovery and want to share your experience of it. It says, too, that you care about your friends.

Most of us have been through similar experiences in recovery and can identify with your discomfort. It's hard to relax if we think we're running the show. We're not really hosts at a party, though, and we're not responsible for how it goes. We have to trust that people we bring to a meeting will hear and respond to whatever they're ready to take in, no more and no less. We can neither predict nor control what that will be, any more than we can predict or control what others at the meeting will share or hear. Other people's experience of recovery is not our responsibility; in fact, it's none of our business. When we surrender the outcome to a Higher Power, each meeting is exactly what it's supposed to be.

Today, I let go of my worries about how a meeting is proceeding; I allow myself to focus on my own recovery.

290

Regret is an appalling waste of energy,
you can't build on it: it's only good for wallowing in.
KATHERINE MANSFIELD

Newcomer
Someone I hoped would be an important part of my life for years to come has left. I'm devastated. I don't know how much of what happened is my fault; I keep thinking, "If only I hadn't said what I said ..."

Sponsor
Human lives are filled with all kinds of separation. Friends, mates, family members—the people in our lives are only lent to us. If they accompany us for some part of our journey, we're blessed. We don't get to control or keep them.

Sentences beginning "if only" can go nowhere but

straight to regret. They support our false belief that we can control what happens in other people's lives. "I should have," "I could have," and "I would have" are all variations on the same theme. They postpone acceptance and necessary grieving.

At times it's we ourselves who do the leaving. We can count it a success, not a failure, when we've had the courage to acknowledge the truth of an ending.

Today, though I may go through some pain as I learn acceptance, I rejoice in the strength and clarity it gives me.

291

It is a spiritual axiom that every time we are disturbed, no matter what the cause, there is something wrong with us.
TWELVE STEPS AND TWELVE TRADITIONS

Newcomer
In reading about the Tenth Step, I get confused when I see the words "we were wrong." That word "wrong" again! I'm working to honor my feelings and build my self-esteem. I've learned in this program that I'm not to blame for everything.

Sponsor
The spot-check inventory isn't intended as a stick to beat ourselves with, any more than Step Four was. It's a practical way to help us evaluate what's going on in the course of our day, to recognize what we ourselves can do to reestablish emotional balance. It reminds us that we have some control over our responses. For example, suppose the check

I've been waiting for doesn't come in today's mail. I may have some anger to discharge or a momentary fear that I won't be able to send out my rent check on time. I may need to take a few minutes to vent my feelings. The feelings pass, and I go on to other things. In the old days of active addiction, I blamed everyone I could think of, from the postal service to the landlord, for the way I was feeling. I usually felt justified in picking up my drug of choice—that was one way that my rage at being frustrated could be quieted.

Step Ten reminds us not to get caught in the cycle of blaming others for the way we feel.

Today, I abstain from blaming. If I'm upset, I practice the "three A's": awareness, acceptance, and action.

 *292*

We use great plainness of speech.
SAINT PAUL TO THE CORINTHIANS

Newcomer

I made a call to someone I'd previously said yes to when I'd really wanted to say no. Without making a big deal out of it, overapologizing and making up elaborate excuses, I just told the truth. I said, "I'm sorry to have to change plans, but after giving it some more thought, I realized that I need time to finish a project I've been putting off. Let's get together another time." My friend was disappointed, but not devastated. She wished me luck with the project.

I felt such relief after this phone call. Instead of being preoccupied by nagging feelings of obligation and wrongdoing, I have energy to do what I need to do and to enjoy myself with a clear conscience.

Sponsor

This is good Tenth Step work you've been doing. It sounds to me as if you've begun developing greater self-trust and an intuitive sense of how to handle situations with people.

Today, I don't let difficulties build up. I act promptly to keep my relationships with others clear and in balance.

 **293**

Though my mouth be dumb, my heart shall thank you.
NICHOLAS ROWE

Newcomer

I've been thinking about some of the things I said to you when I was newer in recovery. I wonder how you put up with me. I was so self-absorbed, and I took for granted that you'd be there for me each day.

Sponsor

Your questions help me to go deeper in my own reading and thinking about the Steps; to stay honest, I've had to deal with some issues of my own that I'd been procrastinating about in recovery. Listening to your experiences reminds me of my own. You help me to stay mindful of my past of active addiction—to remember what got me here, and to feel the importance and the joy of my own recovery.

Sponsoring you has given me an opportunity to show up for another person, to be there consistently, yet honor my need for boundaries—there's such a thing as being too helpful, and that's something I've been getting practice dealing with. I have the same addiction you do, and my issues aren't very different from yours.

Your trust is a gift. Thank you.

Today, I feel gratitude for my ability to give and to receive trust in a relationship with another recovering person.

Any musician who says he is playing better on tea, the needle, or when he is juiced is a plain straight liar.
CHARLIE PARKER

Newcomer

In spite of everything I've been learning about addiction since coming into recovery, I still have an image of artists, musicians, and other creative people as exceptions, as people outside the norm. Some part of me wonders if the ones who drink or use drugs would still be able to do what they do sober.

Sponsor

If you take a good look around at a meeting, you'll find a great many creative people. Listening to them tell their stories has convinced me that addiction got in the way more than it helped. My own myth of the creative vision inspired by drugs has fallen apart as I've heard writers, musicians, and painters tell how, when they were active in their addictions, they lacked the will and attention span to write, make music, or paint. Those who've always done their creative work while using an addictive substance need time in recovery before they are able to create with ease and pleasure again.

We crave the experience of heightened perception and spiritual release that addictive substances and behaviors once provided. We sometimes want to crack open our shells, to forget what others think, to be our spontaneous, unedited selves. We need to explore new ways to let the hidden parts of ourselves out into the light, to allow ourselves the freedom to dance with our demons and angels.

> **Today, I shed some of my inhibition and
> allow more of my real self to come out.**

295

*There are wonderful moments, those rare moments
when there is silence, a tangible silence out there,
a silence deeper than silence.*

DEREK JACOBI

Newcomer
Sometimes I get uncomfortable when there's a long period of quiet in a meeting. It always seems strange to me when people aren't putting up their hands. There's so little time. It amazes me that not everyone wants to speak.

Sponsor
Some of us feel bored or anxious when there is silence. Many people live with the continuous sound of radio or TV in their homes, cars, and even workplaces. I moved from the nonstop noise of the city to a quiet rural village, only to

find that my next-door neighbor left her TV on all night long.

Why is silence so unacceptable? Some of us are filled with excessive concern about others in the room: "They should speak; it would be good for them." Or "Have I done something to alienate them, to keep them from wanting to speak?" For some of us, silence means having to listen to the chaos of our own thoughts and feelings. If we're unwilling to sit with ourselves in stillness, letting thoughts and feelings pass through us, then we also fail to hear what lies beneath them, what some call the voice of our souls. Whether we're alone or with others, when we sit in stillness, we may begin to hear Eternity.

Today, I allow myself some time to sit in stillness.

296

The dogs bark, but the caravan moves on.
ARABIC PROVERB

Newcomer

I read an article that attacked Twelve Step programs. It was the same criticism I once heard expressed crudely by someone I knew who'd tried the program for a short time: "First they suck you in; then they drop the God stuff on you." The article asserted that people in Twelve Step programs don't think for themselves.

Sponsor

Perhaps it's an indication of our widespread success that some people feel compelled to critique us! By now, you know that every suggestion we're offered here is optional. We have no rules, no creed. Most people who want what we have find their own way here.

Like you, I've felt upset when I've seen occasional misrepresentations in the media of how we accomplish what we do here. I've noticed that most of the self-designated experts who are opposed to us aren't people in recovery. I like to think of their "exposés" as something like travel writing—you and I, who live in recovery, can smile at their mistakes. More people need recovery than find it. If someone is persuaded to stay away from us after reading just one magazine article, my hunch is that he or she is still looking for ways to rationalize active addiction.

Recovery is not an abstraction; it makes life today possible. I have immense gratitude that this program was founded and has lasted to the present day. Luckily, it isn't a debating society. We don't have to concern ourselves with petty attacks on the program, from without or within.

**Today, I focus on my experience of recovery,
not others' opinions of it.**

297

Live and let live.
PROGRAM SLOGAN

Newcomer

I saw some people in a public place recently who seemed "high." I reminded myself that what they were doing was none of my business. I didn't have to condemn them, and I didn't have to indulge in my own drug of choice in reaction to them. I can't say that I was completely tolerant, though; my first reaction was judgmental.

Sponsor

I still don't enjoy being around people who are active in their addictions; I avoid it, if possible. But sometimes it happens. Like you, I don't immediately think, "They're suffering from a disease"; instead, impatience and intolerance surface in me. At the end of certain meetings I go to, the speaker asks for a moment of silence "for all those who are still sick and suffering, both in and out of these rooms." This moment of focused attention reminds me that I can open to greater acceptance of others—and of myself.

"Live" is just as important a part of the slogan as "let live." When I'm not preoccupied with others, judging them, becoming obsessed with what I believe to be their difficulties, and trying to "fix" them, then I can embrace my own life with energy and enthusiasm. That's living!

Today, I mind my business;
I stay centered on the pursuits of my own soul.

298

In spite of everything,
I still believe that people are really good at heart.
ANNE FRANK

Newcomer

I get upset and discouraged about what's in the news. So much of it is about violence and tragedy, lying and competition. What's going on out there is so different from what I see at meetings. I wish that everyone had what we have.

Sponsor

Sometimes it does seem as if the world "out there" is on a binge of some kind. And addictions themselves, of all kinds, are still widespread and causing considerable damage. But what about the healing, the taking of responsibility, the turning around of lives? News of recovery, changes in consciousness, spiritual growth, and service is not what sells papers, but it is a real and vital part of what's happening in the world. Twelve Step recovery has been around for less than a century, but its healing principles have entered the awareness and lives of millions of people around the world.

When we think about what our individual lives were like before recovery and what fundamental changes we've been able to make in a short time, it gives us hope and a sense of what's possible.

Today, I'm blessed with hope. I let change begin with me.

⇒ *299* ⇒

My tidiness, and my untidiness, are full of regret and remorse and complex feelings.
NATALIA GINZBURG

Newcomer

Even though I've done steps Four through Nine, my defects haven't all disappeared. Now that I've started doing Step Ten, just taking a few minutes once a day for a "spotcheck," what comes up isn't new. For the most part, it's stuff that

I've had problems with for a long time. Am I ever going to change?

Sponsor

If you think about how much you've changed already, you'll get some idea of what an unstoppable process recovery is for those who stay committed to it.

We may unconsciously cling to some of our defects because of positive things they do for us. Perhaps they keep us in familiar situations, protecting us from having to try new approaches. Perhaps they serve to ward other people off, so that we don't have to face them. Perhaps we're hoping that we won't have to do anything ourselves to address our limiting characteristics—that somehow, in time, they'll just go away.

We can think of our so-called defects as challenges. Our discomfort is a source of information: it reveals that there are things our Higher Power wants us to work through over time.

**Today, I let my daily inventory inform me
of what I want to change. I make small changes today.**

300

Hell has three gates: lust, anger, and greed.
BHAGAVAD GITA

Newcomer

I've really gotten into diet and exercise in a big way, and I'm spending a lot of time working out and preparing health food. I've started going to a weekly spiritual service, too, and getting involved with some community work. I feel as if I'm racing ahead in my recovery.

Sponsor

Each of these things sounds worthwhile, but the number of them and the demand you're making of yourself to "race ahead" make me wonder whether you can sustain so many activities at the same level without burning out.

Take the areas of food and exercise, for example. Transforming the way we eat, becoming conscious consumers, is one of the most radical changes we can make. It involves a surrender, a sense that our Higher Power is in charge of the process of change, rather than a clenched effort to control. When we start thinking in terms of rapid weight change, rather than of a commitment to conscious eating and healthful, moderate meals, then we risk moving into obsession. Gentleness and moderation at the beginning of an exercise program or other demanding new endeavor is a more reliable route to consistent, long-term commitment than an overly demanding schedule we'll soon tire of.

In recovery, while we don't postpone dealing with obstacles to sober living, we don't have to rush to change every detail of our lives at once. We can take time to savor and enjoy new directions.

Today, I don't treat my recovery as some kind of race;
I remember "Easy does it"—but do it.

Nothing is more difficult than competing with a myth.
FRANÇOISE GIROUD

Newcomer

I've been spending time with someone I have a lot in common with. We've spent the last several weekends doing things together; I assumed that I could count on company for a weekend outing that's coming up. Now it turns out that my friend isn't willing to go. I'm really upset; I guess I'm overreacting, but my first thought was that this isn't much of a relationship if I'm going to end up by myself on a weekend.

Sponsor

It sounds as if you have a solid basis for a continuing connection with this person, and that you've reached one of those bumps in the road that occur in all relationships between real human beings. Differences are a part of life; conflicting wishes often have to be negotiated.

Many of us approach both friendship and romance with mythical notions of perfection. When the myth is challenged, we may be tempted to leave and find a "better" partnership, without attempting to resolve the problem. Anger, loneliness, and pain occur in good relationships, relationships that are worth keeping and working on. Sometimes what we've believed to be a relationship problem is instead a problem within ourselves. Exploring these questions usually involves experiencing some discomfort. It's part of any growth process.

Today, I don't expect one person to meet all of my needs, all of the time. I accept that relationships worth keeping have their imperfections and limitations.

> *Never bend your head. Always hold it high.*
> *Look the world straight in the face.*
> HELEN KELLER

Newcomer

Sometimes I still feel shame about having this addiction. It comes up when I'm with nonprogram friends and have to go to a meeting. It comes up when a relative says, "You mean you're *still* going to those meetings?"

Sponsor

The stigma attached to having an addiction has lessened because of widespread awareness of Twelve Step recovery programs and an understanding of heredity and the "disease concept" of addiction. While there may still be some who believe that addiction is a moral deficiency that willpower can eliminate, most of us who are in programs of recovery have let go of this incorrect belief.

Though guilt and shame are often experienced together, they are different. We feel guilty about an incident or behavior; the process of acknowledgment and amends addresses guilt for things we wish we hadn't done. Shame is an attitude we have toward some aspect of ourselves. Few of us are entirely without it. Shaming others is one way that people try to cope with their own shame.

I'm glad that you can talk about this lingering problem. Bringing shame out of darkness, sharing about it in appropriate ways with those we trust, is the path toward healing and freeing ourselves from it.

Today, I face my old feelings of shame.
I'm worthy of love and acceptance just as I am.

I used to trouble about what life was for.
Now being alive seems sufficient reason.
JOANNA FIELD

Newcomer

I keep hearing, "This is a family disease," but I'm not sure I accept the idea that I've inherited it. I know people in this program whose parents and other close relatives don't have it.

Sponsor

Addiction doesn't have to affect every member of every generation of a family the same way to support the idea that it has a powerful effect on the family. Whether or not we believe that biology is where addiction starts, we can see that addictive behavior and coaddictive reactions are often learned in families. Whether a grandparent, parent, sibling, aunt, or cousin is dependent on a substance or compulsive behavior, his or her addiction has an impact on everyone else in the family system. The family is like a spiderweb: if we tug on any one part of it, the entire web vibrates.

We don't have to ask *why* we have this disease. Instead, we can concentrate on developing the habits of recovery. We accept that we must replace our old addictive habits with healthful ones.

Today, I focus on living in the present. Learning how
to have a rich recovery is more important
than wondering why I need this program.

I'm grateful for every drop I drank.
WOMAN IN RECOVERY

Newcomer

I've heard some people in this program say that they think it may be too late for them, that they wish they'd come here years earlier. I've heard other people say that they got here at such an early age that they sometimes wonder if they quit using too soon. I find myself identifying with both groups at different times.

Sponsor

Anxieties about age, laments that we're too old or too young for recovery, are yet another variation on the theme of denial. It took me as long as it took me to get here; I don't think I could have gotten sober one day sooner. Now that I'm here, I intend to stay, to live whatever seasons and whatever days my life consists of, appreciating the richness of life in recovery.

Some days I feel raw and inexperienced. Other days I feel mature and wise. I learn from the experience of those who are older or younger, from the sponsor who got here before me and the sponsee who got here after me.

Whatever age we've reached, we can be of use. We're learning to trust that what time holds for us is good; when we're struggling with some problem, we're not going to leave before the miracle.

**Today, my recovery supports me,
wherever I am on the continuum of my life.**

After distress, solace.
SWAHILI PROVERB

Newcomer

Something I've been deeply dreading for a long time has finally happened. I'm surprised that I'm feeling relief instead of misery. I wish I'd known sooner that I was going to feel this way.

Sponsor

I'm often startled to discover that my Higher Power doesn't have the same deadlines for my happiness that I myself have imagined. When my mother died after a long illness, many things ended, including the chance that she might still, after so many years, nurture me in the ways that I'd wished for. What I'd tried so hard to hold at bay had come. I was powerless, confronted with mortality. As I went through the grieving process, an energy I couldn't have previously imagined began to bubble up in me. I understood, at last, that I didn't have forever to live my own life. I plunged into a period of creativity. I moved to a place that was more congenial than where I'd been living. I went back into therapy to address some unresolved conflicts. I let go of work and relationships that were unsatisfying and made more time for pleasure. My fear was over; I'd gone through the worst and survived. I had a life to live and to celebrate.

What we envision as the end of everything can turn out to be the beginning of a more expansive period in our lives, an opening of perspectives we would have had no access to without going through loss, suffering, or failure.

**Today, changes I've feared do not destroy me;
they open doors to the unexpected.**

When you pray you are opening a window within yourself.
GURUDEV SHREE CHITRABHANU

Newcomer
I don't know if I can pray the way I'm supposed to.

Sponsor
There's no wrong way to pray, no place or time, no posture or language, that's inappropriate. We can pray anywhere. Some of us pray on our knees; some pray while sitting, standing, walking, or performing sacred movements. Some of us use prayers from the religion we claim as ours, some use prayers found in program literature, and some of us write our own. Many prayers are said spontaneously. Some prayers may even be unconscious or involuntary. All are holy.

Prayer can be a medium for expressing gratitude, joy, and acceptance of what is; it can be a cry for help or understanding; it can be a reaching out for relationship, an attempt to find our way to the Spirit, or a means of maintaining contact with our inner guidance. I've heard someone in recovery say that prayer may come before we find out who or what our Higher Power is. Most of us, once we have the habit of prayer, find it a necessity.

Today, I nourish myself with prayer.

After my morning's talk with God I go into my
laboratory and begin to carry out His wishes for the day.
GEORGE WASHINGTON CARVER

Newcomer

How do I know if I'm doing my Higher Power's will? Does my Higher Power really care what I do for a living, whom I associate with, what I eat for dinner? Or is praying for knowledge of my Higher Power's will for me just about morality?

Sponsor

Morality isn't the whole story, but it's part of it. Most of us have a good idea of what ethical behavior is. There are many guides for living, both religious and secular, but few of us need to rely on books for the answers. We know what's right or wrong by consulting our conscience.

It does matter what we do. You mention making choices about food and friends and work. These aren't trivial things; they're the stuff of our lives. Any choice can bring us closer to the truth or further from it, can lead us toward addiction or recovery. Prayer and meditation illuminate these choices. They help us to know ourselves.

My relationship with the Spirit comes from looking within. For me, Step Eleven is a reminder that I have the responsibility to bring my life into alignment with the deepest desires of my soul. Love, joy, gratitude—I've come to believe that these are necessities. My Higher Power's will for me includes nourishment for my spirit.

God's will for me is written in my inmost being.
Today, I read it with ease and joy.

Come what may, I have been blessed.
GEORGE GORDON, LORD BYRON

Newcomer

People are always saying, "There are no coincidences." I
don't know what that really means or what to think about
it. If some Higher Power cares about me, then what about
the years when I was active in my addiction? Where was
my Higher Power then?

Sponsor

Miracles don't all happen instantaneously. The desire to
heal was in me long before I was able to enter recovery, but
I didn't understand or acknowledge it. I didn't even know
what was wrong with me. The process of identifying my
central problem as one of addiction—and of beginning to
hear that there was help for me—didn't happen overnight.

Recovery is such an immense gift in our lives that it's
hard to understand how it happened. Many of us were led
to it with the help of a particular person who seemed to
appear at the critical moment. For some, a seemingly
chance phone call or encounter influenced our decision to
come to a meeting. We may feel as if we were brought here
at exactly the right time. And it's true—we were!

**I thank my Higher Power for this day,
and for every day leading to this day.**

*You gain strength, courage and confidence by every
experience in which you really stop to look fear in the face.*
ELEANOR ROOSEVELT

Newcomer

Everybody in recovery seems to have his or her own prescription for enlightenment: a self-help book or therapist or
meditation group, a guru or religious institution. People are
always telling me what works for them. I've tried so many
things that I'm starting to feel like a New Age cliché. Why
can't I stick with something?

Sponsor

I can hear your hunger for spiritual connection. Once
we've gone through the early stages of recovery, once survival is no longer the primary issue, many of us discover our
capacity and desire for a spiritual path.

This is a spiritual program; that's why it works. It saves
lives. Like you, I'm committed to working the program,
coming to meetings, sharing, giving service, "practicing
these principles" in everything I do. Without this program
as my foundation, I wouldn't have much of a life today.
But, for me, the program is a gateway to spiritual practice,
not the practice itself.

Your exploration of various spiritual paths suggests that
you're searching for a spiritual center. But why the constant
darting from place to place that you've described? Perhaps
you haven't found your "spiritual home" yet. Or perhaps
sitting still and experiencing feelings as they arise may be

frightening. Though facing these feelings may seem overwhelming, they won't destroy you.

All true spiritual paths lead within.

Today, I have the willingness to be still and go within.

310

Be not ashamed to say what you are not ashamed to think.
MICHEL DE MONTAIGNE

Newcomer
I went to an Eleventh Step meeting last night. After the reading, someone shared that a fictional character from a movie had become her Higher Power! Doesn't that prove what nonsense this Higher Power stuff is?

Sponsor
I'm not at meetings to debate issues or shoot down my neighbor's concept of a Higher Power. I'm here to stay alive and in recovery, and to help others to do the same. When I'm practicing my own spiritual path with sincerity, I become less concerned about how others do it.

We don't have to define a Power greater than ourselves as anyone else defines it, but we do have to find and acknowledge what that Power is for each of us. For some, it's the source of life. For some, it's our capacity to take responsibility and make ethical decisions. For some, it's love—our feelings and acts of caring for ourselves and others.

When we hit bottom, some part of us finally gave up on the idea that we had to be our own Higher Power. Understanding that remains essential if we're to live without addictive substances and behavior. Recovery gets sidetracked when we entertain the belief that our foundation is anything other than a Higher Power.

> **Today, I acknowledge my relationship with a Power greater than myself.**

 *311*

> *You have to believe in happiness.*
> DOUGLAS MALLOCH

Newcomer

You've been encouraging me to take the risk of trying new things and thinking about what my personal goals are. I'm confused. If I pray only for knowledge of my Higher Power's will for me, aren't I negating myself? Does being sober mean I can't have any desires or goals of my own?

Sponsor

We know what our lives were like in active addiction; we know what they are in recovery. Something in us can see clearly that the real life, the one we're meant to have, the one our souls desire, depends on staying away from addictive substances and behaviors. Why imagine that the Source of Life wants us to have anything but full recovery, anything less than the ability to make our own sober choices? Would Eternal Truth require us to behave like puppets? Would a Creator want us to stifle the creativity within us?

Our relationship with a Power greater than ourselves includes listening to our own hearts. Underneath fear, underneath shame, underneath rebellion, underneath self-rejection, there is wholeness, joy, and the desire to live. It's here that we find our true purpose and the way to fulfill it.

**Today, I trust the voice of health, sanity,
and self-love that is growing more articulate within me.**

 **312**

*When we trust God with our whole heart, we don't fill
our prayers with "Give me this" or "Take this from me."*
ISAAC OF NINEVEH

Newcomer

I've heard people in meetings talking about God's will for them. What does "Thy will be done" have to do with my life in recovery? It's from a prayer that's part of one particular organized religion. Isn't it passive and old-fashioned?

Sponsor

Through prayer and meditation, through listening to others sharing from their hearts, through listening to our own spirits, we sense the presence of a larger Self, one that includes us and other human beings, but isn't limited to our egos, our individual collections of wants and fears. As we grow in recovery, we begin to feel something working in our lives, something that's more inclusive, wiser, and more completely loving than the litany of thoughts in our limited, everyday minds. We don't have to call it "God's will for us" if we don't choose to. We can reach it by another name or have no words for it at all. We can experience it as a continuing process or presence in our lives, one in which we take an active part.

Once the obstacle of active addiction is removed, we

have the opportunity to begin to know who we are and who we can be. Participating in a deeper, more intimate relationship with our Higher Power is the result of, not passivity or willfulness, but humility and courage.

Recovery is the path of my spirit.
Today, I summon the courage to go more deeply within.

 *313*

Someone once asked me . . . whether I
waited for inspiration. My answer was: "Every day!"
AARON COPLAND

Newcomer
I've been praying for help in an area that is very difficult for me; I feel as if I've hit a wall, and I don't know what to do. The prayers don't seem to be helping. Is my Higher Power listening?

Sponsor
Our reserves of patience are so easily exhausted. We quickly move to discouragement and even despair when we don't get what we want when we want it. Problems may have been in our lives for years, but we are only now becoming aware of them in recovery. How can we expect them to clear up in a few weeks or months? We think that we're at the end of our rope, but perhaps our situation will seem less desperate if we acknowledge that, through prayer, we've made a beginning.

Think of how patient our Higher Power was with us, all those years that we continued to be active in our addictions. Can we be that patient with ourselves, as we make progress in recovery?

Instead of giving up, we can believe an answer will come, and can prepare to recognize it by keeping our lines of communication with our Higher Power open.

> Today, my daily prayers are part of an ongoing
> conversation with my Higher Power.
> I pray with confidence that I am
> in the process of receiving what I need.

314

Fear is an emotion indispensable for survival.
HANNAH ARENDT

Newcomer

I have something to do that terrifies me. I've talked about it with other people, but nothing has taken away the fear. They make it sound easy, but then I hang up the phone, and it's as scary as ever. Other people don't really get it anyway; it's not the kind of thing everyone else is afraid of—it's something that I've always found hard. I wish I weren't such a coward.

Sponsor

We all have fears, and though rational discussion helps some of the time, it doesn't always remove them. What does work is taking the required action. Whether it's taking one of the Twelve Steps, auditioning for a part in a play, making love without drugs or alcohol, or simply making a dreaded phone call, when we begin to take actions *in spite of* the fear we feel, we are changed.

In our old days of active addiction, we missed out on opportunities to grow through doing what we found difficult. We may have avoided challenges by doing nothing, or by using addictive substances to foster numbness or defiance. Without the healthy kind of fear that we need for survival, we may have taken life-endangering risks.

Fear doesn't make us cowards. There is no courage without fear. If we fear nothing, we never have the experience of walking through our fears and letting our spirits expand.

**Today, I walk through a fear;
as I take action, I experience my courage.**

 *315*

*Natural abilities are like natural plants,
that need pruning by study.*
FRANCIS BACON

Newcomer

I'm so discouraged. I used to think I had so much talent. Now I can see that I'm not as good as hundreds of other people. While I was off hiding from reality in my addiction, other people were getting ahead of me.

Sponsor

Neither our talents nor our dreams have vanished. In recovery, we have the chance to explore the question of what kind of education and training we need to support our natural gifts, to help us take steps in the world, and to flourish.

For some of us, this may mean formal education; people in recovery are doing it all the time. Some of us may simply want instruction in a recreational pursuit that brings pleasure and expands our options. Books and articles, a peer support group, or friends with some time for hands-on help may be enough to get us started. The rest comes with experience, patience, and practice.

Still others of us may have had considerable experience and worldly success, but addiction has limited or interrupted our path. It takes courage and the willingness to think like a beginner again to find the way back to what matters to us. Our experience of hitting bottom and embracing recovery has given us insights, attitudes, and habits that enhance the experience of living.

Today, I have the willingness and courage to give myself a second chance at an old dream. I take small steps. I persist, no matter what.

 *316*

It is not true that life is one damn thing after another—
it is one damn thing over and over.
EDNA ST. VINCENT MILLAY

Newcomer
I've been letting go of a habit that I thought of as minor, nothing like the addiction that brought me here. I'm surprised to discover that I'm having some of the same feelings that I had when I first entered this program. I want to indulge myself, cry, run, explode with rage. How can anything so small be such a big deal?

Sponsor

Congratulations on recognizing the importance of this habit and taking an action to change your relationship to it. You're describing withdrawal symptoms; it's likely that this habit has served the same purpose as that served by your primary addiction. Without this "minor habit," you're again face-to-face with reality.

Most of us have more than one way to protect ourselves from realities we believe we can't face. We overlook or excuse "minor" habits for years, until one day the "minor" habit becomes an addiction. Letting go of a "minor" habit may remind us of our experiences in early recovery. If we face our addictive feelings head-on, with our experience in recovery to support us, we'll walk away freer than we've ever felt before.

Let's remember that we don't have to go through physical or mental detoxification, or other major life changes, on our own. Now, more than ever, is the time for sharing. It works.

Today, when addictive feelings arise, I trust that they're getting ready to leave. I assist their passage by talking about them with people in recovery.

⟵ *317* ⟶

It has begun to occur to me that life is a stage
I'm going through.
ELLEN GOODMAN

Newcomer

I've had thoughts and dreams about dying lately. They scare me; I've never thought of myself as suicidal.

We don't have to take our thoughts and dreams about death literally. It makes sense that we'd be thinking a lot about death in our early recovery, when so many old habits and attitudes are in the process of "dying." We may fear that nothing will come to fill the empty space we've created by clearing out self-destructiveness, negativity, guilt, low self-esteem, or grandiosity. We may wonder who we are, who we can possibly become, now that we've divested ourselves of the habits and attitudes that we thought *were* us, those that had occupied so much of our waking time. But there is far more to us than what we've left behind. We're just at the beginning of a lifelong process of communicating with the Spirit that lives within us.

We can have faith that we're in the right place. The life force is present here: our laughter, our stories, and our sharing are full of hope and willingness.

> **Today, I embrace the passages in my life,**
> **trusting the necessity to let old selves die**
> **to make room for the new and vital.**

318

Luck is just a matter of preparation meeting opportunity.
OPRAH WINFREY

Newcomer
Nothing good is coming into my life right now. I feel stuck.

Sponsor
While we don't control what happens in our lives, we do have the ability to articulate our goals. We need to invite

positive happenings by making room for them in our psyches and to recognize and acknowledge the positive when it does show up.

Prayer is one medium for acknowledging the gifts we already have and for affirming faith in the possibilities our lives hold. Writing—which might include making a gratitude list, writing about our current experience of one of the Twelve Steps, or writing down our goals so that they are clear to us—is another tool for cultivating positive attitudes that prepare us for success.

Visualization is another powerful tool. Visualization involves seeing in detail, in our mind's eye, exactly what we hope to accomplish. A writer I know began work on a book by visualizing the entire process of producing it: completing pages, mailing the manuscript, even holding the publisher's check in his hand. He visualized printing presses running, the binder gluing the cover, the distributor making shipments, readers buying the book. This process wasn't willful or magical; it was a tool for creating the mental conditions he needed to believe in himself and to complete his project. Visualization can change our mind-set and prepare us to recognize opportunity when we meet it.

**Today, I rehearse the positive in my imagination,
embracing it when it comes.**

If they try to rush me, I always say,
"I've only got one other speed—and it's slower."
GLENN FORD

Newcomer

I've been working like a maniac, running around like a chicken with its head cut off. And I don't have that much to show for all this effort.

Sponsor

How is it that "slow" got to be a negative word? To me, it holds the possibility of safety, care, thoughtful reflection, and taking pleasure in details. Many things today are supposed to happen at breakneck speed. Fast food, electronic mail, and express flights encourage us to think that we're performing inadequately if we can't proceed at a faster pace than feels comfortable.

In the past, I'd sometimes try to get two days' work done in one, even staying awake all night to meet a deadline. While I sometimes met my goal for that twenty-four-hour period, I'd be exhausted and perhaps ill the next day. I'd lose an entire day catching up with myself. I'd have defeated my purpose of getting ahead and made errors of judgment in the process, too fatigued to see my mistakes.

We're not machines. We may have periods of seeming inactivity and periods of accelerated activity; growth often happens in spurts. But if we set out to be deliberate and consistent, whatever our pace, we will get things accomplished, and we won't burn ourselves out.

Today, I'm not in a race.
I respect my body's signals about pacing.

For it is in dying that we find eternal life.
THE PRAYER OF SAINT FRANCIS, QUOTED IN
TWELVE STEPS AND TWELVE TRADITIONS

Newcomer

A friend in recovery showed me a prayer by Saint Francis. Even though it's specific to a particular religion, I find it beautiful and inspiring, until it gets to the very end: "It is by dying that we find eternal life." I don't know what I believe about life after death, but I can't accept that we're supposed to renounce everything in this life or that happiness begins only with death.

Sponsor

Whether or not our religious beliefs include a literal interpretation of that last line, we can read it figuratively. "Dying" is something that can happen not just to our physical bodies, but also to our egos.

Everything in the prayer that leads up to that final statement is about letting go of ego gratification. When we pray to understand rather than to be understood, we're praying for the kind of maturity that a parent has: as good parents, we listen to children with compassion and good humor; we're confident enough of our own adult "turf" not to have to defend it. We know, too, that offering unconditional love expands and fills our hearts far more than waiting, with a sense of neediness and deprivation, for love to be offered. If we "die" in this sense, letting go of our self-centered demands, then we waken to "eternal life": our souls wake up.

Our bodies don't have to die for this to happen; our self-centered fear does.

Today, I'm willing to let go of my ego so that I can become more open to the presence of a Higher Power in my life.

321

Just about the time you think you can make both ends meet, somebody moves the ends.
PANSY PENNER

Newcomer
Too much is going on today. I was looking forward to a real rest as soon as I'd dealt with a current crisis. Instead of relief, I've suddenly got a whole new problem to handle. Why does everything have to happen all at once?

Sponsor
One of the most comforting sayings I've heard over and over in this program is "God doesn't send us more than we can handle." We're not able to control the timing of crises, nor can we know what unexpected demands will be made on our reserves. We can drain our energy focusing on the cosmic unfairness of it all, or we can accept that we have to change our plans. When we're flexible, we find resources within us we may not have known we had.

When we wonder how we'll manage to keep going in a physically demanding situation—finishing a race , for example, or giving birth—nature provides energy in abundance at the needful moment. Our human spirits, too, find the energy we need to go through whatever is in front of us.

**Today, my Higher Power doesn't send me
more than I can handle.**

 *322*

*True worship is not a petition to God:
it is a sermon to ourselves.*
ABRAHAM JOSHUA HESCHEL

Newcomer

I don't understand why, but prayer always seems to make my day go better. It doesn't matter so much what the prayer is; it's the act of doing it. It's beginning to feel more like a conversation, less like begging.

Sponsor

When we have the courage to connect with our deepest selves in meditation and prayer, we learn who we are. We become aware that we have a purpose in life. Letting go of active addiction was only the beginning.

Continuing the path of recovery requires us to take actions: attending meetings, working the Steps, giving service, and not picking up our addiction are becoming second nature. We pay attention to the requirements for maintaining the health of our bodies and minds. We are no longer afraid to sit still with our feelings. We experience sobriety in our relationships and work lives, showing up for things we find difficult as well as for what seems easy. We begin to address the particular needs of a self that we've neglected and numbed. We no longer deny our souls the nourishment they needs. Prayer can heal, strengthen, and lift our spirits.

Today, any difficulties I may experience are opportunities to turn to my Higher Power for guidance and strength. Prayer gives me courage as I go through the day.

 *323*

It is difficult to stop in time because one gets carried away. But I have that strength; it is the only strength I have.
CLAUDE MONET

Newcomer
I love to start new things—work assignments, artistic projects, even relationships. But then I hang on and can't let go when things are finished. I make up my mind and then change it. I don't know if it's self-doubt or what.

Sponsor
One of the many shapes perfectionism can take is difficulty with completing things. Some of us slow down as we reach an ending. Perhaps we fear that we'll lose the part of ourselves that has been alive and engaged. Or we fear criticism and rejection, both of which we'll risk when we let our work into the world, or when we commit ourselves to a decision. We slow down or even abandon something we've given much of ourselves to, to avoid ending it. Or we keep going when we should stop and redo what is already good enough.

The myth that perfection is possible feeds and is fed by the sense of inadequacy that characterizes our addictions. It keeps us from the pleasure and pain of finishing. It shuts off our connection with our intuition, which usually knows when enough is enough. In recovery, we can receive gratification and self-esteem from finishing unfinished business.

Today, I work toward completion.
I stop when I see that there is no more to be done.

324

Most of the trouble in the world is caused by people
wanting to be important.
T. S. ELIOT

Newcomer

Someone I know finally started coming to meetings. I'd told her about this program months ago; she needs it as much as I do. She came for a while, then stopped attending on a regular basis. I've called her several times, but she always brushes me off.

Sponsor

If you really want to be helpful, do nothing! I can identify with your feelings of concern. In the past, there were many people I forced to listen to my experiences in this program. Most said things such as, "I don't like groups"; "I tried it, but it wasn't for me"; "Maybe someday"; or "I feel sorry for those people; I'm not like them." Still, some of these people stayed in the program, but not because of anything I said. Each of us finds his or her own way to recovery. Telling people what we think they should do seldom makes a difference. It's what they tell themselves that counts.

When I insist on trying to rescue someone who sends clear signals that he or she doesn't want help, when I take on responsibilities that aren't my own, I have to ask myself what my motives are. I've sometimes obsessed about another person's problems while not facing my own, and then feelings of resentment and superiority have reared their heads. I can't fix anyone else's life; my attempts to do that have usually backfired.

It helps to remember that others, like me, have a Higher Power. I can pray for them to find the path that leads to their highest good. And I can let go of having to be right.

Today, I am enough. I have enough. I do enough.

325

If you can't be direct, why be?
LILY TOMLIN

Newcomer

I heard someone who'd gone through enormous losses talk at a meeting recently. I reached out to him, invited him to coffee, and gave him my number. He started calling me, and I've enjoyed a lot of what he has to say. But the calls are always longer than I really want them to be. I don't dislike this man, and I really am willing to be a program friend, if we can set some limits.

Sponsor

Sometimes, out of kindness and the desire to help, you take on more than you can manage, perhaps more than is appropriate. You're not alone; many of us experience some variation of this problem in recovery. Setting and maintaining personal boundaries is a lifelong journey.

In situations like the one you describe, directness is important. When we give something we don't really want to give, when we act as if we're more available than we are, we end up with resentment. Forcing ourselves to give against our will distorts our relationships with others as we feed our egos. To give freely, whether of time, money, work, or material things, is a blessing. We experience our own and others' abundance. We can then feel gratitude for what has been given to us.

Today, my giving is honest. There are no strings attached.

326

I don't want to make money. I just want to be wonderful.
MARILYN MONROE

Newcomer

I talked with someone about this program recently, and she surprised me by saying, "It costs money, doesn't it?" I explained that no one is required to pay anything, that we meet our expenses by passing a basket at meetings. I realized, talking to her, that the program's relationship to money is pretty unusual in this society. If we tried, we could be making a big profit, couldn't we?

Sponsor

Our tradition is opposed to profit-making. As you probably know by now, each individual group supports itself, paying for such expenses as rent, hospitality, and literature from whatever people give voluntarily when a basket is passed for contributions. Once a group meets its basic expenses, it may send a contribution to intergroup headquarters, to help meet administrative expenses. The program as a whole doesn't accept donations from outside sources, and individual groups are discouraged from keeping money in the treasury "beyond prudent reserves." This tradition helps keep us independent and safe from the risk of disagreement and competition that can arise where there are accumulations of money. It helps us to stay focused on our spiritual program.

> Today, I take time to examine my attitudes
> and beliefs about money.

 *327*

When people are still asleep
I hear God best and learn my plan.
GEORGE WASHINGTON CARVER

Newcomer

I'm beginning to have a sense of my own Higher Power. It's not that I can tell you in so many words exactly what I believe. But I do have a feeling of being part of something larger than myself and, often, a sense of comfort and safety that I didn't have before. It surprises me that I've developed the habit of prayer.

Sponsor

Many of us have had the experience of finding a Higher Power as a result of prayer, instead of the other way around. We don't have to resolve questions of belief in order to pray. Like you, we simply take the action of praying. People get to know one another over the course of many, many shared conversations and activities. Why shouldn't we begin to develop our relationship with a Power greater than ourselves in the same way, using prayer as a form of communication? Some of us use the beautiful prayers of the religion we grew up with or have chosen; some of us write our own prayers or speak them spontaneously, aloud or in our hearts. When we apply Step Eleven to our lives, using prayer as a form of daily "conscious contact," our relationship with a Higher Power evolves.

Today, I begin to know my Higher Power better through prayer.

 *328*

Become as resourceful in inspiring yourself to enter your own peace as you are at being neurotic and competitive in the world.
SOGYAL RINPOCHE

Newcomer
Meditation continues to be difficult for me to understand, to do, and to keep doing consistently.

Sponsor
With repeated practice, meditation can be the most intimate and rewarding way to be with ourselves. The key, as with all our practices, is to meditate each day.

Just as with prayer, there isn't just one right way to meditate. We can be artists at daily meditation, finding creative ways to inspire ourselves to enter peace. A city friend whose home is one small room has created an altar on a windowsill with a bowl of water, some lemon leaves, and a candle. Something simple—one stick of incense or a tape of sacred music—may be all we need to bring us back home to our real selves, reacquaint us with the peace at the center of our being.

Or we can go to nature to meditate, letting the sky, a

stream, rain, wind, or sunlight enter our minds. We relax and let our minds expand and be filled with and become what we are looking at: we become the infinite space of sky, the movement of water, the energy of wind, the warmth of sunlight. When we've taken time to greet our spirits in meditation, our minds feel cleansed.

Today, I meet my true self in meditation.

329

Our emotions are neither primitive nor "natural,"
but rather intelligent constructions.
ROBERT C. SOLOMON

Newcomer

I went out for coffee after a meeting with a group I didn't know. Two people, one on either side of me, talked with each other without including me. They chatted about things they'd done together and then made plans for getting together. I felt excluded. I guess I still don't know how to become part of a group. Am I being too sensitive?

Sponsor

Too sensitive? You are sensitive, and that's a gift. You notice what's going on around you. You notice what you're feeling.

Not every get-together makes us feel more a part of things, especially when people pair off for conversations. Many of us in recovery are still learning how to act in social situations, and we're not always open and thoughtful.

If we're having trouble reaching out to others, we need to give ourselves plenty of time. Social and relationship skills aren't learned overnight. And sometimes, no matter how friendly and open we ourselves are willing to be, those we're sitting with just don't seem to want to respond. It happens, both in and out of the program. Our object can be to have as good a time as possible and to decide whether or not we want to try spending social time with these people again.

Today, I'm willing to treat new social experiences as a way to practice skills of relating to others.

330

Let every man be respected as an individual and no man idolized.
ALBERT EINSTEIN

Newcomer

At one meeting I go to, the same two people seem to dominate. Both take service positions every term. Both, when they share, say things that are subtly critical of other people's recovery and all the "new" ways of doing things in this program.

Sponsor

It's a program tradition that we don't have "bosses," but now and then a group gets lazy and allows itself to be led a bit heavy-handedly. Tolerance is the solution for both old-timers and relative newcomers. Rather than criticize the critics, other group members can become willing to take a more active role by attending business meetings, volunteering for service positions, or nominating new officers. When a group is facing proposed changes, a "group conscience" meeting is held; we trust that a Power greater than ourselves expresses itself through the decisions we arrive at together.

Personal styles and common cultural experiences of new generations of people in recovery may be a bit different from those of people who've been here for a while, but the basic principles of this program haven't changed. Sharing our own experience and listening to others with humility is still the way we recover.

Today, I practice tolerance.

331

It is well to lie fallow for a while.
M. F. TUPPER

Newcomer
The person who makes coffee for my home group left me a message at the last minute asking me to sub for him or suggest someone else. I said no—I hadn't planned to attend the meeting. I couldn't find my list of phone numbers, either, so I didn't suggest anyone. I'm feeling guilty. He doesn't know as many members of the group as I do; he has less time in the program than I have.

Sponsor
What's the worst thing that can possibly happen as a result of your not taking on this person's responsibility? Perhaps there'll be no coffee at the meeting this time, but I doubt that anyone will lose his or her recovery over it. More

likely, someone will walk in, see that the coffeepot isn't on, and get it started.

When I can't keep a commitment, I do my best to make phone calls, but I'm not guaranteed that someone else will take it on for me. I start making calls well in advance, if at all possible. I do the best I can to find a substitute. But if no one else is available to help, I let go. I'm not indispensable. I've never known a meeting not to take place because of my absence.

The person who asked you to fill in for him may also need to learn more about keeping commitments; that's one of the reasons for taking on responsibilities in the early months of recovery. If you're there to rescue him whenever he can't make it, he may miss out on learning about reality. Saying no and being said no to is part of life.

Today, I am responsible, not overresponsible.

332

Open your eyes! The world is still intact.
PAUL CLAUDEL

Newcomer
Someone who entered recovery close to the time I did stopped coming to meetings about a month ago. I've just learned that she has relapsed. I called her once, but she said she was busy and never called back. I'm surprised at how betrayed and unsafe I feel. I hardly even know her.

Sponsor
Like you, when someone has a relapse, I feel deeply shaken. Another human life is at stake. Someone who was on my

path, whose presence served as solace and example, has left. He or she may never come back. I'm powerless over another person's decision and over what time will bring. My desire to rescue comes up, and I know I have to let that go—no one can rescue us from addiction. Then I go through feelings of betrayal: how could he or she have abandoned me like this? What if everyone else decides to drop out? Where will I be then? Mixed with this feeling is one of anger: she's getting to have her drug of choice again! I want it too, and I'm furious that I can't have it. After the anger, fear, grief, and loss, I may feel something like gratitude. I understand how deep my own commitment to recovery is, how much I need and want it.

Today, I choose recovery again, for one more day.

333

*If only we'd stop trying to be happy
we could have a pretty good time.*
EDITH WHARTON

Newcomer
What is it about me? A while ago, I finally figured out that I really did feel better on the days I meditated. When I meditate, I like the feeling of being refreshed and alive. But I get impatient with it, and I rebel against doing it consistently.

Sponsor
I've often heard it said at meetings that the definition of insanity is doing the same thing over and over and expecting that things will turn out differently. The same kind of logic

applies here: I try something, I experience good results—so I quit doing it! It makes no sense, unless you're an addict.

The results of regular meditation are subtle but powerful. Over time, a transformation takes place not only in our minds and feelings, but also in the cells of our bodies. It's well established that people who meditate have better-regulated blood pressure, a high level of efficiency and competence at what they do, improved relationships, more zest for living, and greater serenity. It costs absolutely nothing to do, requires no equipment, and takes relatively little time.

We don't have to punish ourselves for what we failed to do yesterday. Today is as good a day as any to begin again. Rather than struggling with meditation, just sit down and allow it to happen.

Today, I do all that I set out to do with ease and pleasure.

➤ *334* ➤

God knows no distance.
CHARLESZETTA WADDLES

Newcomer
Step Twelve begins with the phrase "Having had a spiritual awakening . . ." I'm disappointed to report that I've never had a vision, seen blinding light, or witnessed anything supernatural in recovery.

Sponsor
Let's look at what the whole phrase says. "Having had a spiritual awakening as a result of these steps" reminds us that a spiritual awakening, for most of us, has been a grad-

ual process, a consequence of a whole series of actions that we've taken over time as we've practiced Steps One through Eleven.

Sometimes, instant transformation occurs; perhaps we ourselves, though we may not have heard voices or sensed a divine presence, can remember one particular moment when things seemed to turn around for us. Whether we can recall such a moment or not, the real miracle of recovery is one that has evolved over many days and months, the miracle that we've become willing to grow and are open to doing things differently. I think of the phrase "a spiritual awakening" not as something magically conferred on us by outside forces, but as the waking up of our spirits over time.

Today, the spirit within me is awake.

 *335*

What is a great spiritual practitioner? A person who lives always in the presence of his or her own true self, someone who has found and who uses continually the springs and sources of profound inspiration.
SOGYAL RINPOCHE

Newcomer
In meetings I hear the phrase "To thine own self be true." Does it mean that my true self isn't the part that's addicted?

Sponsor
Being true to myself means many things to me in recovery. The first layer of meaning includes restoring my sense of

right and wrong, taking responsibility for my past actions, acting in the present in a way that allows me to hold up my head as a member of the community. The next layer has to do with discovering my preferences: what do I want my work to be, and with whom do I want close associations? A still deeper layer of being true to myself means coming to know my spirit through prayer and meditation, unclogging the channels, greeting my soul.

Recovery gives us the opportunity to begin to know ourselves, in all our aspects. I've come to know the self that craves addictive substances and behaviors and the self that craves recovery; both are aspects of me. Once you acknowledge your addictive self, you can begin to heal and to know all the rest of who you are.

> Today, I know who I am and what I am here for.
> I am true to myself.

 *336*

I myself must mix with action, lest I wither by despair.
ALFRED, LORD TENNYSON

Newcomer
How is it possible to apply Step Twelve, "to practice these principles in all our affairs"? Does that mean taking all Twelve Steps again?

Sponsor
The Steps can help us live more consciously. Take our relationships with other human beings, for example. How do we handle duties, disappointments, disagreements? Steps One through Three remind me that there are people and

things over which I have no control, and that surrender is more effective than forcing my will. Steps Four and Ten remind me to examine and commit to writing any ways in which I may be contributing to what troubles me. Step Five reminds me of the powerful process of speaking with others. Steps Six and Seven remind me that it's my Higher Power, not me, who's in charge of my healing; Steps Eight and Nine, that I have an effect on others. The Eleventh Step reminds me to tend my relationship with the Spirit with daily practice; and the Twelfth Step, that I'm not in recovery just for myself.

Taking actions in the light of the Steps, whether or not we repeat them formally, is the next phase of recovery. Continuing to attend Step meetings where we hear other people's experience of the Steps in their recovery offers us information and wisdom. We realize that we've learned a great deal about how to live. As recovery progresses, we discover that the simple principles underlying these Steps have become deep-seated commitments.

Today, I have reliable principles for how to live.

337

The more you praise and celebrate your life,
the more there is in life to celebrate.
OPRAH WINFREY

Newcomer
I saw a newcomer, someone who's only been around for a few weeks, putting promotional fliers on the seats before a meeting to advertise a concert she was performing in. I told her that we don't advertise anything here. I was kind of

shocked to realize how much I've come to depend on the fact that no one tries to sell me anything at meetings.

Sponsor

One of our most important traditions is that each of our groups is essentially spiritual in nature. We're here for only one purpose, to carry the message to people who are still suffering from our addictions. We're not here to advertise, affiliate with, or endorse anything.

It may seem harmless, at first, for a person in recovery to use a meeting as a place to advertise something he or she is trying to achieve. But think of what would happen if our traditions permitted advertising. Where would we draw the line? Would sober car salesmen, plumbers, insurance agents, and computer consultants all begin hawking their wares and services? Would we begin to treat the principles of the program as one more thing to buy or pass up?

We are certainly free to share the news of our lives with friends in recovery, but we don't use meeting rooms as a place to promote our careers, religions, or worthy causes.

**Today, I'm grateful that meetings give me
the opportunity to focus my attention on recovery.**

 *338*

People who fight with fire usually end up with ashes.
ABIGAIL VAN BUREN

Newcomer

I feel sad about a relative who has the same addiction problem I do but isn't in recovery. I don't know what to do about it.

Sponsor

We can remember that others, like us, have a Higher Power. We can pray for them. And there's nothing wrong with letting a relative know that we've found a Twelve Step program and have stopped using our addictive drug or behavior.

There's a fine line, though, that's dangerous to cross. We can get into trouble if our ego thinks it's our job, or that it's even possible, to bring another person into recovery. If we share information about our recovery with a family member, we have to be prepared for lack of interest, refusal to hear, or downright hostility. We may have to deal with the impact of the person's denial about our own need for recovery. It helps to remember that we're as powerless over another person's addiction as we are over the addictive substance itself.

Today, my own recovery is my highest priority;
I surrender family members to my Higher Power's care.

 *339*

Ignorance and conceit go hand in hand.
THE TALMUD

Newcomer

Now that I'm in recovery, it's amazing how much active addiction I can see around me. It's all over the place. Friends, family members, co-workers—more people than I realized have the same problem I have. There's one person in particular I wish I could help. Before coming into recovery, I didn't realize that she was on such a self-destructive path.

Sponsor

Once we have an insight into our own addictions, we begin seeing it everywhere. It's not hard to find: addiction is a widespread problem in our culture. We're excited about the changes that we're experiencing in our own lives, and we want to help others.

Many of us, in our enthusiasm, start to diagnose everyone around us. We may be accurate in our perceptions, or we may be mistaken. There are people who can safely do things that aren't safe for us. Or perhaps they have issues similar to ours, but are far from hitting bottom. In our zeal, we may do more harm than good. Spreading the news where it isn't wanted may make others feel uncomfortable about the program, change their minds about giving it a try, or postpone coming to a meeting.

This is a self-diagnosed disease. Who gets sober, and when, is not for us to decide. When we find that we're becoming preoccupied with other people's recovery, it's time to pay closer attention to our own.

Today, I keep the focus on my own recovery.

$\rightarrowtail$ *340* $\rightarrowtail$

I know God will not give me anything I can't handle.
I just wish that He didn't trust me so much.
MOTHER TERESA

Newcomer

I've heard of "Twelve Step calls"—going to people's homes and carrying the message. Is that what we're supposed to do?

Sponsor

"Twelve Stepping" is not limited to situations in which two or more people in recovery go to the home of someone who's ready to get sober, in order to share their experience, strength, and hope. There are many ways to carry the message. Answering telephones, providing meeting information and transportation to newcomers or out-of-town visitors, buying literature for the group, sponsoring—any service we perform that makes it possible for people to attend meetings and to hear the message of the program is a form of Twelfth Step work. The simple act of showing up at a meeting, sharing and thanking others for sharing, is Twelfth Step work. Our willingness and consistency and simply being ourselves send a powerful message.

All of us are qualified to share our own experience, strength, and hope. Our recovery itself is eloquent.

**Today, I perform some form of service
for others in recovery. I give it back in order to keep it.**

341

Love is wiser than ambition.
BRYAN WALLER PROCTER

Newcomer

I thought that nobody was supposed to make any money out of this program. What about the people who work at program intergroups and get paid regular salaries?

Sponsor

We figured out some time ago that certain kinds of work get done more efficiently by paid service workers, rather than by volunteers. Running offices, programming computers, publishing, filling book orders, answering volumes of correspondence from all over the world, preserving historical records—such work requires training, continuity, and consistency.

But our traditions do keep the direct Twelfth Step work of helping other people suffering from addictions forever nonprofessional. We share our experience, strength, and hope voluntarily and freely, to help bring recovery to others suffering from our addictions. Whether we're speaking, performing other services that keep meetings going, answering telephone hotlines, or sponsoring newcomers, we are never paid.

I don't have to question the motives of someone who is giving it away to keep it. The message goes straight from his or her heart to my own.

Today, I'm grateful for opportunities to carry the message. I share my experience, strength, and hope freely and voluntarily, without thought of gain.

342

When someone's life is shattered, there is only humanity.
DIANE SAWYER

Newcomer

There's someone I took a dislike to the first time I saw her at a meeting. From her age and appearance, I assumed that we had little in common. Recently, she was the speaker at a meeting I attended, and I heard more. The sincerity of her sharing touched off strong memories from my own past. After the meeting, I thanked her, and told her how moved I'd been listening to her. It surprised me to find out that my prejudices can still keep me from seeing and hearing people as they really are. It's humbling.

Sponsor

Congratulations on listening in spite of your initial negative feelings. We can learn from people whose lives and personalities are vastly different from our own, people whom we would not necessarily choose as friends or close associates. I once heard a man in recovery say, "If you haven't met anyone you don't like, you haven't been to enough meetings." We aren't required to like everyone we meet here, but we do need to give one another respect and a special kind of attention. As we hear how others' lives have changed, we listen actively for feelings that echo our own. We learn to go deeper than the surface, to see the journey of another's spirit, and we find that we want to celebrate one another's victories in recovery. Our respect for those who speak at meetings has a further benefit. As we learn to see the humanity of those who are recovering in this fellowship, our tolerance for all human beings grows.

Today, I sense the humanity of all those in this fellowship.

343

It is when you give of yourself that you truly give.
KAHLIL GIBRAN

Newcomer

Someone told me that she liked what I'd shared at a meeting and asked me to be her sponsor. I explained that I don't have a full year of recovery yet and that I need to wait until the year is up before taking on a sponsee. I'm flattered that she asked me, but sponsoring someone seems like such a big responsibility.

Sponsor

What a lovely acknowledgment of your growth, your love of the program, and your clarity. Her request that you sponsor her indicates respect for you and your recovery. I trust you can accept the compliment. Sometimes we're not aware of how much we've grown until people who've seen and heard us sharing let us know that they appreciate our words and example.

You are wise, too, to have said no to this particular request. Customs vary from program to program, group to group; in some places, people may begin serving as sponsors before they themselves have completed a year of recovery. But giving ourselves time to go through an entire year of focusing on our own recovery ensures a more solid basis for helping other newcomers. The time will come. Meanwhile, there are many other ways to give service.

Today, I'm aware of the difference my recovery has begun to make in the lives of others.

344

When you take the alcohol out of alcoholism, you still have to deal with the ism.
SAYING HEARD AT MEETINGS

Newcomer

I've had a falling out with someone I'd been spending time with recently. She's been in recovery a couple of years longer than I have, and I assumed that she'd be normal by now or, at the least, more stable than I am. But she is needy and difficult, and I just can't do and be what she wants.

Sponsor

Recovery doesn't give anyone instant maturity, insight, or a gift for stable relationships. Even after we've let go of addictive substances and behaviors, we still have work to do. This work isn't identical for all of us and doesn't follow a prescribed timetable. We've entered recovery at different times in our lives, having had different experiences, and we may face a variety of challenges in addition to our common problem of addiction. Once in recovery, we have the opportunity to address underlying issues; that doesn't necessarily mean that we'll resolve them quickly, or that all of us are maturing at the same pace.

We can't assume that someone's length of time in recovery guarantees that he or she won't have unreasonable expectations of us. Good relationships develop over time, if we have the willingness and ability to take responsibility for our own needs, to communicate with love and patience through periods of conflict as well as harmony.

Today, I have realistic expectations of myself and others.

≈ *345* ≈

If it ain't broke, don't fix it.
SAYING HEARD AT MEETINGS

Newcomer

I know that doing service is suggested, and I've done a lot of it. But I want to take some time off now. You've said before that this program makes suggestions, not rules, so I know there's no rule that I have to keep doing service.

Sponsor

We need to look carefully at our motives. Some of us do a great deal of service early in recovery—chores like setting up chairs, making coffee, and cleaning up. This has kept us busy and helped us get to meetings and stay away from our drug of choice. Perhaps now we want to give other newcomers opportunities to serve the group. Or perhaps we'd like to try something new. These are legitimate reasons for changing service positions. Perhaps, however, we've been harboring feelings of resentment about responsibilities we've taken on. We may feel overextended or unappreciated. Or perhaps we want to pull back from the program. We may even be unconsciously laying the groundwork for a relapse.

Service is essential to recovery. Without it, meetings wouldn't take place, newcomers wouldn't find sponsors; phones would go unanswered. Others' service makes our recovery possible; we do the same for those who want what we have. Each of us is responsible for giving service that's appropriate to our schedules and abilities.

> **My willingness to give service today
> expresses my gratitude for recovery.**

One must talk. That's how it is. One must.
MARGUERITE DURAS

Newcomer

Someone I'm involved with is active in this disease again, after time in recovery. I've felt ashamed to talk with you about it or to share it at meetings. Am I jeopardizing my recovery by staying loyal to this person?

Sponsor

Some of us are already in committed relationships when we enter recovery. A partner, child, or family member may have problems of addiction. We know we cannot give recovery to another person. But it's appropriate to raise the question, as you have, of the impact of this situation on our own recovery.

While we want to avoid gossip, accusation, and blame of those we are close to who are still active, it's essential for our own recovery that we don't keep secrets. At meetings, we can share about the ways that a relationship challenges our own recovery, keeping the focus on ourselves. We can talk in more detail with a sponsor or counselor knowledgeable about addiction. We can avoid any tendency to enable another's addictive habits. We can pay close attention to our own addictive thinking and not let ourselves drift away from meetings and from using the tools of recovery.

While it may be painful and challenging to remain close to someone suffering from addiction, we can maintain our own recovery if we use all the help available to us. We can pray for our own and others' healing, as we continue sober practices that have worked for us.

**Today, I protect my recovery
by honest sharing about any challenges to it.**

 *347*

*Although we know that on some level
we are always connected, our most
common experience is one of estrangement.*
MARGOT ADLER

Newcomer
I've had a huge disappointment in my life recently. The details may be too private to share at a meeting, but not sharing them is making me feel more and more distant.

Sponsor
Our own preferences determine how much detail we feel comfortable sharing at meetings. Numerous details may not be necessary, however, for the process of sharing to help us begin to heal. Simply speaking up is always useful; just sharing a few words about how we're feeling today can accomplish a lot. It's a way of saying, "I'm here today; I'm a part of this group of recovering people; I'm staying sober—no matter what." It can keep us from isolation and self-pity.

It is important to share the details of whatever may be having an impact on our lives in recovery with at least one other person. Conversations with a sponsor, a trusted friend, a therapist, or a spiritual adviser are essential. While such conversations may not give us solutions to our problems, they can be a source of support as we find our own way to solutions. Writing about our experiences and speaking with our Higher Power in prayer can also help us go through challenging events in recovery. We don't have to struggle on our own.

> Today, my sober life includes people
> with whom I can share in depth.

 *348*

Our prayers are answered not when we are given
what we ask, but when we are challenged
to become what we can be.
ABRAHAM JOSHUA HESCHEL

Newcomer

So many things continue to be frustrating for me. I've been working so hard at my recovery, but my Higher Power doesn't seem to want to reward me.

Sponsor

Trust in a Higher Power includes trust that our lives in recovery are unfolding over a long period of time and that, though we can't always foresee where our journey is taking us, we're on the right path. Our work in recovery includes the work of learning patience, gratitude, and trust.

Should we turn our backs on a Higher Power simply because we haven't been given some material thing, some recognition from others, or a relationship we've been fantasizing about? Or because our Higher Power's timetable differs from our own? The true dimensions of our recovery are not always visible to us. If we're feeling frustrated about our progress, it helps us see things in perspective when we remember how far we've come in the relatively short time since we walked into our first meeting. Surely, our recovery will continue to take us far beyond what we can imagine today, just as it's already taken us beyond what we imagined a year ago.

Today, I remember that I'm a work in progress.

349

We say: made with joy. We should say: wise with grief.
MARGUERITE YOURCENAR

Newcomer
I've seen some movies lately that weren't very good, but that had a powerful impact on me anyway. One, a horror movie, really scared me, and one was a sentimental movie that made me cry. Neither film was even very believable, but I got emotionally involved. What's happening to me?

Sponsor
First, let me reassure you that your mind is working as well as, or better than, ever. When we're not dulling or depressing ourselves with addictive substances and behaviors, our thinking becomes clearer and sharper.

However, we may also find ourselves more responsive to emotional stimuli in recovery than before. An event that seems to have nothing to do with us—a film, a news item, another person's triumph or tragedy—triggers tears, laughter, or feelings of fear or anger. Often, this triggering event is not the true source of our feelings. The tears we shed in response to a scene in a film may be releasing some of our old, accumulated sadness. It's nearer the surface, easier to tap into, when we're ready to begin letting it go.

Our feelings are freer to flow, now that they're not blocked by addiction. Emotional release is necessary and natural.

Today, I am in touch with my feelings
and unafraid to express them.

 *350*

there is nothing
between me and my soul but myself.
JANE MEAD

Newcomer

Certain situations in my life are putting a lot of pressure on me. I'm lonely and frustrated. I don't want to act out my addiction today, and I don't want to be preached to.

Sponsor

There are times when recovery seems to be the only thing we can rely on. Nothing seems to be going our way. No one seems to understand. We feel as if we've already heard it all, and well-intentioned advice only makes us feel more alone with whatever is troubling us. We feel self-protective, perhaps somewhat defiant, as we declare in meetings that we don't want any help today. Our declaration, though it's intended to ward people off, is also a way of letting others in recovery know what we're going through; it is evidence of a certain degree of trust in ourselves and others.

Recovery, at such times, doesn't seem to be the source of happiness, joy, and freedom that we've felt it to be. Still, recovery has become so deeply ingrained in us by now that it almost feels as if it *is* us. We know that returning to active addiction won't make whatever it is we're feeling disappear. Some part of us knows that the deep discomfort we're feeling today will prove to be temporary, if we stay in recovery.

Today, I acknowledge the transformation in my life
that has eliminated active addiction as an option.
No matter what happens, no matter what I'm feeling,
I can count on my commitment to recovery.

 *351*

You do not notice changes in what is always before you.
COLETTE

Newcomer

My schedule has changed, and now I'm rarely able to go to the meetings where I got sober. It's been a hard adjustment for me; I'm still not used to it. I know that it's the same fellowship wherever we go, but nothing really feels the same to me as it did in early recovery.

Sponsor

When we make a major change in our lives, we sometimes feel as if we're required to give up everything associated with the past, but there are ways of preserving connections we value. While you are reaching out to new friends, you may want to keep making phone calls to stay in touch with people who've been important in your early recovery.

Even if we can continue going to the meetings we went to in early recovery, things won't always feel the same. Everything changes. As we and those around us grow, we experience meetings differently. We will also face different challenges; the problems we entered recovery with are not likely to be the ones that concern us a year later. Our lives in recovery are full of change, and far more often than in our past, the changes we experience are positive. The less we fight the necessity for change, the more easily we'll go through it.

Today, I accept change as necessary and focus on its benefits. I celebrate the ways I've changed in recovery.

352

To say something nice about themselves, this is the hardest thing in the world for people to do.
NANCY FRIDAY

Newcomer
Someone paid me a compliment recently, and my response was to disagree! I'm surprised; I thought I'd learned self-esteem in this program. But I'm still embarrassed when people call attention to what's good about me, even when I share their opinion.

Sponsor
When I was active in my addiction, my drug of choice sometimes felt like a protective cloak—it kept me hidden from myself, and I somehow believed that no one else could see me, either. In early recovery, I felt self-conscious sharing at meetings and embarrassed to be myself in public. I thought that invisibility—if only it were possible—would keep me safe from criticism. Criticism was what I'd long ago learned to expect from others, and what I most often leveled at myself.

Like so much else in recovery, it takes time to stop the habit of being harsh with ourselves and to learn to accept and love ourselves unconditionally. Celebrating our anniversaries and acknowledging our large and small victories when we share at meetings help us practice living in the open and savoring the joys of recovery. A sense of inner poise gradually grows within us. We develop generosity toward ourselves, as well as toward others. It's part of knowing who we really are.

Today, I view myself with love and generosity.

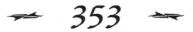

353

Never defend.
SHEILA GRAHAM

Newcomer

I talked with a family member recently who asked, "Are you still going to those meetings?" The tone of the question seemed to imply that there was something wrong with me for continuing to go.

Sponsor

We're not in recovery in order to get understanding and approval from our families and old friends; we're here to treat our addictions—and to save our lives. Nevertheless, it can feel painful when a nonaddict, or an addict who hasn't found recovery, seems critical of what we've come to understand as essential to our health and well-being.

We don't have to engage in explaining or defending our recovery. A smile and a simple answer are enough. If we wish, we can make an "I am" statement, such as, "Yes, I'm lucky that there are so many meetings to choose from, and that such good people go to them." Or, "Yes, it gets even better as time goes on."

Trying to explain to someone who is expressing hostility toward the program or toward us isn't likely to further our recovery or anyone else's—and it can lead to frustration and anger. I've learned, in recovery, to detach gently from any invitations to debate about this program. It's not debatable.

Today, my wholehearted acceptance of recovery keeps me from engaging in arguments about it.

 *354*

All growth is a leap in the dark, a spontaneous, unpremeditated act without benefit of experience.
HENRY MILLER

Newcomer
I've made a wrong decision, and now I'm experiencing the consequences. I'm full of regret and shame—I don't know how I'm going to live with myself.

Sponsor
Whether mistakes concern work, relationships, or any other aspect of our lives, we are not unique in making them. All of us, at times, have done or said things we wish we'd done differently. A cook learns through trial and error how to season a dish; a scientist explores what may turn out to be a blind alley as he or she attempts to prove a hypothesis; a ballplayer sometimes strikes out. Taking risks is

necessary if any of us is to accomplish anything original or worthwhile.

Our mistakes are a part of our education in recovery. If we never made them, we might never know who we are, who we'd like to be, or how we want to act in the future. If our mistake has harmed another person or institution, we can acknowledge the error and do our best to make restitution. If it's our own pride that we've harmed, we can take a deep breath and move on, wiser and more generous than we were before.

> Today, I smile at mistakes, giving myself
> and others room to be human.

355

I graduated first in my class from alibi school.
JEFFREY McDANIEL

Newcomer
I still have the bad habit of overexplaining my reasons when I'm saying no to someone. I feel guilty. I still can't tell the simple truth, if I know that I'm going to disappoint someone.

Sponsor
When we were active in our addictions, shame and guilt were a part of every day, especially where our interactions with other people were concerned. When we acted out our addictions in spite of repeated resolutions and promises, we disappointed ourselves and those with whom our lives were interwoven. It seemed easier to invent excuses than to face our inability to say no, our inability to show up for everything we'd agreed to do.

Now that we're in recovery, we're learning how we want to spend our time and what is realistic to expect of ourselves. Our old habit of providing alibis may not have left us yet, however. We may feel the need to explain and elaborate because we don't yet feel fully entitled to have needs and desires of our own; whatever someone asks of us, we think we should take on.

The need for excuses gradually leaves us as our tolerance and understanding of ourselves grow. We become more practical about what our schedules and energies allow us to undertake, more authentic about what we ourselves want, as we come to know and esteem ourselves in recovery.

Today, I need no alibi for simply being myself.

356

Rage . . . is a hell of an effective mood changer!
GUY KETTELHACK

Newcomer

I'm sick of these people who just do and say whatever they like, in the name of freedom in recovery. There's one character who always tells me I've set the chairs up the wrong way, and another one who regularly comments to me after I've shared at the meeting that I don't sound so good. I've had enough. The next time one of these people attacks me, I'm just going to walk out.

Sponsor

Yes, there are some people in recovery who are overly critical or inappropriate. There are some people who have weak boundaries, people who are intolerant of others, even some who are mentally ill. But they're a small fraction of the people we meet in recovery, just as such people are only a small part of the larger human community.

Anger pouring through us can give us feelings of energy, power, and satisfaction and can compensate for a sense of injustice and powerlessness. But its satisfactions are short-lived and don't offer long-term solutions to our problems. If anger causes us to leave meetings, we may be on a dangerous course that could lead to alienation from the program and a return to addiction. Anger itself can become addictive.

To "Detach with love," as an Al-Anon slogan suggests, is the ideal response to people whose behavior upsets us. If we're not ready to detach with love, we can detach, for now, with whatever feeling arises in us. That doesn't mean cheating ourselves by walking out of meetings. It means refusing to engage in argument. We can abstain from participating, saying simply, "I'm sorry you feel that way," and continue working our program of recovery.

Today, I detach with love from people and situations that trigger my anger.

 *357*

I was praying for rhinestones—when my Higher Power had diamonds in store for me!
WOMAN IN RECOVERY

Newcomer
I applied for something I'm really well qualified to do; it's something I've wanted for a long time. I was rejected in

favor of someone else. I don't plan to relapse over this, but I'm angry and discouraged. It's hard for me to feel generous toward the person who got what I wanted.

Sponsor

I'm sorry to hear of your disappointment. It sounds as if it was intensified by your competitive feelings with another person. Drinking, using drugs, overeating, or engaging in other addictive behaviors only compounds disappointment with feelings of shame and self-rejection.

Whether the context is work, school, community activity, or personal relationships, there are times when each of us has to deal with rejection. But if we value ourselves and our abilities and are not depending solely on someone else's validation to make us feel worthwhile, we can detach from a rejection and move on. We know that there will be other, and perhaps more rewarding, opportunities for fulfillment at the right time. We trust that our spirit has a vision larger than the scope of what we can see today.

We can cope with our feelings of competition by praying sincerely that others will receive recognition and happiness. The love and generosity our prayers create in us will lighten our hearts.

Today, I recognize my own value and am confident
in my Higher Power's plan for me.
I wholeheartedly celebrate others' successes.

You have to sniff out joy, keep your nose to the joy-trail.
BUFFY SAINTE-MARIE

Newcomer

I heard an old-timer say, "You can be right, or you can be happy." What does that mean? When something is wrong, am I supposed to deny what I can see with my own eyes?

Sponsor

This program saying is not meant to encourage stupidity or moral laziness. It's an affectionate way of suggesting that when we obsess about our own point of view or insist on having our own way, we may have our priorities mixed up. It suggests that we be open-minded and tolerant of people with whom we may disagree. It reminds us that self-will is not the path to serenity.

It also suggests that we have a choice about where to focus our mental energies. There is nothing wrong with having our own particular point of view and confidently and persuasively expressing it—that's part of our self-esteem. But we don't have to win arguments and attempt to force people and situations to conform to our own ideas. We can detach from argument, instead of reacting. We can experience the peace that comes from letting go, as we cultivate mental relaxation and serenity as tools of our recovery.

Today, I don't have to be right.
I'm happy, as I live and let live.

What is actual is actual only for one time
And only for one place.

T. S. ELIOT

Newcomer

I spoke at a meeting last night, but I don't feel as if I said much of anything. I feel depressed about it today.

Sponsor

Whatever took place at that meeting, it's now part of the past. In the Serenity Prayer we ask our Higher Power to help us accept the things we can't change. Among the things we can't change are events that have already taken place, whether twenty years ago or just yesterday.

You'll have many more opportunities to speak at meetings as recovery continues. My own experience is that each time I speak is a little different. Sometimes I feel fluent, confident, and in control of my words; sometimes I feel forgetful and shy, or even a bit blank. I've learned to try not to judge my talk as if it were a performance, but to regard it as an offering. My speaking provided a necessary ingredient that kept the meeting going for others (in addition to getting me there). Whatever I say, something will have relevance for someone in the room; it always happens. That's something I can't plan or control; it's part of the flow of things.

Today, I let go of the habit of rating my past performance.

The most exhausting thing in life is being insincere.
ANNE MORROW LINDBERGH

Newcomer

I heard someone sharing about a rather extreme situation. She complained that no one had time to listen to her. I gave her my phone number, and at first, I didn't mind the calls. But every time I suggested a meeting or program tool, she objected: she'd tried everything and had a complaint about everyone. She calls every day now, and I'm always the one to end the conversation. It's too much for me, but I don't want to let her down—she's had too many disappointments.

Sponsor

Our desire to be helpful sometimes backfires. When we're motivated by a need to rescue people, we may present ourselves as more available and able to give help than we really are. When I find that I'm more concerned about someone's growth in recovery than he himself is, I know I've gone beyond the boundaries of appropriate program support.

Part of my work in recovery is learning to accept my limitations. Though some people in the fellowship present their problems to be solved, I recognize that I cannot provide solutions; I can only listen and offer support as others go through the process of finding their own solutions. If people aren't using the tools of the program, offering myself as a substitute actually hinders their recovery. This practice is called "enabling" because it allows others to keep on repeating addictive patterns without challenging themselves. Honesty demands that we withdraw from enabling situations. Recognizing our limits and acknowledging them is essential.

> Today, I don't block others in their search for solutions
> by trying to be the solution.

 **361**

> *I want, by understanding myself, to understand others.*
> *I want to be all that I am capable of becoming. . . .*
> *This all sounds very strenuous and serious.*
> *But now that I have wrestled with it, it's no longer so.*
> *I feel happy—deep down.* All is well.
> KATHERINE MANSFIELD

Newcomer

There are still days when I rebel against recovery—not by using, not even by skipping a meeting, but just by bringing a negative, rebellious attitude. More often, though, I've begun to sense the awesomeness of the journey I've undertaken. It's then that I experience recovery as a miracle, and I feel at peace.

Sponsor

Life doesn't have to be a bed of roses for us to feel happy. Our happiness comes, not from external circumstances, but from a place deep in ourselves. Self-knowledge and self-acceptance are growing inside us, strengthening the core of our being. As people sharing the experience of recovery, we have the chance to return over and over to the sense of the miraculous. I sometimes think, "By rights, I shouldn't even be here. My addiction eventually would have killed me, if I hadn't quit." I'm flooded with a sense of the mystery of recovery, and of gratitude for this second chance at life.

In recovery, we have the opportunity to discover and fulfill our Higher Power's purpose for us. We know that it has something to do with caring for ourselves and others, with giving service and being the best that we can be.

> Today, whatever is happening on the outside,
> I sense that all is well.

 *362*

Be yourself, that's all there is of you.
RALPH WALDO EMERSON

Newcomer

There are some major decisions I made about my life years ago that I'm now beginning to question. It scares me to think that I may have made some mistakes about who I am and want to be. I wonder if I have the courage to change, after all this time, and if I'll live long enough to find fulfillment.

Sponsor

As recovery progresses, many of us find that we have questions about life choices that we made long ago, or that we let others make for us. We've allowed these choices to define us, and now we're not entirely sure they fit. Even if we wished in the past that we'd taken other options, we may have lacked the willingness and energy to take ourselves seriously. Now that we have had some sober experience, we may find that we have questions about former life decisions.

We've learned in recovery not to make hasty decisions based on our desire to stifle a moment's doubt or anxiety. But we've also learned that we can go deep within, listen to our own spirit, and honor what we find there, even if it doesn't conform to other people's expectations or to our own preconceptions about who we are supposed to be. We know we can survive upheaval and complexity—we have already done it. We know how to ask for support today and how to discuss our uncertainties and hopes with trusted friends and counselors as we arrive at the truth of our deepest dreams.

> Today, I'm making my own map
> and becoming willing to follow it.

363

Freedom breeds freedom. Nothing else does.
ANNE ROE

Newcomer
Now that I'm getting close to a year in recovery, I have this crazy feeling sometimes. I say to myself, "What am I doing without my drug of choice? It's been too long!"

Sponsor
We've talked together in the past about "anniversary anxiety." It's natural for doubts to arise at a point in time when we're about to celebrate a success. Some of us may wonder, "Do I really deserve all this? Is this really me?"

Fortunately, we don't have to act on a crazy feeling any more. We recognize that though recovery is a relatively recent phenomenon in our lives, it's rooted in us now, and it's essential to our survival and growth. We make a point of sharing our doubts and fears at meetings, where others in recovery will help us remember where active addiction took us and laugh with us at our doubts about recovery.

Active addiction is not, as we've sometimes believed, an essential part of our identity. It is an obstacle to discovering and nurturing that identity.

Today, I renew my commitment to recovery.

364

There is a love like a small lamp, which goes out when the oil is consumed; or like a stream, which dries up when it doesn't rain. But there is a love that is like a mighty spring gushing up out of the earth; it keeps flowing forever, and is inexhaustible.

ISAAC OF NINEVEH

Newcomer

The changes I've been through in recovery so far are beyond anything I could have predicted when all I imagined was getting some control over my addiction. I never expected to let other people into my life. I never expected to find a Higher Power.

Sponsor

Our Higher Power has been with us from the beginning. Beneath our craving for an addictive substance or behavior, there has always been a craving for connection with our deepest selves.

In recovery, we have begun to know ourselves at the level of soul. We've experienced our connection with the rest of humanity and prayed to be useful to others. We've forgiven ourselves and others for being imperfect. We sense the mystery of the recovery that was offered to us, and we're beginning to know something about gratitude. I've heard an old-timer in recovery sum it up this way: "It's just love. All of it is about love."

We know the love that flows from a Power greater than ourselves when we look at the faces and hear the words of other recovering people. We can tap into this unending stream of love whenever we go to a meeting.

Today, I open myself to the love in this program.

 *365*

Trust in experience. And in the rhythms.
The deep rhythms of your experience.
MURIEL RUKEYSER

Newcomer
At a recent meeting I realized that I wasn't feeling critical of myself or others. I noticed the sounds around me and felt myself accept that the world is just as it should be. I felt peaceful, happy. I listened to people sharing, without my usual objections. I could appreciate each person's contribution. I don't know why this happened or if these feelings will stay with me.

Sponsor
At times, we're aware of a breakthrough. A habit or out-look suddenly shifts for no apparent reason. But, in fact,

you've been doing the work of recovery for some time now. When we keep showing up, progress sometimes seems to leap ahead. We may not always love everyone; old problems may arise. But once we've had positive experiences of recovery like the one you've described, we have memories to draw on for inspiration.

Today, I trust my positive feelings and experiences.

366

Life is an exciting business and most exciting when it is lived for others.
HELEN KELLER

Newcomer

I can hardly believe that it's been a whole year. A year of recovery! When I first got here, I couldn't imagine living through a day without my addiction. I don't think I would have gotten through it without your friendship and support. I wanted someone to care enough to listen; you've done that and more. I know it hasn't always been easy for you. How can I ever pay you back?

Sponsor

Congratulations, from the bottom of my heart. It's been a year of recovery for me, too, and you've helped me significantly with it. Your willingness to show up, ask questions, take suggestions, go through the hard days as well as the easy ones—you've been a joy, and a power of example. Like you, I need to keep learning how to have relationships with other human beings by engaging with them in real ways.

You've challenged me to be as honest as you have been. When we've had conflicts between us, you've showed up and done your part in the process of resolving them.

You don't have to "pay me back"; your allowing me to participate in your recovery has been a gift. But I know that you want to keep on giving service to the program, and that you're going to be a wonderful sponsor.

A year of recovery is something to celebrate; I'm looking forward to hearing you speak at meetings to share your achievement. Then, let's each take a deep breath and move on, and see what a second year in recovery holds, one day at a time.

Today, I feel gratitude and joy.

Appendixes

APPENDIX 1

The Twelve Steps of Alcoholics Anonymous

1. We admitted we were powerless over alcohol—that our lives had become unmanageable.
2. Came to believe that a Power greater than ourselves could restore us to sanity.
3. Made a decision to turn our will and our lives over to the care of God *as we understood Him.*
4. Made a searching and fearless moral inventory of ourselves.
5. Admitted to God, to ourselves, and to another human being the exact nature of our wrongs.
6. Were entirely ready to have God remove all these defects of character.
7. Humbly asked Him to remove our shortcomings.
8. Made a list of all persons we had harmed, and became willing to make amends to them all.
9. Made direct amends to such people wherever possible, except when to do so would injure them or others.
10. Continued to take personal inventory and when we were wrong promptly admitted it.
11. Sought through prayer and meditation to improve our conscious contact with God *as we understood Him,* praying only for knowledge of His will for us and the power to carry that out.
12. Having had a spiritual awakening as the result of these steps, we tried to carry this message to alcoholics, and to practice these principles in all our affairs.

The Twelve Steps of AA are taken from *Alcoholics Anonymous*, 3d ed., published by AA World Services, Inc., New York, N.Y., 59–60. Reprinted with permission of AA World Services, Inc. (See editor's note on copyright page.)

The Twelve Steps of Al-Anon

1. We admitted we were powerless over alcohol—that our lives had become unmanageable.
2. Came to believe that a Power greater than ourselves could restore us to sanity.
3. Made a decision to turn our will and our lives over to the care of God *as we understood Him.*
4. Made a searching and fearless moral inventory of ourselves.
5. Admitted to God, to ourselves and to another human being the exact nature of our wrongs.
6. Were entirely ready to have God remove all these defects of character.
7. Humbly asked Him to remove our shortcomings.
8. Made a list of all persons we had harmed, and became willing to make amends to them all.
9. Made direct amends to such people wherever possible, except when to do so would injure them or others.
10. Continued to take personal inventory and when we were wrong promptly admitted it.
11. Sought through prayer and meditation to improve our conscious contact with God *as we understood Him,* praying only for knowledge of His will for us and the power to carry that out.
12. Having had a spiritual awakening as the result of these Steps, we tried to carry this message to others, and to practice these principles in all our affairs.

The Twelve Steps of Al-Anon are taken from *Al-Anon Faces Alcoholism, 2nd Ed.*, published by Al-Anon Family Group Headquarters, Inc., New York, N.Y., 236–37. Reprinted with permission of A.A. World Services, Inc.

The Twelve Steps of Narcotics Anonymous

1. We admitted that we were powerless over our addiction, that our lives had become unmanageable.
2. We came to believe that a Power greater than ourselves could restore us to sanity.
3. We made a decision to turn our will and our lives over to the care of God *as we understood Him.*
4. We made a searching and fearless moral inventory of ourselves.
5. We admitted to God, to ourselves, and to another human being the exact nature of our wrongs.
6. We were entirely ready to have God remove all these defects of character.
7. We humbly asked Him to remove our shortcomings.
8. We made a list of all persons we had harmed, and became willing to make amends to them all.
9. We made direct amends to such people wherever possible, except when to do so would injure them or others.
10. We continued to take personal inventory, and when we were wrong promptly admitted it.
11. We sought through payer and meditation to improve our conscious contact with God, *as we understood Him,* praying only for knowledge of His will for us, and the power to carry that out.
12. Having had a spiritual awakening as a result of these steps, we tried to carry this message to addicts and to practice these principles in all our affairs.

Adapted from the Twelve Steps of Alcoholics Anonymous, reprinted with permission of A.A. World Services, Inc., New York, N.Y.

The Twelve Steps of Overeaters Anonymous

1. We admitted we were powerless over food—that our lives had become unmanageable.
2. Came to believe that a Power greater than ourselves could restore us to sanity.
3. Made a decision to turn our will and our lives over to the care of God *as we understood Him.*
4. Made a searching and fearless moral inventory of ourselves.
5. Admitted to God, to ourselves and to another human being the exact nature of our wrongs.
6. Were entirely ready to have God remove all these defects of character.
7. Humbly asked Him to remove our shortcomings.
8. Made a list of all persons we had harmed, and became willing to make amends to them all.
9. Made direct amends to such people wherever possible, except when to do so would injure them or others.
10. Continued to take personal inventory and when we were wrong, promptly admitted it.
11. Sought through prayer and meditation to improve our conscious contact with God *as we understood Him,* praying only for knowledge of His will for us and the power to carry that out.
12. Having had a spiritual awakening as the result of these steps, we tried to carry this message to compulsive overeaters and to practice these principles in all our affairs.

From *Overeaters Anonymous* ©1980 by Overeaters Anonymous, Inc., Torrance, Calif., p. 4. Adapted from the Twelve Steps of Alcoholics Anonymous in *Alcoholics Anonymous* 3d ed., published by AA World Services, Inc., New York, N.Y., 59–60. Reprinted with permission of AA World Services, Inc. (See editor's note on the copyright page.)

The Twelve Steps of
Sexual Compulsives Anonymous

1. We admitted we were powerless over sexual compulsion—that our lives had become unmanageable.
2. Came to believe that a power greater than ourselves could restore us to sanity.
3. Made a decision to turn our will and our lives over to the care of God *as we understood God*.
4. Made a searching and fearless moral inventory of ourselves.
5. Admitted to God, to ourselves and to another human being the exact nature of our wrongs.
6. Were entirely ready to have God remove all these defects of character.
7. Humbly asked God to remove our shortcomings.
8. Made a list of all persons we had harmed and became willing to make amends to them all.
9. Made direct amends to such people wherever possible, except when to do so would injure them or others.
10. Continued to take personal inventory and when we were wrong, promptly admitted it.
11. Sought through prayer and meditation to improve our conscious contact with God *as we understood God*, praying only for knowledge of God's will for us and the power to carry that out.
12. Having had a spiritual awakening as the result of these steps, we tried to carry this message to sexually compulsive people, and to practice these principles in all our affairs.

From *Sexual Compulsives Anonymous: A Program of Recovery*, published by International Service Organization of Sexual Compulsives Anonymous, New York, N.Y., page 2. Reprinted with permission. Adapted from the Twelve Steps of Alcoholics Anonymous in *Alcoholics Anonymous* 3d ed., published by AA World Services, Inc., New York, N.Y., 59–60. Reprinted with permission of AA World Services, Inc. (See editor's note on the copyright page.)

The Twelve Steps of Gamblers Anonymous

1. We admitted we were powerless over gambling—that our lives had become unmanageable.
2. Came to believe that a Power greater than ourselves could restore us to a normal way of thinking and living.
3. Made a decision to turn our will and our lives over to the care of this Power of our own understanding.
4. Made a searching and fearless moral and financial inventory of ourselves.
5. Admitted to God, to ourselves and to another human being the exact nature of our wrongs.
6. Were entirely ready to have these defects of character removed.
7. Humbly asked God (of our understanding) to remove our shortcomings.
8. Made a list of all persons we had harmed, and became willing to make amends to them all.
9. Made direct amends to such people wherever possible, except when to do so would injure them or others.
10. Continued to take personal inventory and when we were wrong, promptly admitted it.
11. Sought through prayer and meditation to improve our conscious contact with God *as we understood Him*, praying only for knowledge of His will for us and the power to carry that out.
12. Having made an effort to practice these principles in all our affairs, we tried to carry this message to other compulsive gamblers.

Adapted from the Twelve Steps of Alcoholics Anonymous, reprinted with permission of A.A. World Services, Inc., New York, N.Y.

APPENDIX 2
Twelve Step Groups

The following is a partial list of Twelve Step groups:

Alcoholics Anonymous World Services, Inc.
P.O. Box 459
New York, NY 10017-9998

Al-Anon Family Group Headquarters, Inc.
1600 Corporate Landing Parkway
Virginia Beach, VA 23454-5617

Debtors Anonymous
General Service Board
P.O. Box 400
Grand Central Station
New York, NY 10163

Gamblers Anonymous
P.O. Box 17173
Los Angeles, CA 90017

Narcotics Anonymous
P.O. Box 9999
Van Nuys, CA 94109

Overeaters Anonymous
6075 Zenith Ct. NE
Rio Rancho, NM 87124

Sexual Compulsives Anonymous
P.O. Box 1585, Old Chelsea Station
New York, NY 10011

Index

JOAN LARKIN is the author of three collections of poetry (*Housework*, *A Long Sound*, and *Cold River*) and a prize-winning play (*The Living*). A teacher of writing for many years, she has served on the faculties of Goddard, Sarah Lawrence, and Brooklyn colleges.